LEADING GLOBAL DIVERSITY, EQUITY, AND INCLUSION

A Guide for Systemic Change in Multinational Organizations

ROHINI ANAND

BK®
Berrett–Koehler Publishers, Inc

Berrett-Koehler Publishers, Inc.
1333 Broadway, Suite 1000
Oakland, CA 94612-1921
Tel: (510) 817-2277
Fax: (510) 817-2278
www.bkconnection.com

ORDERING INFORMATION
Quantity sales. Special discounts are available on quantity purchases by corporations, associations, and others. For details, contact the "Special Sales Department" at the Berrett-Koehler address above.
Individual sales. Berrett-Koehler publications are available through most bookstores. They can also be ordered directly from Berrett-Koehler: Tel: (800) 929-2929; Fax: (802) 864-7626; www.bkconnection.com.
Orders for college textbook / course adoption use. Please contact Berrett-Koehler: Tel: (800) 929-2929; Fax: (802) 864-7626.

Distributed to the U.S. trade and internationally by Penguin Random House Publisher Services.

Printed in Canada

Berrett-Koehler books are printed on long-lasting acid-free paper. When it is available, we choose paper that has been manufactured by environmentally responsible processes. These may include using trees grown in sustainable forests, incorporating recycled paper, minimizing chlorine in bleaching, or recycling the energy produced at the paper mill.

Library of Congress Cataloging-in-Publication Data
Names: Anand, Rohini, author.
Title: Leading global diversity, equity, and inclusion : a guide to systemic change in multinational organizations / Rohini Anand.
Identifiers: LCCN 2021033506 (print) | LCCN 2021033507 (ebook) | ISBN 9781523000241 (hardcover) | ISBN 9781523000258 (adobe pdf) | ISBN 9781523000265 (epub)
Subjects: LCSH: Diversity in the workplace. | International business enterprises—Personnel management. | Organizational change. | Multiculturalism.
Classification: LCC HF5549.5.M5 A5235 2021 (print) | LCC HF5549.5.M5 (ebook) | DDC 658.3008—dc23
LC record available at https://lccn.loc.gov/2021033506
LC ebook record available at https://lccn.loc.gov/2021033507

First Edition
26 25 24 23 22 21 10 9 8 7 6 5 4 3 2 1

Book producer and text designer: Happenstance Type-O-Rama
Cover designer: Rob Johnson, Toprotype, Inc.

For my father, who believed
in this book before I did

CONTENTS

FOREWORD

MAJOR UPHEAVALS CAN LEAD TO UNEXPECTED PROGRESS in the longer term. Crises give rise to drastic changes in ways of thinking and in behaviors that have the potential to spawn innovation and accelerate transformations. We have seen this historically. In 2020, for instance, the devastating consequences of the Covid-19 pandemic and civil unrest in the face of racial inequality caused organizations the world over to take action: ad hoc appointments were made; commitments to policy changes were taken in order to address issues of social justice. These crises serve as a reminder that we must accelerate the pace of change in our workplace and communities and be bolder in our ambition to make them more diverse, equitable, and inclusive.

This raw urgency is a prerequisite for driving deep-seated change. Societal disruptions provide a unique opportunity to anchor diversity, equity, and inclusion (DEI) principles and practices as businesses reinvent themselves and assume greater responsibility for addressing societal inequities. But how do you bring about the kind of swift and thorough cultural transformation needed to truly shift mindsets, especially in multinational organizations that exist in locations with vastly different legal, cultural, and social norms? That's where Dr. Rohini Anand can guide us.

This comprehensive book speaks to the intricacies, complexities, and nuances of cultivating DEI in global organizations. As a leader of a company with 420,000 employees and operations in more than 60 countries, I have witnessed first-hand the essential value of a well-conceived and executed global inclusion change strategy that fully delivers on its promise. It takes significant insight, personal experience, and commitment to truly get it right, and that is precisely what Rohini brings to the conversation. Most recently, she has served as the Senior Vice President Corporate Responsibility and Global Chief Diversity Officer at Sodexo, and she is recognized as a thought leader and subject matter expert who has supported many organizations in their inclusion change efforts.

Through engaging storytelling, Rohini lays out five key principles for building an effective global DEI strategy. She addresses everything from localizing efforts and aligning them to business goals, to the necessity of leadership transformation, establishing governance, and developing metrics and accountability. Rohini has the unique ability to speak both to the head and to the heart: in explaining each core principle, she leverages research, data, field experiences, best practices, and vivid anecdotes that bring the principles to life. She enriches her own experiences with insights from other global executives.

An inclusion journey requires organizations and their leaders to go through their own transformation. Rohini sets a clear example by candidly sharing her missteps and her own journey of introspection and awareness. Intentionally highlighting multiple perspectives, the book is packed with stories, lessons, and frameworks to guide change agents in the urgent work of advancing a diverse, equitable, and inclusive culture in their organizations.

Rohini is a bright, passionate, and inspiring leader who quite simply makes you want to follow her. Working closely with her has been an eye-opener, and her vision has spurred my own commitment on this crucial topic. Our relationship has helped me grow. And now, she pours her unique brand of insight, tenacity, resilience, and vision into a book that can guide you as you pursue the vital work of bringing about a more equitable workplace, business, community, and society.

Regardless of where your corporation is on the journey, this must-read book will give you a solid foundation to achieve the vision of a truly diverse, equitable, and inclusive organization.

—Sophie Bellon
Chair
Sodexo's Board of Directors

PREFACE

I WAS EXCITED ABOUT GOING TO INDIA to launch diversity, equity, and inclusion work for Sodexo, a French global food services and facilities management company that I was employed with in the US. I was born in India, had spent my formative years there, traveled to India at least once a year, and spoke several Indian languages. In my mind, I had a good understanding of the culture.

In a small room in the Sodexo India offices in Malad, a suburb of Mumbai, I sat with twenty women who were employed in entry- to mid-level management positions. They wore brilliantly colored *saris* and *churidar kurtas*. A few wore trousers. They were all delighted to have been selected to participate and were eager to engage. I was focused on implementing initiatives to advance women since the representation of women in the Sodexo India workforce was approximately 20 percent. We had seen the success of mentoring and leadership initiatives in the US and elsewhere, and I was convinced that we needed a similar approach to broaden opportunities for women in India.

The women sat patiently and quietly waiting for me to start the conversation. After a round of introductions, I told them why I was there. "I want to understand what your challenges are and how the company can help you advance in your careers," I said. And then I started giving them examples of efforts that we had successfully implemented elsewhere. I talked about the benefits of leadership development and mentoring. I was met with blank stares. I could tell that I was just not connecting with them. I tried a few Hindi phrases to break the ice and to signal I was one of them . . . still no reaction.

I had the best of intentions; I was trying to help them. After all, having grown up in India, I, more than anyone, understood what they needed. But something was not working! It was only when I paused to ask the women what would be helpful in advancing their careers that one of them gingerly raised her hand and said, "Rohini, ma'am, we live with our in-laws and have to take care of them and of the house and our children. If we stay late at work to finish our project, our mother-in-law gets angry." The other women nodded, and then another raised her hand and said, "And even if our mother-in-law is home all day, we still have to take care of our children and cook the evening meal when we get home." They were on a roll—clearly this topic had struck a chord. Another chimed in, "And they don't care what we are doing at work; they just want us to make a salary and do all the housework."

Wow! I had completely forgotten the multigenerational joint-family dynamic in India where many couples live with the husband's extended family and the daughter-in-law is expected to take care of all the housework! I had forgotten the role of the Indian woman, not only as a mother and wife, but also as a daughter-in-law. And, I had forgotten my own limitations as a multidimensional being—focused on one aspect of my shared identity with these women and overlooking the many differences.

I was at a loss as to the solution to this dilemma until, once again, I asked them how we could help. Again, these women came through and offered up a solution. They asked us to host a recognition day with awards and to invite their extended families. I have to say that the awards day was a highpoint in my diversity, equity, and inclusion (DEI) work in India! The extended families were so proud of their family members who worked at Sodexo, and the women were beaming. Did it shift the dynamic at home? I learned that it did, slightly; many of the women could occasionally stay to finish a project without feeling conflicted, and sometimes they even came home to meals prepared by their mothers-in-law!

One of the earliest lessons I learned through this experience in my self-discovery journey is that it is not useful to export initiatives that may have worked "at home" to other parts of the world where they have little relevance. This experience drove home to me a stumbling block in global inclusion transformation work—the temptation to assume that I understood a place without checking out my presumptions. Clearly, I needed to do my own work as a change agent—we all do. This takes self-awareness. If I was going to be successful in changing mindsets and behaviors, I could not stop investing in my own discovery work. Instead of dispiriting, I found these flashes of insight into myself exciting. I was on the edge of my learning curve.

In leading global DEI for over thirty years, I have come to increasingly appreciate the complexity of the work. I have caught myself applying my own limited, one-dimensional worldview to make sense of situations that are unfamiliar to me, which is antithetical to the very outcome that we are seeking. For me, the journey has been as much about doing my own work of self-discovery as it has been about guiding leaders through their respective DEI journeys to inclusive leadership. Eventually I learned that my success was predicated on being able to draw on perspectives from multiple cultural contexts.

A Few Notes on Terminology

I use DEI as an acronym for diversity, equity, and inclusion throughout this book. I define *diversity* as a demographic mix of people, including those from marginalized or underrepresented groups; *equity* refers to eliminating systemic barriers that inhibit full participation and equal access to opportunities; and *inclusion* is the act of creating a work culture in which individuals can participate fully because systemic barriers have been removed. The outcome of an inclusive culture is one in which employees experience a sense of belonging and their uniqueness is embraced.[1] The ultimate goal is to embed DEI at all levels within organizations and society to ensure social justice. I have found that being able to draw on various perspectives and act on them is what makes DEI successful. This starts even with the very words that we use to describe this work. I may use DEI, but leaders in disparate organizations and in different parts of the world use a range of words. For example, in parts of Europe, some organizations prefer to say "inclusion" and "non-discrimination" rather than "diversity" as these concepts resonate more. Others might add "belonging" and drop "equity" altogether.

I have chosen to capitalize Black, White, and Brown. In writing this book, I constantly caught myself normalizing Whiteness as a default and as a result not racializing White in the same way I was doing for Black. Following the lead of the National Association of Black Journalists and some Black scholars, I have decided to capitalize White. Eve Ewing, a Black sociologist at the University of Chicago, wrote in an online essay, "When we ignore the specificity and significance of Whiteness. . . . we contribute to its seeming neutrality and thereby grant it power to maintain its invisibility."[2]

Why This Book?

Why is this book different and why write it? In doing global transformation work, I yearned for a book that addressed the unique challenges of DEI change in a global organizational context. Although there are several academic books on global DEI, this book is a view from the trenches—a view from someone who has had to pioneer a way forward without any real map. I decided to write this book because in my DEI career I've learned some hard lessons. I want to give back what I've acquired from this work to you, leaders in global organizations who want your DEI efforts to matter, to stick, to last, and to make a difference.

Do any of these scenarios sound familiar?

- You come to the US on a business trip and are surprised by how openly US Americans talk about personal experiences with race. You are uneasy about inviting any US facilitators to your country to talk about DEI in case they don't understand the sensitivities in discussing race.
- Your women's employee resource group has been very successful in creating a sense of community and belonging for women, and you've tried to replicate this in other countries. But in some places, women don't seem to be interested and, at times, are even openly hostile to the idea.
- You can see that there are no Black managers in the office in Europe but are told that you cannot collect data on race.
- You give a presentation featuring the business case for DEI and you hear feedback that some people were offended that the company was trying to capitalize on diversity with no mention of it being the right thing to do.
- Your global CEO is very committed to advancing DEI, but several of the country executive teams are dismissive. They see no value-add to the business, and they believe DEI is a US fad.

I know many of you reading this book have experienced the same challenges of global DEI work as I have. Each time I speak at conferences and events, global DEI draws the most interest. And based on what I hear from the audience, it has caused the most frustration. Given repeated appeals for more guidance on global DEI, I knew that sharing my professional journey in DEI would help global change agents.

I've written this book for leaders and change agents in all types of multinational organizations, including for-profit, nonprofit, and the public sector. This book is for executives, line managers, human resource professionals, and DEI practitioners. You will also find value in this book if you lead single-country organizations.

As I started writing, I realized that it was more important to readers to learn about the informative story behind the "how to"—the missteps and lessons I had learned. Because it's the challenges that brought me the greatest insight and, ultimately, the most lasting change. Believe me, it was sometimes frustrating. But mostly, and ultimately, it has been an incredibly rewarding journey of learning and change. After all, DEI work is about how we disrupt our own worldviews in order to bring about transformation in others.

Throughout the book, I cite examples from a range of companies, drawing from over sixty interviews. I mention them not because they are necessarily exemplar, but because they have replicable, interesting practices at a point in time.

If we want our businesses, organizations, and society to become diverse, equitable, and inclusive, we need to embark on a journey of change—not solely for policy and systems, but for people, as well. Ultimately, transformation happens at the intersection of the personal and systemic, and it is work that is ongoing. DEI must be a personal and professional journey for each of us if we want to become part of the plotline for true, lasting change toward diverse, equitable, and inclusive organizations.

INTRODUCTION
From Class Action to Best in Class: A Personal Journey

To be aware of a single shortcoming within oneself is more useful than to be aware of a thousand in somebody else.

—THE DALAI LAMA

IT WAS A BEAUTIFUL SPRING DAY IN PARIS IN 2007. We were sipping espressos and savoring the buttery croissants during a leadership meeting break at the *Palais des Congrès* in Porte Maillot. I stood at a high-top table, the only female among five White French male executives from Sodexo. I was excited. Building on the DEI success we had in the US, I had just stepped into a new role to establish and lead diversity, equity, and inclusion (DEI) globally.

We talked leisurely. The men chatted about their trips to India and how they loved travelling there. They knew I had just returned from a trip to India to visit my parents. They were knowledgeable and curious about India's foods, religions, and politics.

Despite the fact that I had lived in the US for close to thirty years by then, it was clear that they saw me as Indian and not US American. So, they were completely comfortable confiding in me their thoughts about their US colleagues. The "Americans," as they referred to them, focused on flashy presentations, while the French focused on substance. They were perplexed at how people from the US were so politically correct and shied away from discussing politics. One asked me why they did not have challenging discussions during meetings. (Like so many around the world, they referred to "Americans." They, like me before I started doing global work, weren't aware that the use of this term to describe a US American can be offensive to some—particularly to people from other countries in the Americas.)

Looking for an entry point to bring up DEI, I tested the waters very gingerly by raising the importance of DEI to a global organization like Sodexo. After all, my new role as Global Chief Diversity Officer (CDO) was to ensure that we advanced DEI globally, and here I had a ready audience.

The easy banter stopped abruptly. Two executives walked away, ostensibly to smoke. Another executive went out of his way to explain how Sodexo was already diverse. Look at all the nationalities we employ across eighty countries, he pointed out.

Another executive declared that issues of race don't exist in France. As evidence, he cited that some of his friends were married to French women of Algerian or Tunisian origin. When I challenged them about the lack of women in leadership, they promptly replied that women don't want to take executive positions because of family obligations. Their response to the lack of Black French people in management ranks was that they did not see color. And when I very tentatively mentioned the lesbian, gay, bisexual, transgender, and queer (LGBTQ) population, the response was, "That's a private matter that we don't bring into the office."

"Diversity is a very American thing, Rohini. It does not apply to us in Europe as we already have so many nationalities here," concluded the first executive. As we walked back into the meeting, my head was spinning. I realized that as soon as I had engaged my colleagues on DEI, they saw me as an "American" and a barrier came up between us. They pushed back because they perceived that I was imposing a US construct on them.

Their reactions caught me off guard. We had made tremendous progress in advancing diversity in Sodexo USA since I had joined as CDO for North America in 2002. I had reported to the global CEO, Michel Landel, and he had positioned DEI for success in the US.

These executives were comfortable navigating business globally and saw themselves as global citizens. Thanks to their candor, I was now becoming acutely aware of the challenge that lay ahead. I knew I had to help them to first recognize the challenges encountered by people who are marginalized, powerless, or underrepresented in the workplace. Then they needed to see the benefit of diversity to their teams. I was initially taken aback by how their perception of me had shifted so quickly in the conversation. But then, it was a reminder of my own identity-shifting journey to North America decades earlier.

A Personal Journey

On a sweltering, hot, and humid monsoon night, my entire family—parents, siblings, grandparents, a few cousins, and friends—had come to see me off at the airport in Mumbai. I was nervous and excited. Excited because I was finally going to graduate school in North America and nervous because it was my first trip on an airplane.

The farewell was a turmoil of hugs and kisses, tears and advice. "Make sure you eat well." "Write often." "Send pictures." "Don't get an American accent." And from my grandfather: "I am looking forward to seeing you get your PhD."

As I geared myself up for the long flight, I was bursting with anticipation for the next phase of my life. I was ready for this adventure but had no clue of what lay ahead. I recalled stories my father had shared. He had come to the United States as a young man and, throughout my childhood, had told me wonderful stories of the land that nineteenth-century Chinese American pioneers had called "Gold Mountain" or the land of opportunity where fortunes could be made. After completing his university studies and before returning to India, he had worked in Hollywood with the likes of Cary Grant. Not exactly the "typical" immigrant experience.

To provide some context, in the 1970s few single Indian women traveled to the United States to study. This was at a time when women in India generally completed their undergraduate degree as a qualification for a "good" arranged marriage. Yet, despite the prejudices he'd encountered in traveling through the southern US in the 1940s, my father encouraged and supported me to go to North America for my master's degree. I'm glad he didn't dwell on the negatives. He afforded me the opportunity to be open to my own journey.

The underlying expectation was that I would return to India as he had and "settle down." But the aerograms from my grandfather, an academic, urged me to complete my studies and become financially independent. I often reflect on how life would have been different had I been swayed by the cultural assumptions of me as an Indian woman.

I grew up in Mumbai, India. Moving to North America was an inflection point in my life. Growing up in India, almost everyone looked like me. I belonged to the majority religion, Hinduism. Surrounded by others like me, I had the privilege of not having to think about my identity. I was acutely aware of class privilege, however, as I grew up in an upper middle-class home where we spoke English, and I went to an international school.

That was my identity before I flew to North America. In my own naïve way, I saw myself as a citizen of the world. But in the hours and days after I passed through customs, that fantasy gave way to another reality. My identity shifted from being a person who saw herself at the center of her world, part of the educated elite, to being a minority—an immigrant—and yes, a foreigner. And I was totally unprepared for that.

Yet, like millions of people before me, upon arriving in this new land, I took on a new identity. Or, more accurately, identities. My India-to-North America journey crystalized how I perceived myself, how others saw me, my response to their perceptions, and subsequently, how I reacted to the world around me. Even in transit to North America I had my first taste of this. As I waited in Heathrow airport for my connection, I was aware that the only other South Asians I saw were the women in colorful *salwar kameezes* cleaning the bathrooms. Would I be lumped together with them? In that flash, so many things came into focus—my skin color, my accent, the fear of diminishing my own class privilege, and more. It was a brand-new awareness of myself and others' perceptions of me that took years to unpack and fully understand.

This multilayered, cross-cultural experience became the core of my graduate research and today is at the center of my work. The change to being identified as a minority made me realize the privileges that came with being part of a majority. I was part of the majority growing up in India and I had not recognized or reflected upon my privilege in that way. More importantly, I was unable to, until I was perceived as a minority and I experienced things differently. The realization that identity is situational and fluid still informs my work.

So, this vocation is very personal to me. And I've come to realize that the personal journey of understanding what it means to be perceived as a minority—an outsider—in disparate contexts is at the heart of DEI. It's not abstract. It's embedded in how people see themselves, others, and their world.

As I think about DEI and the way it impacts the world around us, there is no denying that diversity and inclusion—or, more commonly, the lack thereof—has been at the core of many societal and corporate missteps. DEI is inherently about change. And change doesn't always come easily. It often comes with, or because of, challenges. Change came to me because of challenges, and it was challenge that eventually made Sodexo a more inclusive company.

Beginning with Trust

Thirty minutes into my interview with Michel Landel, the Sodexo North America CEO in 2002, I knew that I wanted to work for a company he was leading. Sodexo's workforce presented an incredible opportunity for fostering a diverse and inclusive culture. It was a microcosm of society with multiple races and ethnicities represented, particularly in entry-level roles. I would be charged with establishing and executing a DEI strategy and positioning it in the business—initially in North America.

In my pre-interview research, I had learned that Sodexo had several private lawsuits pending, as well as charges issued by the Equal Employment Opportunity Commission (EEOC), the agency that investigates discrimination complaints in the US. "But what large company doesn't have some litigation they're addressing?" I thought, not realizing the seriousness of one of these lawsuits. In March 2001, African American managers had filed a promotion discrimination case against Sodexho Marriott Services, Inc., Sodexo's predecessor company.

The lawsuit was certified as a class action lawsuit in 2002, six months after I joined the company. And on August 10, 2005, the court approved a settlement agreement between the company and the plaintiffs. In addition to the US $80 million monetary settlement for approximately 3,400 current and former African American managers, Sodexo agreed to continue to make enhancements to its systems, policies, and practices. These included equal employment opportunity (EEO) and diversity training, a new performance management process, a validated selection process and open postings for all positions, an office to investigate and resolve internal complaints of employment discrimination, and the establishment of an independent panel of monitors to oversee the implementation of the nonmonetary provisions of the decree. The decree monitor panel was active until 2010. This was a difficult time for the company, and it was clear much work needed to be done in North America before Sodexo could take on any global challenges.

My First Steps: Listening and Learning

After joining the company, my first meeting was with senior African American leaders who had come together to form an employee resource group (ERG) to address the advancement of African Americans and to create a sense of community in the company. ERGs are formed by employees around like identities to address opportunities relevant to their identity group. This was my first official week at the company and I was to lead and present at the meeting. I was acutely aware of my Asian American identity in that room full of African American business leaders. I came to understand the important struggle that lay ahead—there I was, in 2002, an Asian American, very aware of the need to build trust with these leaders in the only way that I knew how: by being authentic and transparent.

Building Trust through Candid Conversations

In the US, issues of race have centered on Black and White, especially as we confront the systemic racism that infuses US history. So how did I fit into this narrative? Was I seen as a management spokesperson by the African American community in the organization? Despite being a fellow *person of color*—a term used in the US to refer to Asian American, Hispanic,[1] African American, Native American, and other people who are not classified as White—was I seen as someone who could not possibly understand the experiences of African Americans?

I began to question the company's judgment in hiring a non-African American, when there was so much at stake. While 13 percent of the US workforce is African American or Black, 26 percent of cases filed with the EEOC are for race discrimination against Black employees.[2] It was natural that organizations tended to appoint people of like identity for positions like mine; they are perceived as understanding the issues.

I had my share of experiences of being stereotyped, of being told to "go back to where you came from," of being told with surprise that I spoke English well. I was also aware of the life experiences of my African American colleagues. But I had not lived their experiences of being marginalized and discriminated against within the potent historical context of enslavement in the US.

Building trust began with candid conversations; I acknowledged that I did not know but was willing to learn and to listen. It began with admitting that this was an extremely difficult time for the company and that, while we were not perfect, we were committed to trying. And it began with cultivating relationships and developing allies among my African American colleagues—allies who would give me candid feedback and coach me. These allies helped me keep my ear to the ground, alerting me if I needed to attend to situations. I know that I would not have been successful without the generosity of spirit of the Black employees at Sodexo and their willingness to trust me.

Tackling Resistance

Building relationships with African American employees and allowing space for sharing stories was a critical first step, but it was far from enough. I also had to build credibility with management and establish a reputation as someone who knew what she was doing and could deliver. I had to find a practical way to encourage the commitment needed to make the culture more diverse and inclusive, while aligning it with the realities of a low-margin business.

I was fortunate to work with a French CEO, Michel Landel, who had gone through his own journey to understand race in the US and who fundamentally believed that DEI was simply the right thing. I know this is not the case in many organizations. With his trust and sponsorship, we launched a multiyear strategy to address all internal systems and processes and to raise the awareness and competence of senior leaders.

Engaging a predominantly White male executive team and getting their buy-in was one of my first priorities. They had to overcome their view that DEI was simply a legal requirement and irrelevant to the business. They also had to be convinced that it was a way to attract and engage the best talent. And they had to see DEI as a market differentiator and an enabler of business success if we wanted a truly diverse, equitable, and inclusive organization as an outcome.

To get there, the executives had to take ownership of their own learning journeys. I had to influence these leaders, chipping away at their resistance, so that ultimately, they demonstrated their inclusive leadership. While a necessary first step, engaging the executive team alone was still not adequate to transform the culture to be more equitable and inclusive. We had to examine the systems and processes at each stage of the talent process in order to eliminate bias. This required partnering across the organization.

Embedding DEI in Company Systems

In 1998 Marriott International's foodservice division merged with the North America division of Sodexo (then Sodexho) to form Sodexho Marriott Services. In 2001, Sodexo acquired all of the share capital of Sodexho Marriott Services, growing exponentially from a smaller regional player to a leader in the food and facilities industry in North America.

The rapid growth and decentralized nature of the business meant there were few consistent practices; the priority during the merger months had been on establishing basic procedures to get people paid and ensuring they had their benefits. This transition presented an opportunity for the legal, human resources, and DEI teams to collaborate on developing consistent systems and policies to eliminate any possibilities of bias in the talent lifecycle.

Our approach was to ensure that DEI was not an isolated program or initiative disconnected from the business. In order to eliminate any bias in the employee lifecycle, DEI had to be integrated into all talent processes and policies from recruitment to development, promotion, retention, and succession planning. A diversity scorecard held leaders accountable for being inclusive.

A critical step in the inclusion journey was launching, what we later called at Sodexo, the employee business resource groups (EBRGs). In other organizations they are called employee resource groups (ERGs). The African American Leadership Forum (AALF), formed in 2002, was the first EBRG and was followed by several others. Contrary to the early resistance premised on the perception that the EBRGs would create silos and become "gripe" sessions, these groups provided a sense of community and belonging, and they seeded the organization with local DEI champions. Regular internal surveys revealed that EBRGs were considered an important investment by the company. They were credited with being a key reason that talent stayed with Sodexo and were a driver of employee engagement.

With investment and an immense amount of work, by 2010, the company had seen tremendous benefits from DEI both to its culture and to the business. Leadership became visibly more diverse, with women and people of color leading large and profitable segments of the business, and the culture became more inclusive as evidenced in survey results. Women and people of color had increased access to job opportunities and more rewarding careers. Surveys showed that they felt included and committed to the organization. Kenneth Johnson, an African American AALF leader, said, "This was an exciting time in our company! I saw leaders like myself in executive positions and in the C-suite. We talked openly and constructively about difference as part of our self-discovery. We were engaged and we felt a sense of belonging to the company!"[3]

With these advances, Sodexo gained stature as a thought leader in DEI. Sodexo's leadership, who had previously considered DEI merely a legal requirement, now saw it as an asset to the company. The legal requirements became an irrelevant threshold that the company far exceeded as they realized the benefits. When the consent decree monitoring committee expired in 2010, the leadership decided to appoint an external DEI advisory board for several years after to ensure Sodexo continued to remain intentional in addressing DEI and had an external perspective to inform that commitment.

The Power of Clients and the Community

As with any business, customers and clients are integral to the external ecosystem. Initially, I was intimidated by Sodexo's size and decentralized nature, which I assumed would make it challenging to establish a foundation for cultural transformation. How do you create an inclusive culture when 97 percent of your employees physically work at client locations like schools, universities, and hospitals and often identify with and assimilate to that culture? How do you foster a sense of belonging to Sodexo? How do you ensure that the client has the same values around DEI as you do?

Rather than being an inhibitor, this client connection became an enabler that fast-tracked the DEI engagement of middle managers, who are usually a barrier in most organizations. As Sodexo started being seen as a leader in DEI, clients began to ask Sodexo for assistance with their DEI efforts. Seeing their clients seeking out Sodexo's help created a sense of pride in the mostly White, male, mid-level managers. It engaged them in DEI, and they chose to diversify their teams, participate in the client's DEI councils, share best practices from Sodexo, and help clients with their own DEI efforts. As Sodexo leaders became more aware of the benefits to client relationships and to the business, the support for DEI deepened.

What had changed to catch clients' attention? Not only was the top management and leadership more visibly diverse, but clients noticed the positive impact on the service to their diverse customers—a result of training and mentoring initiatives. Sodexo became more visibly active in communities of color, partnering with clients to improve the quality of life in these communities. Prestigious organizations like Catalyst, a renowned global nonprofit that accelerates women into leadership, and DiversityInc, a US organization that ranks the top companies for diversity based on a survey, recognized Sodexo's cultural transformation with multiple awards.

With this recognition, not only did DEI make good business sense, it had become an integral component of Sodexo's brand promise, driving differentiation and competitive advantage. Sodexo's leaders saw that addressing equity and inclusion for its employees was compatible with business growth as clients and prospects were drawn to the brand because of the DEI actions Sodexo had taken. The DEI reputation enhanced Sodexo's overall image and Sodexo was increasingly perceived as a strategic partner.

I have always been acutely aware that organizations have to focus on truly making their cultures diverse, equitable, and inclusive before they can share their work externally in a way that is authentic. Although organizations can go from class action to best in class, without intentionality and focus, it is easy to slide back. Addressing DEI is continual and relentless.

Lessons Learned in Going Global

Soon after Michel Landel transitioned to his global CEO role, he asked me to replicate the US successes globally. In the US, we had moved from raising awareness through targeted trainings, to developing diverse talent through sponsorship, mentorship, and other initiatives, and ultimately integrating DEI into company processes while engaging external communities and clients. We followed a similar process globally.

In 2007, Sodexo was in over eighty countries, had 342,380 employees worldwide, and was the nineteenth largest corporate employer in the world. So where to start? We decided to begin by looking at hiring and career progression of women, since this was something that cut across all geographies and could be measured globally. Outside North America, the organization was far from ready to have a conversation about nonbinary gender identities, which is defined by Helen Friedman, a US clinical psychologist, as an "umbrella term for anyone who doesn't identify exclusively as male or female."[4] Our work on global inclusion of transgender and other nonbinary employees evolved a few years later, when we introduced other identity dimensions like disabilities, LGBTQ, generations, and cultural origins.

My early experiences with my global colleagues taught me lessons that shaped the work I did, and I continued to learn as I went.

The first two lessons came early on in the global DEI work. In 2007 in Paris, I organized a meeting to provide insights on the status of women at Sodexo. Michel Landel personally invited the most senior Sodexo women from around the world to attend a half-day session. The objectives were to identify "enhancers" and "barriers" to the advancement of women and, based on the output from this session, educate senior management about women's perceptions of Sodexo's culture.

As expected, some attendees pointed to the masculine culture and stereotyping of women as problematic. However, many of the European women in attendance raised sharp critiques of the meeting and the process. They had managed to overcome these barriers and, therefore, they felt that a special session focusing on challenges encountered by women was counterproductive. Several of these senior women said they would rather not be part of a meeting comprised of only women and that they only participated because they received a personal invitation from the CEO.

Quite a few expressed that they were in their positions not because they were women, but because they'd earned the job. They were adamant that they did not want to be "called out" based on their gender, opining that gender was not a relevant factor. Ability was all that mattered. I was surprised and, frankly, caught off guard by the resistance to a women's-only body, as it was perfectly acceptable in a US context at that time.

Lesson one was that I could not assess situations with a limited, one-dimensional worldview.

Some DEI practitioners, like me, are involved in large-scale efforts to change people's behaviors and mindsets as well as retooling systems. And yet we frequently approach the work with our own limiting worldviews, which are antithetical to the very outcome that we are seeking.

DEI change agents who are steeped in the work in the US tend to approach global tasks with a mindset that is influenced by US civil rights history—a movement by African Americans and allies to end institutional race discrimination. This means US DEI practitioners might think the issues of race and color that they see in other countries need similar solutions to those employed back home. Meanwhile, some leaders in Europe may view diversity in the US through a multiculturalism lens and underestimate the potency of race dynamics. Change agents from Latin America might approach the work through a class lens. While each of these approaches is influenced by the context in their region, the singular worldview is limiting and antithetical to a true global perspective. Bringing our specific lens to the work, while teaching others to be unbiased, is a contradiction that has led to much frustration—both for the DEI practitioner and for those the efforts are intended to serve.

To continue with the story of the women's gathering, a French-speaking US American facilitator led the session and the non-US participants dismissed her and the topic as being "too American." It was clear that using a US facilitator, even though she was a French speaker and very good at her job, was not a smart strategy.

Taking what we had learned from the US journey where we had effectively leveraged Sodexo's clients, I thought that bringing testimonials from other companies, particularly clients, might help. But I compounded the "too American" critique by presenting testimonials from US organizations. I thought it would be okay as the executives who presented were not all US American, but that was not the case. Instead, my choice of client testimonials reinforced for Sodexo's mostly French male executive team that DEI was merely relevant for US companies and buttressed their perception that we were foisting a US priority on a French global company.

I still needed to learn not to impose US experiences on the rest of the world. This was my second lesson.

The resistance to US facilitators and even references to examples of what had worked in the US initially surprised me. I had assumed that the success in the US with DEI was something that would be embraced. However, I soon realized we could not export what had worked in the US. We had to resist coming across as US imperialists on a DEI mission or risk being dismissed.

Another lesson I learned early on was the central importance of relationships. I had to understand where the leaders were on their own DEI journeys. What were their starting points? This involved being a cultural listener in order to build trusting relationships and to effectively nudge them on their inclusion journey. The work was not easy as it was personal and struck an emotional chord for people, including me. I had to learn not to personalize the resistance but instead take in the information as an observer, synthesize it, and engage in a conversation. I slipped up many times and got triggered, learning the hard way to pace myself, while holding on to the conviction about my values and what I wanted to accomplish. Ultimately, I had to remember my own DEI journey and how my understanding of privilege had unfolded.

For the change to be lasting, every leader has to travel their own road in their own way. **The fourth lesson I learned is that leaders have to know that the wins are their wins and that they are the heroes of the story.** They have to feel that progress in DEI is their victory. As their guide, I needed to try to stay grounded and not seek affirmation or credit. Not easy!

If we were to build an inclusive global company, we had to do it in a way that resonated culturally, while catalyzing change. The solutions had to emerge locally, and I had to step back and understand the context and the power dynamics. I constantly encountered the tension between pushing for change and accepting cultural norms. To what extent should I accept that race might not be a relevant construct outside the US, for example, when there was evidence that discrimination and racism clearly existed?

The fifth lesson I learned was that I had to understand the cultural context while not shying away from the challenging issues.

Race and ethnicity are highly charged because of historical contexts and need to be framed appropriately. It is not easy to find the right balance between both understanding the context and pushing for change. I did realize that there is value, however, in being an outsider to the culture as it allowed me to offer a divergent perspective, enriching the discourse with cross-border exchanges. Outsiders can be catalysts for change, if they are well grounded in understanding the cultural context and lean on local allies to guide them.

The sixth lesson that I learned was that things take much longer when doing global work. Global work takes patience and progress is not linear. At meetings we had prolonged discussions at the expense of outcomes. I would come into those early, multiday, in-person, global meetings with a tightly scripted agenda. In the first two hours, I'd realize that we would not even get halfway through the agenda by the end of the meeting because I had not allowed enough time for input from all voices and for storytelling.

This experience was echoed by Wema Hoover, a US American former Global Head of Inclusion, Diversity, and Culture at Sanofi, a global French pharmaceutical company, when she said,

> When I joined Sanofi in Paris, I decided to come up with a 90-day plan, because that's what we do in the U.S. But I quickly realized that something was wrong, and I sought out feedback. I was told that I needed to just listen for 6 months. "Six months!" I thought. But I realized that you really have to allow for this dance with everyone pontificating and being able to have their opinions expressed and philosophizing. But that is also what is needed for people to feel a level of comfort and trust. It is about having the opportunity for voices to be heard, people being able to contribute and feeling that their opinion, their perspective was heard. And having the respect to allow that to happen, to give voice to all, which is very different from an Anglo-Saxon, American standpoint.[5]

These early lessons enabled me to become more self-aware and a better leader. They gave shape to the principles in this book that guide the important and challenging global DEI culture change work.

Global Diversity, Equity, and Inclusion Principles

Given the complex and dynamic nature of the work, there is no quick checklist or playbook for global DEI culture change. It's not enough to have the right initiatives, strategy, or best practices.

In my own journey and in my effort to figure out how to advance DEI culture change globally, I've come to recognize some principles that provide a through line in working in divergent cultures.

Each principle is a simple statement. In this book, I provide insights on each principle, drawing from my own experience, as well as anecdotes and hard-won successes of colleagues who have done this work in other multinational organizations. In this way, the simple statement of the principle can serve as a reminder or a kind of capsule that is imbued with the fullness of this gathered experience.

These principles are simple, yet disruptive. They are not intended to provide standards, or plug-and-play templates based on what has worked in the US. In fact, this has been one of the foundational mistakes in global DEI work. What makes them powerful and useful is they can be applied with sensitivity to any culture. The significance of a principles-based approach is that it empowers global leaders to develop their own solutions organically, rather than mimicking any one country's experience. The principles show up differently in disparate global contexts. The ability to both recognize how they are expressed and translate them appropriately in the cultural context requires us to draw on multiple cultural frameworks.

The chapters of this book are organized around these principles for advancing DEI. Although they are numbered for the purposes of this book, the principles are not discrete, sequential, or linear. Instead, they are iterative and work in concert with each other as a holistic ecosystem (see Figure 1).

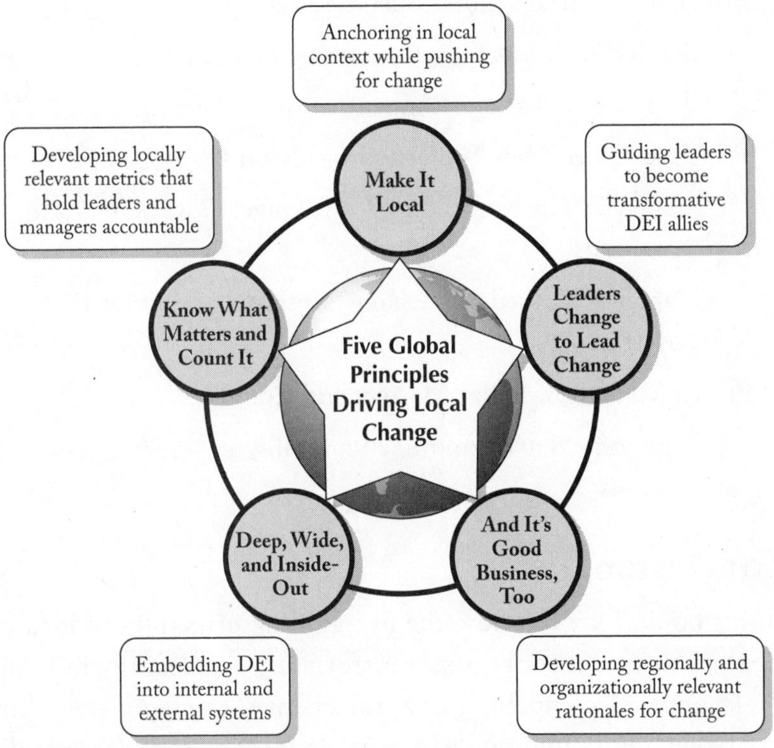

Figure 1: Global Diversity, Equity, and Inclusion Principles

The chapters devoted to each principle delve deeper into an understanding of that principle in different geographic contexts and discuss how the principle is applied. Here is a brief outline:

Principle 1: Make It Local

Chapter 1: Localizing a Global Strategy

Chapter 2: Understanding Race and Ethnicity

Principle 2: Leaders Change to Lead Change

Chapter 3: Transformational Leadership across Cultures

Chapter 4: Dealing with Resistance

Principle 3: And It's Good Business, Too

Chapter 5: Compelling Rationales for Change

Chapter 6: Creating Competitive Advantage through DEI

Principle 4: Go Deep, Wide, and Inside-Out

Chapter 7: The Scaffolding for Change: Governance and Champions

Chapter 8: Embedding Change: Internal and External Ecosystems

Principle 5: Know What Matters and Count It

Chapter 9: Metrics and Accountability

Conclusion

In this book, I lay out how the five guiding principles of localizing the strategy, encouraging transformative leadership, building a relevant and compelling case for change, engaging the entire ecosystem, and holding leaders accountable can successfully guide global change efforts. It's important to note, however, that these principles are not simply academic ideas or abstract, untested strategies. They arise from and through my own journey, my story.

Yes, this professional journey could be seen as one going from class action to best in class (recognizing that *best* is always a moving target). That said, the professional journey would not be possible without the personal one. At its heart, this work is about people. And it will change you.

Principle

1

MAKE IT LOCAL

FOR GLOBAL DEI CULTURE CHANGE TO BE EFFECTIVE and sustainable, it must be anchored in an understanding of local contexts. This principle suggests that any global framework for DEI change must be rooted in local particulars, informed by the history, culture, language, and laws of each place.

Chapter 1, "Localizing a Global Strategy," suggests that diversity change is more likely to succeed when an overarching global strategy is adapted to local dynamics. In order to do this, we must consider how identity is defined, expressed, and perceived in different parts of the world. We must be aware of power structures and identify the dominant and subordinate groups in each setting. Understanding how these aspects of diversity are approached in the local context is the first step in finding strategies to advance underrepresented groups in different circumstances. Awareness of our own role—sometimes as that of an outsider to a particular context—can help us discern when and how to challenge resistance and to serve as a catalyst for change. The chapter provides examples from a variety of organizations that have successfully bridged this tension.

Chapter 2, "Understanding Race and Ethnicity," focuses on racial identity and racism globally. Race can be one of the most difficult identity dimensions to address in varying contexts. There is something both universal and extremely specific about it. While discrimination based on skin color clearly exists in many parts of the world, race and racism are fluid and shaped by culture and history. Even the way that demographics are measured varies across contexts making global target setting challenging. If we expect racism to be expressed in a manner we are familiar with, we are likely to miss important entry points. When we understand how racism plays out locally, we are better equipped to push for change.

1

LOCALIZING A GLOBAL CHANGE STRATEGY

Confined by the walls of the valley,
the river runs freely, finding its own course.

—RAY BRIGGS, *The Tao of Relationships*

EVERY COUNTRY HAS ITS OWN LEGACY OF HURT. Every place has its history of exclusion, its discrimination, its web of attitudes and systems that fuel and justify marginalization. Every country has dominant and subordinate groups and unhealthy power structures. As I began the work of rolling out Sodexo's DEI initiatives globally, I learned that one of my most important tasks was uncovering and seeking to understand those legacies.

Identity—the way it shows up and even the ways we define it—can differ enormously from place to place. I learned that I needed to strike a balance between rolling out a global initiative with a universal vision while at the same time allowing enough flexibility for that vision to be contextualized and take root locally. By doing this, we were able to open space for effective insider-outsider partnerships—allowing outsiders like me and other leaders to play the role of catalyst, while relying on insider change agents and the local ecosystem to determine the best pressure points and rhythm for change.

To make organizations more diverse, inclusive, and equitable, we need to be willing to disrupt the status quo. Making our work local does not mean backing away from the difficult challenges, but it does require that we develop a global mindset, listen to local diversity champions, and constantly fine-tune our own self-awareness and intellectual curiosity. If we do those things, we will be better positioned to grasp the dynamics of a complex interconnected world and find ways to ensure that our efforts resonate locally and contribute to lasting change.

Power Dynamics

Natasha Winkler-Titus, President of the Society for Industrial and Organizational Psychology in South Africa, told me of an international mining company that set up mining operations in South Africa.[1] They invested billions, negotiated with the local chief to operate in the area, and completed the first two phases of development. But they were forced to halt the project due to local protests about the placement of the mine, corruption by the chief, and the lack of economic and job opportunities trickling down to the community. Although they had done thorough research and mapping of natural resources, what they hadn't realized was that the local chief was not acting in the best interests of the community. Without taking the time to listen to a broad variety of voices, they stumbled into a trap of reinforcing harmful power inequities. Perhaps they believed they were respecting local customs by negotiating with the chief and did not probe further to get more well-rounded advice about how best to navigate the crosscurrents and history of the place. At its essence, the company's approach was top-down: it imposed its overarching objective without taking time to unpack the local dynamics. Ultimately, the mining company tried to be local but failed because its attempt was too superficial.

For me, this story epitomizes the dilemma of localizing a global change strategy. How do we understand and respect local values and simultaneously push for change? To what extent do we adapt to each context? If our initiatives are purely locally driven, might that not perpetuate the unhealthy power dynamics that already exist, as it did in the mining example in South Africa? Is it better then to enact a more universal, centralized approach to inclusion change efforts? So, if an organization comes with a top-down DEI agenda—in the same way the mining company started without true local buy-in—don't we risk those initiatives being at best ineffective, and at worst sabotaged? And what happens when a global organization's values come into conflict with local ways of doing things, or even with local laws?

A Transversal Approach to Global Diversity Management

Mustafa F. Özbilgin, a Turkish-born British sociologist and Professor of Organizational Behavior at Brunel Business School in London, talks about three different global diversity management approaches. The first is a universal approach that rolls out a centralized top-down policy across varying countries and contexts. The second is a local approach that is designed in-country and tailored to a specific context. The third is a blend of the two. Özbilgin calls this a transversal approach in which there is a global framework that shapes and guides the work, along with the flexibility and autonomy to adapt it locally.[2]

A Local, Universal, or Transversal Approach?

I found the transversal approach was most suited to implementing a successful global change initiative. Although a universal approach seeks to save time and money by using commonly developed tools and strategies, organizations can struggle to get their initiatives embedded and embraced locally. For example, a global food and package delivery company encountered challenges when the company's US-headquartered lesbian, gay, bisexual, transgender, and queer (LGBTQ) employee resource group (ERG) asked that all employees around the globe be given a Pride rainbow badge to display in celebration and support of LGBTQ staff.[3] This seemed like a powerful way to make allies visible and to create safety zones for employees who may not be open at work about their sexuality. But employees in Egypt balked. Same-sex relationships were illegal there. LGBTQ employees had learned to be discreet for their safety. No one wanted to carry the burden of a visible label that might endanger them.

In contrast, Subarna Malakar told me that when he led global DEI at Ahold Delhaize, they had a very local DEI strategy, in keeping with their overall segmented business model with twenty-two distinct local brands.[4] Ahold Delhaize, a Dutch company, is one of the largest food retail groups with supermarkets and convenience stores that have local brand recognition—such as Albert Heijn in Europe, and Giant, Stop & Shop, and Food Lion in the US. Subarna said that to appeal to local consumers, the shops hired people who live within a five-mile radius. They didn't have global hiring targets; rather, needs were determined with a view toward reflecting the communities they serve. The idea was that if the staff reflects the community, the shop would cater better to its customers. This meant that, for example, in a heavily Muslim neighborhood of Amsterdam, most employees were Muslim, and the shops sold halal food that appealed to the community.

This type of local approach is very appealing, but implementation can be inconsistent without broader accountability measures in place. If it is not a part of an overall global strategy, it may not benefit from tried-and-true interventions nor be enriched and stretched by cross-regional exchanges, best practice sharing, and networks.

A transversal approach customizes strategies to local environments while ensuring a consistent global brand and broader accountability. It is a delicate balancing act between not reinventing the wheel and, at the same time, avoiding the imposition of cookie-cutter tactics that risk replicating the very dynamics of cultural imperialism that DEI seeks to challenge. Imposing aspects of a dominant culture onto another less-powerful community is an easy trap to fall into.[5] It takes more time and up-front investment, but ultimately a transversal approach benefits from being informed by best practices without imposing them and thus has the greatest potential for lasting success.

The Transversal Approach in Action: Barilla

A transversal approach provides a frame, but also ensures that any global DEI process is consultative. Barilla Group is an Italian family-owned food company with a presence in over one hundred countries. In 2013, Guido Barilla, the chairman, made a homophobic comment on an Italian station, Radio 24. He said, "I would never do a commercial with a homosexual family, not for lack of respect, but because we don't agree with them."[6] The comments sparked outrage as people accused Barilla of homophobia and called for a worldwide boycott. Harvard University in the US pulled the pasta from its dining halls and celebrities pledged to shun the brand. This was a wake-up call for the company, and it began on a long journey to repair the damage and build a more inclusive culture.

Part of their response—and I will be exploring their approach in more detail later in the book—included establishing internal employee resource groups that were organized around particular identity groups. These were first launched in the US with great success, and so Barilla decided to replicate the approach in Italy, and then worldwide. "When we wanted to expand our ERGs outside the US, we learned very quickly that you cannot cut and paste," Kristen Anderson, Barilla's Global Chief Diversity Officer, told me.[7] When over a hundred employees came to a high-profile launch event for an LGBTQ ERG at Barilla's headquarters in Parma, the levels of enthusiasm and support made Kristen expect a large core group to sign up to take the new ERG forward. But by the end of the event, only twelve people had registered.

"And we said, uh oh, we have a problem," Kristen remembers. "When we interviewed employees, we discovered that it was not a problem about not wanting to work on LGBTQ inclusion and be an ally. It was more not knowing what ERGs are. There was cultural insensitivity on my part in not understanding that although in America, we're very comfortable in this idea of forming community to make some change, in other cultures, it's something new. And we took a step back and basically spent a lot of time educating employees about ERGs: the benefit for you as an employee and the benefit for the company."

Kristen and her team provided clear guidelines and governance structures; but they also ensured that there was freedom to decide the focus and the approach in each context. In fact, while in the US they had had success in developing ERGs along singular dimensions of diversity—such as LGBTQ, Black, or Latino/a inclusion—in some of Barilla's smaller branches, they decided to form hybrid ERGs that address multiple identities, tackle issues relevant to the region, or rotate areas of focus.

For example, an ERG named *Respeito* (Respect in Portuguese) in Barilla's operation in Brazil focused one year on LGBTQ inclusion and the next year on race and ethnicity. In spite of the fact that Afro-Brazilians make up the majority of the population, it is surprisingly rare to find race addressed directly and substantively by companies in Brazil. This fluid focus of the ERGs offered an entry point into some difficult arenas in Brazil and elsewhere. In Canada, *Inclusivo* (Inclusive in Italian) rotated its focus on different cultures that represent the main immigrants into Canada. And Greece's *Armonia* (Harmony in Italian) concentrated on integrating refugees, particularly pertinent given the surge in refugees coming into Greece at that time. Russia's ERG focused on LGBTQ one year and then looked at breaking down hierarchical divisions—encouraging managers to work for a day on the factory line and factory workers to come to the office.

Russia's example is a reminder that our DEI initiatives can miss important dimensions and that staying open to local adaption can go a long way in correcting that. In "every major economy in the world," according to Paul Ingram, social-class origin has a major impact on career progression, but it is taboo in some cultures (such as the US) and therefore rarely makes its way explicitly onto DEI change agendas.[8] But some societies, such as the UK and some parts of Asia and Latin America, are much franker about class divides. Flexible ERGs leave room for the very typology of our DEI work to be stretched and strengthened.

Kristen's outsider perspective allowed her to share and even push for a strategy she believed would work well. Combining her outsider status with a flexible approach that listened to, enabled, and empowered insider diversity champions resulted in some surprising and even radical initiatives. It allowed local changemakers to judge the pulse and rhythm of what transformation might be possible, with a clear platform and firm support from Barilla's leadership.

Through its ERGs, Barilla introduced a way to address identity, but through collaboration with local staff, they discovered this new flexible and multiple dimensional approach. The overall impact of the ERGs has been extremely positive for Barilla. *Voce*, the LGBTQ ERG in Italy, now has over 250 members. The diversity and inclusion scores in their biannual employee engagement survey have gone up. Barilla's leadership credits the ERGs as playing a key role in creating a more inclusive organizational culture.

In recognition of their global progress in DEI, Barilla received the prestigious 2021 Catalyst Award for initiatives that have elevated inclusion.

For a transversal approach to be effective, it's critical to

- take the time to understand how identity is expressed in each location,
- listen to local change agents,
- build collaboration between those change agents and the organization's outside influencers,
- be willing to disrupt the status quo when necessary, and
- remember the enablers and obstacles in the larger ecosystem.

Identity in Different Contexts

The type of reluctance Barilla encountered in Italy to form an ERG can be influenced by culture and history. Some societies are organized around group identities and therefore might be very comfortable with identity-based ERGs. To others, just simply naming, much less gathering around, group identity can be threatening.

My colleague Laura Shipler Chico told me about her time working within the Myanmar democracy movement. She noticed that many people introduced themselves by their ethnic organizational affiliation before even offering their personal name. In 2006, just twelve years after the Rwandan genocide, she organized a visit from two Rwandan women peacebuilders to the Thai-Myanmar border to meet with women activists in the Myanmar democracy movement. The Rwandans—one of whom had lost most of her family in the genocide and the other whose husband was imprisoned, accused of committing acts of genocide—were horrified as they realized how Myanmar society was organized around ethnic groups. In Rwanda it is now taboo to refer to someone as Hutu or Tutsi and the Rwandan guests warned their hosts that what they were hearing could be a precursor to genocide in Myanmar.

Identity Is Fluid

Barilla's hybrid approach to ERGs also allowed for the intersectional nature of identities. Identity is "relational and socially constructed, not innate and fixed," and it can shift depending on the situation.[9] I might identify as Asian American in the United States. In India I'm seen as a US American and I see myself that same way. But as soon as I go to France, I am considered Indian—until, that is, I start talking about diversity, and then I am suddenly viewed as a US American again! The truth is, I am all those things and more. Identity is multifaceted—and it responds to the external ecosystem of how others perceive you. Mary-Francis Winters and Andrés T. Tapia, two thought leaders in DEI, suggest that DEI work has what they call a "fundamental genetic flaw," a "one-dimensional view of difference."[10] This is true in the United States, and it is particularly important to remember when working globally, where a visible identity, such as gender or race, is often closely intertwined with language, region, religion, caste, class, or color.

Identity Is Linked with Power

In every society, we will find dominant and subordinate groups based on identity. Sometimes these power systems travel with people across borders.

In June of 2020, a discrimination lawsuit—the first of its kind—was filed against Cisco in Silicon Valley. Two former managers, both upper-caste Indians, were accused of discriminating against a Dalit (lower-caste) employee. In the social stratification system that divides Hindus into rigid hierarchical groups, Brahmins are the highest caste and Dalits are considered "untouchables." After the suit was announced, Equality Labs, an advocacy group for Dalit rights, reportedly received over 250 similar complaints from Dalit tech workers in the span of three weeks from Facebook, Google, Microsoft, IBM, Amazon, and more.[11]

While some power dynamics remain fixed as they cross borders, a change in context can also shift identity power relationships. When a colleague of mine travelled to Ghana many years ago to volunteer for a Habitat for Humanity project, she found that her Whiteness trumped her womanness; she was allowed to work with the men, doing the easier job of bricklaying rather than the grueling women's task of carrying water from the stream to the building site. An African American from the US travelling to Europe might be treated poorly out on the street, but in the boardroom, they could be viewed as an instrument of US cultural imperialism, with all its associated privilege and power, and in stark contrast to their marginalized position back home. This means that we may unknowingly carry privilege or disadvantage into a new cultural context, and that can impact our access to decision makers, the receptivity to our messages, and the candor with which local change agents might be willing to share their insights. Doing global DEI work requires that we understand not only the local dynamics, but also how we ourselves are perceived as we cross borders. Those perceptions shape how we are heard and will impact how we can best use ourselves as instruments for change.

Outsider-Insider Collaboration

One of the benefits of the transversal approach is that it allows outside influencers to serve as catalysts for change while at the same time empowering local change agents to ensure that the work is relevant and has the best chance for success.

Tackling Race in Germany

In 2017 Lawrencia Quarshie moved from Ghana to Ingelheim, Germany, to work for Boehringer Ingelheim (BI), the German pharmaceutical company.[12] She was part of the Afrika Kommt! program launched by nineteen leading German companies in 2008. The program brings to Germany future managers from Africa and gives them the experience of working at German companies.

Arriving in the small town of Ingelheim, Lawrencia was acutely aware of being an outsider because of the color of her skin. People would stare at her. She remembers one woman, who upon seeing her BI badge said, "'You should know my friend. She works in the kitchen [at Boehringer Ingelheim.]' It gradually dawned on me that this lady actually thought that I worked in the kitchen," Lawrencia told me. "And when I told her that I didn't, she was visibly shocked and kept staring at me afterward for a long time." Despite her visibility in a mostly White society, Lawrencia felt that race was not acknowledged or discussed explicitly, even as she often felt implicitly judged. "I was tired of self-editing all the time," Lawrencia told me, "of having to over-justify because everything from Africa is seen as substandard."

Given her experiences, she decided to launch the African Heritage ERG at Boehringer Ingelheim. She wanted to create a safe space for others like her to share experiences and to support each other. At her invitation, about thirty BI employees of African descent began meeting informally every other week in the cafeteria. They came not only from all over Africa, but from all over the world including places like the US and the UK. Lawrencia's face lit up as she told me about the energy and laughter at those lunches and how they shared information on hairdressers and supported each other through challenges, swapping stories of how they felt in the aftermath of the killing of George Floyd in the US in 2020.

Advocating for Women's Rights in Saudi Arabia

Outsiders often have the freedom to raise issues that are difficult to broach from the inside. They can really make a positive difference, but they need to balance their enthusiasm with a careful consideration of where and how to enter the conversation. Outside influence works best when it empowers and amplifies the work of local diversity champions within the organization and in the society at large. When my colleague Alain Morize arrived in Saudi Arabia in 2011 to head up Sodexo's Energy and Resources work there, he was conflicted. Alain is originally from France but is truly a global citizen—he has lived in Boston, Los Angeles, Puerto Rico, Angola, Indonesia, and even on a ship that travelled around New Caledonia in the Pacific. "I was a guest in the country," Alain told me as he remembered his time in Saudi Arabia, "so not there to change or judge. But I was not comfortable with what I experienced with women, as it did not align with my values or Sodexo's values."[13]

Saudi Arabia is ranked 146 out of 153 countries in the World Economic Forum's 2020 Global Gender Gap report.[14] For years, Saudi women were considered legal minors and subject to a far-reaching male guardianship system that required permission to travel, work, and more.[15] Alain happened to move to Saudi Arabia during a time of great change. In 2011, a royal decree allowed women to vote in the 2015 elections.[16] By 2016, a mass feminist movement was campaigning for the end of the male guardianship system.[17] Although feminist activists have been arrested and harassed, they also succeeded in earning women the right to drive (2017), the possibility of winning custody of their children after divorce (2018), and the right to travel abroad alone (2019).[18] Labor laws began to slowly shift, incrementally allowing women to work in some private-sector jobs.[19]

As Alain noticed things opening, he made a move to hire more Saudi women. He began reaching out—and there was no lack of qualified women. Saudi women have a high education level, and a 95.3 percent literacy rate.[20] He found that many women were eager to advance their careers and to work hard. According to Sharia law, they had to work in a separate room with the door closed. They were not to be seen by male colleagues, and they had to communicate via an intercom. Men could not enter the space where they were working without announcing themselves, and if women were to stray from that area—say for a work meeting—they needed a male Muslim chaperone.

Viewed through a Western feminist lens, these working conditions would be absolutely unacceptable. Outside change agents using a universal approach might be tempted to draw the line and insist that women be integrated fully into the workplace, but setting such a top-down ultimatum in this context would be counterproductive. With those ultimatums in place, women would not have been able to work for Sodexo at all. Instead, now that he had increased the number of women on staff, Alain used his outsider status carefully, opting for slowly stretching and disrupting the status quo from within, taking care not to impose his own views.

At first the women were slow to speak up, but eventually, as they gained their footing and saw they had leadership support, they began to express themselves. They suggested leaving the door open so they could interact with male colleagues more easily and feel part of a larger team. Soon it became clear that the women would occasionally need to meet with male colleagues. But conservative men on staff pushed back; they felt it was not acceptable for women to have work meetings with men without a Saudi or Muslim man to accompany them.

Alain put the dilemma back to these men, saying, "Okay, we have a business; they have to talk to people, how do you want to resolve this? You can accompany them to every meeting if you want, but if that is not realistic, you come up with a solution." Eventually these conservative men proposed that women could meet with men, as long as they were sitting on different sides of the desk and the door was open.

Alain's approach disrupted the status quo—as an outsider he had the freedom to push for increased hiring of women—and then he invited the insiders, those with local knowledge, even those most resistant, to propose fundamental changes to women's career opportunities.

Be Disruptive—It's Okay

In Saudi Arabia, Alain was able to work within the laws and still push for change, but sometimes the local context is extremely hostile. In 2019, homosexual activity was still illegal in seventy countries, including thirteen in which it was punishable by death.[21] This means that initiatives promoting the rights of LGBTQ employees can be extremely dangerous for those employees and can sometimes risk organizations' right to operate in a particular context. Sylvia Ann Hewlett and Kenji Yoshino outlined three models of engagement used by organizations in the face of these restrictions.[22] The first they called the "When in Rome" model—organizations keep their heads down and adhere to the laws.

The second is the "Embassy" model in which companies extend policies and protections to their own employees but do not try to change the society. In Singapore, for example, Aviva—a British insurance company with a presence in sixteen countries—has made sure that its employees with same-sex partners have equal benefits, but when I spoke with Anuradha Purbey, Aviva's People Director for Europe and Asia, she was quick to recognize the limits of this approach. "This is not challenging your belief system," she said of the policy's impact on employees' awareness, "but it is just to make sure that we are aligned with how we show up at the workplace. That's all."[23]

Barclays, a British bank, has tried to follow Hewlett and Yoshino's third "Advocate" model, which seeks to influence the society and laws. Along with Google and several other multinational companies,

Barclays was one of the first corporate sponsors of Singapore's Pink Dot festival, celebrating the local LGBTQ community. These *outsider* companies used their status, influence, and money to support local *insider* change agents who were trying to carve out a safe space within their country. By the time the government banned foreign organizations from sponsoring Pink Dot in 2017, enough momentum had built up that over one hundred local companies came together and were able to keep it going.

In Uganda, Barclays chose a less public approach while still trying to influence country policy. In 2012 Ugandan lawmakers proposed a bill that, if passed, would make homosexuality punishable by death. Barclays had major operations in Uganda and was known for its pro-LGBTQ stance around the world. However, a provision of this new legislation said any company proven to be promoting an LGBTQ agenda could lose its business license. The legislation sparked global outrage. Employees signed a public petition asking Barclays what they were doing to address the situation in Uganda. Barclays quickly issued a statement that tried to navigate the delicate balance between maintaining its business, influence, and connections in Uganda and its support for LGBTQ rights worldwide.

At the time, Mark McLane was Managing Director, Head of Global Diversity and Inclusion, based in Barclays' home office. He remembers that it was an extremely sensitive situation. At one point, Barclays' staff had to stop all email communication about the bill with colleagues inside Uganda for fear of the repercussions on local staff should the bill pass. Barclays' employee networks elsewhere were concerned, and Mark realized that it was as important to communicate clearly with Barclays employees globally as it was to find a way to influence things in Uganda. This was made more difficult because the details of Barclays' lobbying efforts were not necessarily visible to the larger world, and those coming at the issue with a fixed, justice-oriented human rights mindset were frustrated with Barclays' stance.[24]

This is a common dynamic in which a social justice approach can come into conflict with a culturally or locally driven approach, but it doesn't have to be either-or. In fact, DEI embodies both of these values like no other area of work. International organizations can support local change agents and find safe and effective ways to be disruptive. Navigating this complicated terrain, however, can be very tricky, especially when there are competing stakeholders and high levels of risk to employees or to the business. In Uganda, Barclays continued to work quietly behind the scenes. Ultimately, the bill was passed, substituting life imprisonment for the death penalty, but it resulted in international boycotts and was eventually overturned by the constitutional court, although homosexuality remains illegal in Uganda.[25]

Conclusion

The work of localizing need not be too daunting. I found that there are two key ingredients to success. The first is to **ask questions and listen to local change agents:**

- Who are the dominant and subordinate groups and what is their history?
- Who are the local change agents and what are their goals and strategies?
- What are the specific obstacles to inclusion?

The answers to these key questions will lead us to finding the best entry points and approach. And they will allow us to tailor solutions to the specific obstacles in each context.

Every society has people working toward greater inclusion from within, whether they call themselves change agents or not. Find those people—those with local knowledge who you trust to talk to you candidly and help you understand what is going on. Effective global change efforts build on the knowledge and energy of those people, supporting and enabling them to broaden their sphere of influence.

The second tactic, as Wema Hoover of Sanofi said so well, is to **find the "freedom within the frame."** A clear global vision and framework provides the necessary structure for implementation and accountability, but it should never be rigid. Creativity, flexibility, and local ownership are essential elements of any successful DEI initiative.

While a transversal approach allows us to adapt our strategic DEI efforts to the local context, it takes more upfront investment and more time. It relies on the messy work of relationship building between outsiders and insiders. It requires a nuanced understanding that power dynamics and the way people construct their sense of identity shift according to context and the unique cultural, religious, historical, and legal setting.

Making our DEI work local is essential if it is to take root and grow. The next chapter will zoom in on race and ethnicity. This dimension of diversity is one for which a local understanding combined with a global commitment is key if we are ever going to succeed in creating organizations that actively oppose discrimination based on race. When grappling with race and ethnicity in various parts of the world, listening and flexibility are indispensable tools—especially because these two aspects of identity can be so rife with hidden undercurrents, sharp and historic pain, and political implications.

2

UNDERSTANDING RACE AND ETHNICITY

What people look like, or, rather, the race they have been assigned or perceived to belong to, is the visible cue to their caste. It is the historic flash card to the public of how they are to be treated, where they are expected to live, what kinds of positions they are expected to hold, whether they belong in this section of town or that seat in the boardroom . . . whether they may be shot by authorities with impunity.

—ISABEL WILKERSON, *Caste: The Origins of Our Discontent*

I FOUND RACE TO BE THE MOST DIFFICULT DIMENSION of diversity to tackle when we started to roll out our DEI initiatives globally. Race—this socially constructed notion that we can categorize human beings based on visible physical differences[1]—is extremely sensitive, politically charged, and often talked about in code or not at all. If we are new to a country, we need to find local allies who can help us understand these nuances.

In France, Brazil, and elsewhere, I was told, "We don't have racism here. That is a US American thing." And yet, I could see that management and leadership in these countries were almost exclusively

White. Discrimination based on skin color clearly existed. Something about it was both universal and extremely specific. Racial identity and racism are fluid, shaping themselves to each country's contours of history and culture. Even the way demographics are measured or not measured varies greatly, making it more difficult to set global targets or evaluate impact. This means we cannot use a cookie-cutter approach to dismantling racism. Each initiative needs to take into consideration the unique dynamics of each context including how race is tracked, expressed, and defined.

The only way I saw to begin to chip away at this dimension in Europe was through refugee employment programs that aimed to provide opportunities but also to expand empathy and understanding in the workplace. This provided an entry point to the discussion on race because refugees frequently belong to visibly nondominant groups. I'm proud of that work, but it is one of my greatest regrets that we didn't make further headway in our antiracism work around the globe while I was at Sodexo.

As I did the research for this book, I discovered that I was not alone. DEI professionals all over the world have felt stymied about how best to address race-related bias in their companies, and very little has been done. There are few global examples of best practices to look to and it can be difficult to know how to start this sensitive and demanding work. This chapter helps us begin on this journey—not with answers, but with the questions we should be asking of local change agents and of ourselves. When we understand how racism may play out in a particular place, we are better equipped to challenge the status quo and to cope with the resistance we will inevitably encounter.

The Birth of a Global Movement

When George Floyd was murdered by a police officer kneeling on his neck for nine minutes in 2020, protests exploded not only throughout the US, but also around the world in Australia, Brazil, Canada, France, Germany, Italy, Japan, South Korea, Turkey, the United Kingdom, Senegal, and more.

In Australia, New Zealand, and Canada, Aboriginal and Indigenous people suffer brutality routinely at the hands of the police.[2] In Brazil, the reaction to George Floyd's death was a call to action—killings by police of Afro-Brazilians were so commonplace as to have almost become normalized.[3] In France, George Floyd's murder touched a nerve. It reminded people of the 2016 death of twenty-four-year-old Malian-French Adama Traoré while in police custody, triggering fresh demonstrations in 2020 throughout France from Marseilles and Lyons to smaller cities like Dieppe and Avignon.[4] In Berlin, Black Lives Matter (BLM) organizers planned for 1,500 people to show up, but instead an estimated 15,000 protested in the city center.[5] Aida Sock, a Senegalese singer and artist involved in a small protest in Senegal, said, "It was not just about Black Americans, it was about Black people, it was about Africans, it was about anybody . . . going through oppression."[6]

This global movement triggered new responses in companies. It opened up space that was previously closed, offering a platform from which to grow organizational transformation when it comes to race. But while there is clearly an experience that connects us, one of the most difficult things about addressing race globally is its specificity to its context.

Race: A Shifting Social Construct

Racism is commonly defined as the potent mixture of racial prejudice combined with power—whether that power be personal or systemic. While we certainly see similarities in how racism is expressed—for example, through police brutality—if we expect racism in other countries to be a mirror image of the context we know, we are likely to miss important entry points and misunderstand the resistance we encounter.

Historical Legacies

Racism in the Americas region is steeped in its history of slavery, but not all countries share that past. Europe's long history of racism is expressed through its colonial legacy and its immigration policies. The trauma of World War II continues to shape how European countries approach race; they have seen what happens when extreme bigotry is allowed free reign.

We often think of the minority as being the disenfranchised group, but in Brazil, the *preto* (Black) and *pardo* (mixed) population combined is well over 50 percent, and they still experience discrimination. In Africa and Asia, often the population is primarily one race, but divisions along ethnic lines are deeply entrenched. Exacerbating these divisions, the colonial strategy of divide and rule means that in many contexts, it is in fact the minority population that holds the higher positions in government and industry and has had access to better education. Sometimes diversity is about handing power over to local nationals rather than perpetuating an unequal global north/south dynamic by populating all senior leadership roles with Western expats.

Migration Patterns

Migration patterns and regional conflicts play a role in determining the groups who are racialized. In Germany, Turks have experienced discrimination for decades—so much so that the first ERG to launch within German car manufacturer Daimler AG (commonly referred to as Mercedes Benz) was a Turkish network called Daimler Türk Treff. A Mexican executive I spoke to told me that when he moved to Germany on an assignment, he often preempted any possible judgments about his heritage by saying, "I speak Spanish," as part of most introductions.

In Qatar, migrant workers from Nepal, Bangladesh, and India make up large swaths of the labor force and they, along with workers from East and Central Africa, are subjected to dangerous working conditions, withholding of pay, racial profiling by police, and more. A 2020 UN Special Report referred to the situation in Qatar as "a *de facto* caste system based on national origin."[7] Latin America has a history of classifying people based on skin color, rather than racial heritage. This comes from sustained state *blanqueamiento* policies that promoted European immigration and mixing to "whiten" the population.[8] In China, the dominant Han race represents 92 percent of the population, but with fifty-five ethnic groups, there can be tensions between regions and language groups, as well as distrust of "outsiders."[9] The tension between Han and Uighurs, a mostly Muslim minority ethnic group, has been brewing for decades, and has only recently come to international attention as China faces growing scrutiny over its treatment of Uighurs.

Intersectional Identities

One of the greatest challenges in developing a cohesive global approach to counter racism is that race is often tangled up with many other identities as well—ethnicity, religion, language, region, class, and caste. While in the US, race and racism have been a driving social force, in many other regions, race is one of several identities that divide and may play a less prominent role. This means that if a diversity initiative were to focus exclusively on race, along with the other conventional dimensions of diversity such as gender, LGBTQ, and so on, it might miss entirely that Roma are the largest ethnic minority in Europe and among the most disadvantaged.[10] It might miss discrimination against the lowest caste and religious minorities in India or the ethnic undertones that are instrumentalized in Kenyan politics.

Visual Cues

Colorism—"prejudice based on skin tone, usually with a marked preference for lighter-skinned people"[11]—is rampant throughout the world and is often a thread running through this multilayered tapestry. From Nigeria to Pakistan, men and women alike report discrimination in their careers, marriages, and more due to skin color.[12] The skin lightening cosmetic industry reached US $4.8 billion in 2017 and is growing.[13] Colorism, like race, is a result of imported cultural imperialism, but it is also very local. In many places, it may not be so much a question of race, but rather class or caste. Fair skin indicates that you have not had to work under the sun, and therefore implies wealth, just as a tan on White people in the United States can subconsciously signify that you have the money and leisure time to travel to a sunny holiday spot. The historical roots may be hidden now under a commercially perpetuated standard of beauty, but they have played a part in shaping that aesthetic.

We also tend to forget to treat Whiteness as a race as much as any other. Even though I work in this field, and I, myself, am not White, I catch myself normalizing Whiteness and falling into the trap of not racializing Whites in the same way that I call it out in other groups. This is so deeply ingrained into our psyches that we must constantly be interrogating our own assumptions and how we are framing our questions.

Crossing Borders

Our racial identity, like other identities, can shift depending on where we are in the world. A high-caste Indian can find herself at the bottom of the hierarchy in Singapore where Indians are second-class citizens. A Latin American who considered himself White can suddenly be labeled a "person of color" when he moves to the United States and is identified as Hispanic.

And just because people may look the same, it does not mean they have the same experience of race. When Lawrencia Quarshie convened the African Heritage ERG at Boehringer Ingelheim in Germany, she and its other members found many commonalities among them. But Lawrencia was also struck by the differences in their experiences. "For the colleagues from the US, I personally realized that they found themselves in this place where they take their identity—their Black identity—as something sacred . . . Those who come from Ghana, Nigeria, or from Senegal—our experiences were completely different . . . I am Ghanian, I am African. Black is not something that I associate myself with because it wasn't an issue until I stepped out of my country . . . [In Ghana] your skin is not on trial wherever you go."[14]

In my conversation with Mark McLane, he told me a story from his time as Managing Director, Head of Global Diversity and Inclusion at Barclays that perfectly illustrates how perceptions of race shift as we move across borders.[15] Barclays had hired actors in London to help conduct an unconscious bias training. When one of the actors travelled to South Africa to help Barclays with training there, she was identified not as Black (as she was in the UK), but as colored due to her fair skin and mixed-race heritage. This came as a shock to her, and Mark remembers that she said to him, "I wasn't enough in London. I'm too much in South Africa. I have never identified as anything other than Black and I'm now in a country saying you're not Black."

Power: Dominant and Nondominant Groups

At its heart, DEI work addresses historical inequities. To do that, we must understand the dominant and subordinate groups in each context.

Redressing Past Wrongs: Australia

When I worked at Sodexo, my colleagues in Australia developed a very specific range of strategies tailored to address racism against

Aboriginal and Torres Strait Islander people, who make up 3.3 percent of the population. Australia has a brutal history of forced removals, interrupted education, and racist barriers to Aboriginal employment. Over a sixty-year period, from 1910 to 1970, an estimated 100,000 mixed-race children were kidnapped from their families to be raised as White, with many put in institutions plagued by widespread abuse.[16]

Sodexo had a number of sites on traditional lands belonging to local Aboriginal and Torres Strait Islander peoples, and as such had land use agreements in place to ensure that the community benefited from Sodexo's presence. So, Sodexo had a strong incentive to develop excellent working relationships and truly contribute to the local community in which they found themselves. My colleagues began by hiring a national Indigenous team, including two full-time Indigenous Recruitment Specialists. One of these specialists, Darryl Rae, explained some of the challenges they faced: "We didn't become citizens of our own country until 1967," he said. "A lot of people don't have birth certificates, so therefore no passports or driving licenses. Then there were people who were taken away from their birth parents. That creates mistrust. People worry that if they register their baby, the government will come and take their baby away, so they don't have the paperwork."[17] To combat this, Darryl and his colleagues worked with human resources to build their understanding of the obstacles. They also grew relationships with elders, communities, and job candidates to help them navigate the recruitment process and support their career development.

When It Is Dangerous to Talk about Race: Rwanda and Burundi

In Australia, government policies provide incentives for companies to promote Aboriginal and Torres Strait Islander rights, but in many parts of the world, it can be dangerous to raise issues relating to race and ethnic identity. Even seemingly similar contexts can vary enormously. For example, Rwanda and Burundi are small, neighboring, landlocked countries in the heart of Africa. Unlike most countries in the region, their residents all share one common mother tongue. Both countries have three ethnic groups—Hutu, Tutsi, and Twa. The Hutu are the majority; the Twa are a very tiny minority (1 percent).[18]

Both countries were colonized first by Germany and then by Belgium. It is near impossible to tell Hutu and Tutsi apart by sight, or by name. In fact, lore has it that if someone owned more than ten cows, they were classified by Belgian colonizers as Tutsi. Others say that Tutsis are taller and bear a stronger resemblance to their Ethiopian and Somali neighbors. Whatever the history, these classifications persisted, and the colonists favored the minority Tutsi (14–15 percent)—giving them educational opportunities and governing responsibilities as a means to control the population.

After independence, the two countries' paths diverged. Hutus eventually came into power in Rwanda and in 1994, almost a million Tutsis and moderate Hutus were killed over the course of one hundred days. A rebel army composed mostly of Tutsi exiles stopped the genocide and took power, putting in place a government that outlawed any further identification by ethnicity. Is the government still primarily Tutsi dominated? We don't know, because it is forbidden to ask, to measure, or even to pose this question. Those who do are accused of being "divisionist" and risk imprisonment or worse. Meanwhile, Burundi suffered decades of civil war. Tutsis maintained control of the government, but Hutu rebels controlled much of the country. Massacres happened on both sides, claiming an estimated 300,000 lives. Finally, a peace accord helped the country transition to a power-sharing arrangement that mandated ethnic quotas of 60 percent Hutus and 40 percent Tutsis in the government, military, and police.[19]

The government extended this quota in 2017 to all international nongovernmental organizations (INGOs) working in the country.[20] What is striking are reports of the differing responses by INGOs. Journalists Vince Chadwick and Christin Roby were told by a European diplomat that "most organizations that are based in the US or financed by the US were told [by donors or organization head offices] that 'for us, positive discrimination [i.e., affirmative action] is not a problem.'"[21] In contrast, many European funders and governments warned their grant recipients that they might not be eligible for future funding if they provided individualized ethnic information about their staff to the Burundian government.[22] If this is true, it suggests that at least some US funders might have been viewing the latest government requirements through the lens of historic discrimination and affirmative action, while European agencies could have interpreted the policy through a lens of past experience with the Holocaust and the dangers of classifying individuals in the face of ethnic conflict and increasing authoritarianism.

The political and social context of each country determines not only what specific nondominant groups to support but also the methods we use. We need to listen carefully and discern standard resistance from very real political danger, particularly if we are approaching inclusion work as an outsider to a country that is new to us. This can be even more challenging in places where the discussion of race is taboo, and we might not be told candidly about the pitfalls to avoid.

Language and Talking in Code

Every country has its own subtle and coded ways of referring to race, and these contextual signals can be completely missed by an outsider. Because race and ethnicity are so often politically charged, many cultures do not confront the question head on.

In Rwanda, one would never ask someone directly if they were Hutu or Tutsi—but this could be inferred: if someone fled to Congo in 1994, the chances are they are Hutu. If they point to a church along a highway and say their uncle died there, that is an indication that he was a victim of a church massacre during the genocide and the family is most likely Tutsi.

Caste in India is this way. Although Brahmins, India's highest caste, tend to have fairer skin, while Dalits tend to have a darker skin color, generally we cannot tell caste by someone's complexion. India's regional differences make it even more complex as all castes in southern India tend to be darker skinned. But if someone was raised a vegetarian or has a particular last name, that's a hint that they might be Brahmin caste. Or sometimes, men will pat each other on the back to see if the other is wearing a ceremonial thread worn by some Brahmins under their shirts.[23]

Even when we can easily tell someone's race by sight, conversation about race is rife with euphemisms. The words we use to talk about race can be very emotive—they change over time and can differ considerably even between countries who share a common language.

For example, *people of color* is not a term often used in the United Kingdom. In fact, it has been, at times, confused with the more dated term *colored* and has caused considerable offense. In the UK, the common term is *BAME*—which stands for Black, Asian and Minority Ethnic, although not everyone embraces that acronym, and it now may be slowly falling out of favor. *Minority* is used frequently in the UK, while in the US it is increasingly being replaced by other terms, such as *BIPOC* (Black, Indigenous, and People of Color). In Latin America the term *negro* is the Spanish word used for Black, but in the United States, the United Kingdom, and many other English-speaking countries, that term is reminiscent of a history of slavery and segregation.

When Race Is a Bad Word: France

The word *race* itself can elicit visceral reactions. In 2018, France removed that word from its constitution,[24] and it is illegal to collect race-based demographic data. When I first encountered this refusal to talk about race in France, I found it frustrating and interpreted it as a device to obstruct meaningful attempts to eradicate race-based discrimination. But as I got to know the country, I realized that it was more deep-seated than that. *Race* in French refers not only to people but can also be translated as *breed*—as in animal breed—and it is deeply abhorrent to many French.

In spite of the strong underground resistance movement, France's Vichy government was complicit with the Nazis during World War II, playing a part in rounding up Jews and sending them to concentration camps.[25] In the process of rebuilding the country after the war, France tried hard to redefine itself as "indivisible"[26] meaning, among other things, that never again would it ask for racial or religious information about its citizens and use that as a justification for state action.

For many people, this means that any race-conscious policies or even conversations are too reminiscent of that shameful past. French "universalism" and the accompanying values of *liberté*, *egalité*, and *fraternité* are at the very foundation of French society, and they promote the belief that individuals should not be judged by community affiliation, but rather held to a universal standard that applies to all. Race in France is widely considered a harmful social construct that does not truly exist. It's difficult to talk about race in France—so some people began using an English word, especially once Black American celebrities increasingly appeared on their TV screens.[27]

Since the 1980s, it has been common to use the English term *Black* to refer to Black people in France. When the slogan "Black is Beautiful" took off in France as well as in the US, it was initially a term that many Black people in France embraced, and in 1990, the term *Black* officially entered the French dictionary—this in a country that guards its language closely. But recently, some Black people in France have started asking people to call them *noir*—the French word for black. Using the English term Black externalizes race somehow—making it less intrinsic to France and the French experience. But that otherness is exactly what some object to.

So how was I as a DEI change agent based in the US to make headway in this arena in France? It helped me to understand that the history of complicity with the Nazis instilled a deep aversion to racial classification, but if the reluctance to talk about race becomes a cloak to evade action, then is it not avoidance and resistance? It is very difficult for an outsider—especially someone informed by the civil rights history in the US—to understand the difference and to find ways of working constructively. And the French might be impatient with the US American soft and euphemistic language of inclusion. While it's uncomfortable in France to speak of *race*—people do speak of racism and discrimination and have tough laws against hate speech that would make most US American First Amendment enthusiasts balk.

Coded Discrimination

Like many countries, including the US, France does not live up to its ideal. Hidden behind race-blind government policies and thinly veiled euphemisms, racism is alive and well.

Adecco—a large recruitment firm headquartered in Zurich but with over 1,000 offices in France—was slapped with a lawsuit in 2001 for systematic racism in its recruitment practices for fifty major companies, government agencies, and schools, including L'Oréal and Disneyland Resort Paris. When Adecco recruiters interviewed candidates, they were instructed to use a code to indicate their race: BBR, signifying *bleu, blanc, rouge* (blue, white, red for the colors of the French flag), was used for White candidates while NBBR indicated Black or Brown candidates. Adecco's justification for this was that their clients would specifically indicate that they didn't want Black candidates—usually for public-facing jobs. Tristan d'Avezac, spokesman for Adecco, told the *Washington Post*, "A client doesn't say, 'I don't want Blacks.' He says, 'I want people who are not from the suburbs. You know what I mean?'" The *Washington Post* article explains that the suburbs are where most of Paris's subsidized housing is located.[28]

As part of an effort to get their house in order, Adecco hired actors to test for discrimination in hiring practices and committed to make the results public. The process revealed that Adecco recruiters favored candidates with the name "François" over candidates with the name "Ibrahim." In response to these findings, Adecco conducted in-house anti-bias training for its recruiters.[29] Twenty years after these allegations first came up, Bruce Roche, Adecco's Director of Social and Environmental Responsibility, shared with me that Adecco had also helped lead a coalition to develop antidiscrimination guidelines for their industry, which offers strong advice on how to address race and racism.[30]

His advice to me was interesting. He said, "Maybe we should be careful on words. So you have some convenient words [and] diversity is one. Inclusion is another one. People are not explaining these words. It's really much easier to give an explicit definition of discrimination and exclusion. Diversity is a softer word. Equality is easier to understand with the French background."

Measuring Race

Equality may be a core value in France, but with legal restrictions against collecting data on race, religion, and ethnicity, there is no way to measure whether the country is living up to its aspirations. The constitution prohibits "measuring personal data revealing directly or indirectly the racial or ethnic origin of people, as well as the introduction of variables on race or religion."[31] The focus is on "objective" criteria such as citizenship and migration background rather than race and ethnicity.

Club 21e Siecle is a membership organization in France that conducted a survey of French companies to demonstrate the positive correlation between a company's diversity and its productivity. In order to gather data, Secretary General Reza Hariri and member of the board Batoul Hassoun explained that they ask two questions, among others—where your parents and grandparents were born, and if you perceive yourself as contributing to your organization's diversity. They were surprised at the pushback they got from some US American board members who were asked to complete the survey. These board members would have been accustomed to answering direct questions about their race, but somehow being asked about their parents and grandparents' origins felt invasive or misrepresentative. For the French respondents, however, a direct question about race would not only be illegal, but it would be acutely uncomfortable, even for Reza and Batoul, who were conducting the survey.[32]

And France is not alone—many countries in Europe use a demographic identity model based on the idea that the state should interact with the individual only, not communities or groups, in order to give equal treatment to everyone. In Spain, the government believes that collecting data on race or ethnicity results in discrimination. In Sweden, the terms used are *foreign origin* and *Swedish origin*, but the actual size of racial and ethnic minority groups—especially mixed and third-generation immigrants born in Sweden and legally counted as being of Swedish origin—is not known because the data cannot be collected.[33] Geographic origin and immigration are used as a proxy for race, and race, therefore, is not measured.[34]

These constraints on data collection can thwart US change agents who often find it frustrating to encounter, for example, Black populations disproportionately represented in entry-level positions in the workplace and yet be limited by the law from capturing evidence that demonstrates the scale of the problem. They feel restricted in discussing issues of race, especially as it can be perceived as forcing a US American paradigm onto the rest of the world.

"We Don't Have Racism Here": Brazil

My Latin American colleagues often told me that racism is a US problem. "We don't have racism here. Look at how many intermarriages there are." And they had a point. While the US was outlawing interracial marriage, much of Latin America was busy promoting it.

But what is often lost in the discussion is that these countries were not promoting mixing because they were pursuing a post-racial ideal. They were promoting mixing as a means of whitening the population. In fact, many Latin American countries instated aggressive White-only immigration policies—investing public funds to advertise their countries in Europe, and even offering land grants, free transport, and other incentives to Europeans considering a move across the Atlantic.[35]

This *blanqueamiento* project had varying degrees of success, and where policy makers believed they fell short of their goals, they then moved to actively encourage interracial marriages to further whiten their demographic.[36] In stark contrast to the US "one-drop rule," which categorized anyone with even one Black ancestor as Black—something that was codified into law in some states in the early twentieth century[37]—most Latin American countries manipulated their census data, to "understate the presence of persons of African descent" in an attempt to further whitewash the image they tried to project to the world.[38]

Brazil, realizing that it would never have a completely White nation, then turned to building its national identity as a "racial democracy"—instilling into Brazilians' psyche the notion that the country does not discriminate on the basis of race or even see race. And at first glance, it is easy to believe in this romanticized portrait. In a survey conducted in 1976, when asked to describe skin color, respondents gave 136 different shades—including "honey-colored white," "somewhat like cinnamon," "sea blue," and "deep-dyed, very dark."[39] However, Brazil has one of the largest wealth gaps in the world and rates of poverty are closely correlated with skin color.[40] Black and mixed-race people make up well over half the population—ship records show that 3.6 million enslaved people were brought to Brazil from Africa, seven times more than the estimated 500,000 who were sent directly to North America.[41] Today Whites in Brazil earn an income that is almost twice that of non-Whites, and Afro-Brazilians represent less than 5 percent of top management in the top 500 companies in the country.[42]

An Innovative Approach to Leveraging Racial Diversity: Natura & Co. in Brazil

Natura & Co., a Brazilian cosmetics group that includes Avon, Aesop, and The Body Shop with a presence in seventy-three countries, launched an innovative approach called *CorageN*. The goal was to hire a diverse group of interns to drive innovation for their business. Natura understood that if they kept conventional requirements that interns have an elite university education, speak English fluently, and have international experience, they would have very few *preto* (Black) and *pardo* (mixed) candidates due to educational disparities that fall along color lines. Instead, their criteria valued life experience and an entrepreneurial mindset. They also understood that if they simply posted job advertisements through their usual channels, the candidate slate would not be racially diverse, so they used every channel and network they could think of. They went to *favelas*—low-income settlements in Rio—and suburbs to advertise the opportunity.[43]

Their call for applications yielded 22,000 candidates for just twenty slots. The recruitment process asked candidates to complete two tests. One test assessed how the candidates would fit in with the company's ethos of equality and teamwork. Natura wanted to attract people who would work well within the company's ecosystem; they wanted people who cared as much about *how* they worked as they did about their results. The second tested their innovative mindset, creativity, and problem-solving skills. Of the twenty people they ultimately hired to be a part of the CorageN internship program, 85 percent came from underrepresented groups. This group of twenty was mighty—most of them did not have a university degree, but the program gave them access to Natura's top leadership, and they generated four new viable business ideas, three of which are now part of the business strategy. Seventeen of the twenty CorageN members have gone on to be hired by Natura.

Conclusion

Addressing race in differing contexts is not easy. **Racism is a shape shifter**—definitions of race, racial categories, and how racism is expressed all adapt to their context—and therefore DEI initiatives must be flexible enough to do the same. I've learned that **racism is both universal and highly specific.** Every context has its dominant and nondominant groups. These power dynamics are often informed by broader global forces of colonialism, slavery, and cultural imperialism—but also shaped by local and regional conflict, migration patterns, and history. Therefore, it is not possible to effectively confront racism with a one-size-fits-all initiative across the globe.

To further complicate things, **race is highly emotive and politically charged** and can be dangerous to talk about openly. It means that each context usually develops a code and euphemisms that refer to race. As outsider change agents, **we need local allies to help us understand** the language being used and any resistance we encounter.

Understanding the context can help us better understand that resistance. While in France, it could be connected to a collective memory of the atrocities of the Holocaust, in Brazil it is more likely to be tangled up with a deep-rooted national identity as a "racial democracy." When we understand the nature of the resistance, we are more effective at developing strategies to transform leaders and organizations.

Principle

2

LEADERS CHANGE TO LEAD CHANGE

TRANSFORMATIVE LEADERSHIP IS KEY to embedding DEI within an organization's culture. Without commitment from leaders, it is very difficult to fully embed DEI in the systems and values of an organization. When organizations are led by people who truly embrace DEI with purpose and passion, the benefits are clear: people from disadvantaged groups have opportunities to succeed and thrive in a culture where they feel they can belong.

To lead authentically, leaders need to internalize the benefit of DEI to themselves and to the organization. For most leaders, this requires a disruption of their worldview and a change in mindset—a change that only happens as a result of the often-painful work of introspection. Leaders must embrace multiple perspectives and acknowledge their own unearned privilege. They have to recognize that they have certain advantages purely due to their particular identity, and that this social reality impacts the lives of marginalized people. Even leaders who are not part of a dominant group have privilege in some aspect of their lives, and every leader is responsible for broadening their outlook to include and understand a multitude of experiences.

Leaders who travel this path become genuine allies—lending their privilege to those who do not have it and taking action to change power structures. This is in stark contrast to transactional leaders, who say or do the right things out of self-interest and solely for appearance's sake.

Chapter 3, "Transformational Leadership across Cultures," tells the story of three leaders who took this journey in three disparate cultures—India, France, and the US. Their change in perspective and the road to get there are expressed in a variety of culturally bound ways and may be missed if we look for a familiar expression based on a one-dimensional perspective.

Chapter 4, "Dealing with Resistance," acknowledges that leaders can be at different points in their DEI journey. As not all leaders seek out disruptive experiences, the chapter provides change agents with head and heart strategies to provide transformative experiences for leaders so that they can lead with commitment, authenticity, and inclusivity.

3

TRANSFORMATIONAL LEADERSHIP ACROSS CULTURES

Now more than ever, [we're] open to listening, understanding, and lending our voice—as a company that connects the world—to take action for social and racial equity.

—ERIC YUAN, CEO, Zoom
in a memo to employees on May 31, 2020
following the killing of George Floyd

SODEXO'S NEWLY APPOINTED CEO FOR NORTH AMERICA, Dick Macedonia, left his meeting with the African American Leadership Forum (AALF), an employee business resource group (EBRG), fuming, upset, and demanding to know, "How can they ask me these questions?"

Dick was a White street-smart businessman and a native of Pittsburgh, Pennsylvania. He had worked at Sodexo for thirty years. He rose to CEO in 2005, the year Sodexo signed a consent decree settling a class action promotion discrimination lawsuit filed by the company's African American managers.

Given the lawsuit, eight members of AALF leadership asked to meet with Dick to personally assess his commitment to DEI. I sat with them around the boardroom table along with Dick and James Taylor, a senior African American executive assigned to the Office of the CEO. As AALF's leadership asked pointed questions about his views and commitment to diversity, I saw that Dick was defensive and uncomfortable. He tried unsuccessfully to match his tough, urban childhood against the stories of his Black colleagues. Tensions lingered in the room and the meeting ended abruptly.

The Journey toward Transformative Leadership

DEI change agents know only too well that a commitment to inclusive leadership at the senior-most level is fundamental to ensuring that DEI is a sustained part of the culture and the business. When companies are led by people who truly embrace DEI with purpose and passion, the benefits are clear: people from disadvantaged groups have increased career opportunities and thrive in a culture in which they have a sense of belonging and feel engaged and validated for who they are.

Leaders set the tone and direction locally and globally. This requires transformative leaders who combine inclusive mindsets and behaviors with concrete action. Leaders' personal behavior has the power to demonstrate their conviction, and taking action signals the level of their commitment to strengthening DEI within their organizations. It also requires intentionality to prioritize DEI as they would any other business imperative.

To lead authentically with genuine purpose and passion, leaders have to go through their own transformation journey in order to truly internalize the benefit of DEI to them personally and to the organization. Robin J. Ely and David J. Thomas, highly respected academics, suggest that, "to dismantle systems of discrimination and subordination, leaders must undergo the same shifts of heart, mind and behavior that they want for the organization as a whole."[1]

What is it that gets leaders to the point where they view diversity, equity, and inclusion as a *passion imperative* rather than merely a brand-builder or checklist activity? To truly change power structures in their organizations and make them inclusive and equitable, they must be willing to make DEI a personal, driving force. A Catalyst study found that often the "commitment to fairness ideals was rooted in very personal and emotional experiences."[2] To get there requires self-transformation; "leaders must 'disrupt' themselves—their thoughts, their values, their actions" to be successful.[3]

As Joanna Barsh, director emerita at McKinsey & Company and author of *How Remarkable Women Lead*, says, "Many leaders accept accountability, but few truly understand that this kind of disruptive cultural change starts from within."[4]

Change agents often have to deal with leaders' resistance to the value of DEI. Few leaders take responsibility for seeking out transformational experiences that prompt introspection and a shift in perspective. Change agents often play the role of guiding leaders through transformational experiences drawing on a robust arsenal of strategies calibrated to the individual, as well as their cultural context. This takes energy, skill, resilience, and emotional intelligence. It also requires awareness of the different ways that transformation may be experienced and expressed in different cultural settings.

This chapter explores stories of leadership transformation expressed in three cultural contexts—the US, India, and France. It sets the stage for understanding the key head and heart strategies discussed in the next chapter—strategies that are essential for presenting leaders with opportunities to shift their worldview so they can lead with purpose and passion.

Transformation in an Informal Cultural Context: The US

To best describe the process of perspective shifting, it's worth returning to Dick's story. Prior to becoming the CEO, he headed one of the two largest business segments at Sodexo. When AALF was choosing their executive sponsor, they decided to interview three executives including Dick. They chose Dick as their executive sponsor because, as Keysa Minnifield, a member of the AALF leadership, said, "Dick was sincere. He did not come in with numbers and a prepared corporate-speak script saying, 'This is what I have done.' He was not cavalier. He was genuine."[5] As their sponsor, Dick started informally mentoring some of the members. Selecting Dick was clearly a strategic choice that AALF made. He headed one of the largest business divisions and, as an influential leader, they realized that his approach to DEI could impact many employees. Keysa and her colleagues made a conscious decision to work with Dick as they appreciated his transparency.

Although Dick had served as AALF's executive sponsor, he was not prepared for the shift in his relationship with AALF in the context of the lawsuit. Now, as the CEO, he was held to a higher standard of accountability for the entire organization. Following the tense meeting with AALF, James, who was at the meeting with us and worked closely with Dick, shared his own experiences outside Sodexo. He explained things like why he always wore a tie and jacket even in dress-down situations. He said he had to look professional at all times to avoid being mistaken for the help at a restaurant or being followed in stores or being stopped by police. As these stories got closer to Dick's world, he listened with newfound interest.

Dick asked to meet with AALF again. Recently, when I asked him what prompted him to reach out after that first difficult meeting, he said, "We were being attacked externally (by civil rights organizations) and I had to bring the organization together internally; so, I had to be open to listening."[6] After experiencing Dick's initial defensiveness, the AALF leadership was skeptical, but they reminded themselves that they had a prior relationship with Dick as executive sponsor. It took fortitude, generosity, and optimism for them to agree to a second meeting with him. AALF's leaders, Keysa Minnifield and Kenneth Johnson, told me that when Dick was their sponsor, they had seen that he cared about people and was willing to learn and ask questions. "He was not trying to hide behind anything. So it was worth investing time in helping him," Kenneth said.[7]

This time, Dick came ready to listen. "Help me understand your experiences as I haven't walked in your shoes," he said. The AALF leadership told Dick about their reality, inside and outside Sodexo. They shared, and Dick heard them and asked more questions. In that exchange—with AALF investing in Dick by sharing their stories and with Dick expressing genuine interest—a connection was made. The AALF leaders eventually became Dick's strongest champions. Dick said to me, "The best thing that ever happened was being asked to be AALF's executive sponsor. It was a great honor."[8] Upon that foundation of trust, together with the AALF leadership, we built a plan to create an inclusive culture across the company's North American business operations.

With AALF's engagement, Dick became a transformative leader, determined to make the culture at Sodexo more inclusive. He began with his leadership team, creating opportunities for them to shift their perspectives—a critical first step in transforming the culture. He allocated resources, held teams accountable through an incentive compensation linked to diversity objectives, and invested resources in advancing the careers of women and people of color. During his tenure, women and people of color headed significant business portfolios and their engagement increased dramatically as evidenced by employee surveys. Even the named plaintiff in the class action lawsuit chose to stay with Sodexo because of the positive changes she was experiencing.

The AALF leadership made some very strategic choices to help Sodexo get to this point. They could have written Dick off after the first meeting. Instead, they decided to focus on Dick's potential as an ally by building on the authenticity they had experienced in Dick as their executive sponsor. Sharing stories of repeated indignities and discrimination takes energy and can be emotional and fatiguing. Too often people in marginalized groups are pressured to "educate" without dominant group members taking responsibility for their own learning. But Dick was ready to be vulnerable, and AALF saw an opening. They hoped that sharing their journeys would help Dick along on his own journey of transformation that would lead to change in the organization. They made an active decision based on the belief that Dick could change. They examined their options through a lens of abundance—allowing Dick the space to grow. In doing so, they exerted their agency and exhibited generosity of spirit. And it paid off. Keysa told me, "AALF provided us a sense of community where we could seek support. As one of AALF's early leaders, it also gave me visibility. With the support of inclusive leaders, I took on increasing responsibility as an HR leader. As the culture became more embracing of difference, I finally felt that as a Black woman, I could belong and succeed!"[9]

Dick said, "I have to be a role model. I have to hold people accountable, but I also have to be vulnerable, and I have to listen. And it was in being vulnerable and in the listening that I had my 'aha' moment."[10] When Dick retired from Sodexo, he joined DEI advisory boards exclusively. He said, "I came late to the party, but once I realized on a personal level the importance of an inclusive organization and what it means for the business, I became zealous about my commitment. I see this as my greatest legacy to the organization." Dick shared his transformation narrative publicly as a way to motivate, galvanize, and lead by example. Not only do change agents influence a leader, but leaders in turn influence their organization and other organizational leaders, as many leaders went on to do in their new roles outside Sodexo.

US Cultural Patterns

While individuals certainly differ, cultural patterns can inform how a leader understands and expresses their transformation. In the US, openly sharing personal information, including deeply personal stories, is fairly commonplace.[11] In this example, African American leaders were willing to share their experiences of race discrimination and Dick was open about sharing his transformation to embracing DEI. In the US, many White leaders publicly expressed stories of personal transformation following the murder of George Floyd in 2020. As we will see, this is not the case everywhere.

In France, for example, workers rarely have personal pictures in their workspace. Augusto Muench, who is Mexican and Boehringer Ingelheim's Country Managing Director for Mexico, Central America, and the Caribbean, said, "In Mexico we had a group of work colleagues and we would meet once a month . . . in our homes to play cards; you make that part of your life. In Germany, office is your office and private life is your private life. German friends will be loyal and share but to get to that point takes longer."[12] In private cultures, personal stories may not necessarily be shared openly, and therefore the strategies used by change agents might differ.

High- and Low-Context Cultures

US work culture tends to be informal, encouraging input from employees. Given this context, it's not surprising that Dick was open to having his subordinates challenge him and ask questions that would have been unacceptable in a more hierarchical culture. Management structures in the US are often relatively flat, with the power distance between the boss and the subordinate fairly low. With more hierarchical cultures, distance between the boss and the subordinate is greater and status is important.[13] In India and France, I found the work cultures to be more hierarchical and formal.

One way of understanding different cultures is to classify them as either high or low context. In *low-context cultures* like the US, communication is usually direct with the messenger explicitly spelling out details rather than relying on circumstance or context to complete the meaning. Erin Meyer, a professor at INSEAD, a leading international business school, explains that in low-context cultures, "messages are expressed and understood at face value."[14]

By contrast, in many high-context cultures, messages may be communicated implicitly, which requires reading between the lines and a shared understanding between the sender and receiver to decode the message. If you expect that all communication will be precise, explicit, and understood at face value only, you are likely to miss indirect stories that hint at a leader's transformation.

Given the more direct context in which Dick operated, he conveyed his thoughts overtly; when he was annoyed or disagreed, he clearly articulated his concerns. AALF felt that they could trust Dick because what they saw was what they got. Precisely because he was open with his resistance, they were more likely to trust his expressions of transformation and he was received as authentic and transparent. In another cultural context, the resistance would not have been expressed so openly, and if it were, it may not have been received as an indication of authenticity.

Transformation in a Hierarchical Culture: India

Rishi Gour is an Indian CEO of Theobroma, a family-owned Indian company with cafés and baked goods. He was CEO of Sodexo India from September 2015 to December 2019 and worked previously for well-known brands like Accenture and Citigroup in India and the UK.

Rishi successfully raised the percentage of women in the Sodexo India workforce of over 48,000 employees from 15 percent to 20 percent before he left Sodexo at the end of 2019. “In India the problem was fundamental; it’s a complex problem but a simple problem,” Rishi said. “We had to get the numbers of women up. If we have no women, inclusion has no meaning. I saw it as a business problem similar to getting profits up. I put it as a core business parameter. Like any other change agenda, I gave my team targets, helped them understand what I was trying to do, had clear expectations, and if they did not deliver, they had to explain why and face the consequences.”[15]

He often spoke about deliberate change. “If you say that it’s important, you have to allocate time to it. The moment you do not stay focused on DEI, there is slippage. Just like any other business outcome, you need intentionality.” Rishi hired women in roles with responsibility for profit and loss, an area where they were underrepresented in Sodexo. He invested his personal time to coach and guide them to be successful.

Rishi admits that DEI was not on his radar professionally until he stepped into his CEO role at Sodexo India. Two things laid the foundation for his transformation. The first was personal, something he does not discuss publicly. Prior to joining Sodexo, when he had to relocate with his job to London, he had expected his wife, also a professional career woman, to give up her job and follow him—which she did. Later, when he realized the personal cost to her and the difficult choices she had to make, he returned to India, where her career took the lead. “I never had to face this choice between my career and my personal life as my wife had to,” Rishi said. Her career experiences opened his eyes to the discrimination women experienced in the workplace, especially once they had children. This learning through his wife was profoundly disruptive for him, but he has never shared it openly with his teams.

The second transformative experience was his involvement with SoTogether, Sodexo’s internal global gender advisory board. Given the size and importance of the India business and therefore Rishi's role, I needed him to be an active champion of DEI. I invited him to participate in SoTogether in 2015 hoping that the experience would have an impact. "I recall the first meeting I attended in Rotterdam," he told me. "I was one of the few men with twenty-five women in the room. It was a very intimidating experience for me and I thought that this is what women must feel like when they are mostly in rooms full of men."[16] Each time he returned to India after a meeting, he felt renewed pressure but also motivation to take action.

Publicly and to his teams, Rishi talked passionately and compellingly about the business case with data to back it up. Getting the best talent was an important driver as Sodexo India struggled to recruit and retain women. He talked about Sodexo as a leader in DEI on par with the best global brands and how it raised Sodexo's profile. "Clients personally told me that they admired what we were doing in DEI, and I know that on the margin it made a difference in getting and keeping clients," he told me. Sodexo India hosted several DEI forums with clients, and his teams actively participated knowing it was important to Rishi.

Rishi's transformation was expressed very differently from Dick's. India is a hierarchical culture in which leaders are expected to be experts, to provide clear direction, and to not be vulnerable or admit mistakes that might diminish respect. Status is important and leaders are shown deference and held up as subject matter experts.

Given the cultural expectations and his positional power in a hierarchical society, he drove DEI from the top down through data, metrics, and accountability. Rishi was expected to demonstrate expertise with facts, statistics, or other evidence. He focused his team on the business benefit and talked with conviction about the business case in external forums and with clients. He leveraged Sodexo's leadership in DEI as a competitive advantage with clients.

Rishi never discussed his personal story about his wife's difficult choices and sacrifices, a story he relates very emotionally in private. Neither does he discuss the impact and growth he experienced through his involvement in SoTogether. In the social and cultural context, such revelations may have undermined his ability to forge change, particularly among those, like him, with power.

If I had expected a visible personal transformation story, as with Dick in the US context, I might have come to the erroneous conclusion that Rishi had no disruptive experience and consequently no transformation at a deep level. In truth he had, but it was expressed in keeping with the cultural expectations of a leader in the Indian context—with data and facts. Understanding this allowed me to expose him to the experience of participating in Sodexo's gender advisory board. Rishi's transformation was evident in his driving DEI like any other business objective and holding his teams accountable over the long term.

Anchoring Inclusion in High-Context Cultures: France

Michel Landel, a White French male, spent his early years in Morocco and started his career at Sodexo in 1984 managing operations in Eastern and Northern Africa. In 1986, he was promoted to manage Sodexo's business throughout Africa. In 1989, he was named CEO of Sodexo North America.

Michel had studied, worked, and lived in Europe and Africa and was attuned to cultural differences. However, one of his many learning moments came soon after he became CEO of Sodexo North America. While visiting Sodexo clients in California, he visited a school where Sodexo provides meals to students from kindergarten to high school. Given his exposure to media portrayals of US society, he had expected to see mostly White students in the schools. He was surprised when he looked out across a lunchroom packed with students of color and only a smattering of White students—in stark contrast to the images he had formed.

"It made me realize that even in North America our customer base is diverse and that the future talent in our workforce will reflect this diversity. We are in the business of serving others. So, if we are not able to understand our customers, then we are not able to adequately serve them," Michel said.[17]

He also credits extensive conversations with his wife, Marie-Yvonne Landel, a White French woman, and his Chief HR Officer, Ollie Lawrence, an African American man, about their own experiences of discrimination. Michel was not familiar with the history of race relations in the US, but he listened deeply to Ollie's stories, including the experience of being mistaken for a caddy at an elite golf club where he was a member.

The promotion discrimination lawsuit filed by African American managers and certified as a class action in 2002 was a jolt to the company and to Michel personally. He said that he thought that Sodexo had the right values and mission, but the lawsuit was a big wake-up call. He realized that racism was a significant reality in the US. "Unless we make it a priority, nothing will move. It was my responsibility to make sure that everyone had the opportunity to be successful at Sodexo," Michel said. "I had to challenge myself personally. I did not know what I did not know. The journey ultimately made me a better person and us a better company for all employees."

The lawsuit gave him an additional impetus to do what he knew had to be done to stay competitive in the complex global economy. At a meeting of over 1,500 senior leaders at Sodexo, Michel said, "I want Sodexo to be the reference and the benchmark in diversity and inclusion not only in North America, but globally." Needless to say, with Sodexo early in its DEI journey at the time, his remarks were met with skepticism.

He galvanized the organization with the consistency and sincerity of his behaviors and actions. On one occasion, a client asked that Sodexo not "promote" its support of LGBTQ employees on its website and in other communications. Without a minute's hesitation Michel said, "We can do without clients who don't respect our values. We have to be consistent, or it is a slippery slope. Who will they tell us not to support next?" He believed in a purpose-driven organization and in treating diversity as a value that creates a strong brand promise and business outcomes.

Michel was determined to replicate the DEI success in North America in the rest of the world where Sodexo had business. He personally sponsored women from around the world, many of whom went on to lead large business portfolios. During succession planning discussions, he challenged leaders to identify women successors and to share their plans to sponsor and advance women. He would push recruiters to identify female candidates on interview slates. Michel frequently said about DEI, "You can't take your foot off the pedal for a minute, or the organization will slide back."

At Sodexo, I initially reported into HR. In a bold move to underscore the importance he placed on diversity and inclusion, Michel broke with most traditional corporate structures and established an independent DEI department, reporting directly to him, initially in the US and then to the global CEO. By appointing the head of DEI to the senior leadership team, Michel signaled the importance of DEI. He allocated resources and ensured that the DEI budget remained intact even during financial challenges. He held managers accountable for DEI by linking a percentage of their incentive compensation to DEI objectives. Under his leadership, DEI became one of the strategic principles of the business, and every business review included an update on DEI. The result was an increase in women executives globally and an organization-wide culture in which women were highly engaged, as measured through an employee engagement survey.

Vijay Sharma, a leader of Sodexo's Pan Asian Network Group (PANG), said,

> I am convinced that transformational leadership was the single determining factor that propelled so many of us from middle management to senior executive and even C-suite positions—a tangible and palpable change that we aspired for became real and within our grasp. During my thirty-five-year career in Sodexo, the growth I achieved in the last ten would never have been possible without the fundamental, effective, and lasting culture change.[18]

As a French man, Michel's transformation showed up very differently from that of a US American leader. His influences—including how he had internalized his experiences from working in Africa, the class-action lawsuit, and his relationships with his wife and with Ollie Lawrence—were cumulatively disruptive. They led to self-reflection and deep internal work that enabled his shift in perspective. But he never talked openly about, what to him, were very personal experiences.

In the French cultural context, the public domain is far smaller than the private, with a clear separation between what is considered personal and impenetrable and what is considered public. This had a strong influence in Michel's discomfort in talking publicly about the personal influences that shaped his approach to DEI.

Wema Hoover, formerly at Sanofi, captured French privacy when she said, "I am sure you have heard the saying that Americans are like a peach and the French are like coconuts. The French feel that Americans reveal and open up much too quickly, and it's somewhat uncomfortable for them how much we share up front and how open we are. The French are quite the opposite; it's very difficult to break in, but once you do, it is a lifelong connection."[19]

For Michel, the proof was in the actions he took as an inclusive leader, not his words. While neither Rishi nor Michel were public about their own journeys, Michel signaled his commitment by talking philosophically and indirectly about bias and racism and the need to be open to learning. He frequently referred to DEI culture change as being "complex" and needing constant focus. Layers of nuanced thinking about bias, the deep emotional response DEI elicited, and the role of leadership were bundled into that statement. He had a high-context style of implicit and subtle communication. Rishi, on the other hand, was more explicit in private about the influences on him. And while Michel talked minimally about his own transformation, it was clear by his actions that he had been deeply affected.

Conclusion

Leadership commitment is critical to the success of a DEI change effort. Leaders who are serious about diversity, equity, and inclusion must be committed to embedding DEI at the very deepest levels of the organization's values and culture, and this requires transformative, committed leaders. It requires leaders to develop a clear and unobstructed vision for how DEI adds value to the business, and perhaps more importantly, how it helps them uncover a personal passion for championing it. To lead DEI authentically and with conviction and fortitude, leaders must do their own work of disrupting their worldviews.

Dick, Rishi, and Michel are all leaders I had the privilege of working closely with during my eighteen years at Sodexo. Each of them came to be role models of DEI through their own transformative journeys—journeys that were expressed differently in keeping with the cultural milieu in which they operated.

I am aware that I've only talked about male leaders here—and it is true that in their contexts they were each part of the dominant and most privileged group. But, although there are certainly exceptions, this is often the case with leaders, and it will stay that way until our DEI efforts really take root and make change at the very top.

Not all leaders—whether they are from the dominant group or not—seek out these disruptive experiences for themselves. Many are resistant to DEI and need to be shepherded by change agents. What is the best way to break through that resistance and guide leaders through this transformation process? How do we know they are ready? How do we know that they have, in fact, been impacted enough to lead DEI authentically and with personal passion and purpose? There is no one-size-fits-all approach to effective transformation. So, the question becomes, how does one disrupt a world view to shift one's perspective to lead DEI with purpose and passion?

4

DEALING WITH RESISTANCE

There is only one way to look at things until someone shows us how to look at them with different eyes.

—PABLO PICASSO

EACH LEADER HOLDS A KIND OF ECOSYSTEM of beliefs—conscious and unconscious—around issues at the heart of DEI. It's important to tease them out in order to develop a responsive approach that stirs the leader's growth and transformation.

It is well established that commitment and role-modeling by senior-most leaders is critical to embedding and sustaining a culture that is diverse, equitable, and inclusive so that all employees are valued and have rewarding career trajectories. To be genuinely passionate about their commitment, leaders have to internalize the importance of DEI to the organization and to them personally. This takes deep work of perspective shifting. Not all leaders seek out transformational experiences that prompt the necessary introspection. My colleagues often share that they struggle with leaders who are resistant to the value of DEI. Change agents have to be strategic in how they expose leaders to experiences that are disruptive so that they can lead DEI with conviction.

As we worked to advance DEI globally at Sodexo, I found that one of the first and most important steps was to secure support from country leaders. The challenge was that they were at different starting points and operating in different cultural realities with varying degrees of resistance. It's helpful to understand the range of perspectives that a leader may start out with in order to calibrate strategies that support the necessary leadership transformation.

Common Beliefs and Mindsets That Impact a Leader's Approach to DEI

Some common beliefs and perspectives can impact how a person sees diversity and inclusion in the workplace. Why are a person's beliefs important? Because beliefs contribute to a person's worldview, predispose them to take certain actions, and, ultimately, influence results. Progress in creating diverse, equitable, and inclusive organizations starts with how people think, how people understand the world, their point of view. Lasting change requires a shift of heart and mind, a shift in thinking and perspective. When you understand the beliefs or point of view a leader may hold, you are able to design targeted experiences to shift or expand their mindset on these topics.

The following common mindsets related to diversity and inclusion can give us insight into a leader's thinking. Figure 2 illustrates how these mindsets are expressed as a continuum from least supportive to DEI (left) to most (right). A leader may be anywhere on that continuum.

1. *Deny Systemic Barriers → Acknowledge Systemic Barriers*

   Leaders who dismiss systemic barriers believe that we have a level playing field for all and that the "cream rises to the top." Such leaders might think, believe, or say, "I don't see color as we are all equal with equal chances of succeeding if we just work hard." They make excuses such as "We cannot find any qualified . . ." or "Women are leaving because they have little children."

Those who acknowledge barriers that impede advancement of underrepresented populations look for ways to address it in the systems, policies, and behaviors within their organizations. They address gaps by unpacking underlying root causes and harnessing the best of what a diverse workforce can offer.

2. *Diminishing Returns Mindset → Expansive Mindset*

   Leaders with a diminishing returns mindset see a zero-sum game: "They are just hiring women; my career is over because I am a man." Or "We cannot invest in DEI as we have other business priorities." Those with an expansive mindset can envision how DEI will help grow the business by targeting specific consumer groups or leveraging diverse talent for innovation. They see the benefit to their employees resulting in innovation and higher productivity for the organization. Typically, a diminishing returns mindset shows up toward the beginning of an organization's or individual's DEI journey. If organizations are truly committed to DEI, movement on this scale has to occur early in the process.

3. *Solve for Today → Vision for the Future*

   Leaders who want to "solve for today" see DEI as an immediate, short-term problem—perhaps a lawsuit or a performative response to the Black Lives Matter movement—that can be solved by hiring a few women or members of other underrepresented groups or by giving isolated charitable contributions. These reactive responses can result in "diversity-washing" without furthering their commitment by addressing inequities more systemically. Leaders with a vision for the future see beyond the burning platform du jour. They strategically endeavor to become an industry benchmark for DEI rather than level off at compliance standards.

4. *Closed Mindset → Receptive Mindset*

   Leaders with a closed mindset dismiss experiences of others. This might manifest as "I don't believe that racial profiling occurs," or "I am not sure what you mean by privilege. I grew up in a poor Caucasian family and made it by pulling myself up by my bootstraps." Inclusive leaders approach DEI with a sense of humility and a genuine desire to learn—a receptive mindset. They admit to what they don't know and are open to listening deeply without denying other's experiences.

5. *Diverse Talent Is a Risk → Diverse Talent Is an Asset*

   All too often leaders hire people like themselves, where there is an immediate bond, comfort level, and trust. They see talent different from themselves as a "risk" they would rather not take. An inclusive leader sees value in diverse talent, fostering candidates' potential contributions to innovation, future growth, and ability to reduce groupthink.

Leaders will be at various points on this DEI beliefs continuum, requiring a range of strategies to move them toward being transformative inclusive leaders. Their place on the continuum may also depend on their belief about an identity group. For example, they may have a receptive mindset on race but still have a journey to develop awareness of LGBTQ inclusion. Leaders may also be influenced by their cultural orientation. For example, a leader in a future-focused culture might generally solve for tomorrow, and this would in turn influence their orientation to DEI.

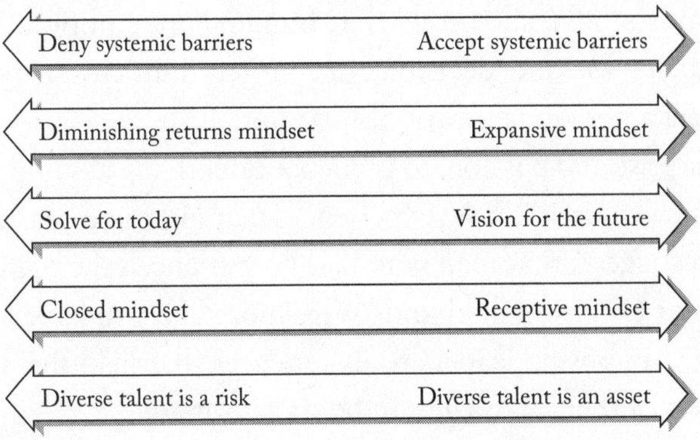

Figure 2: Continuum of Common Beliefs and Mindsets Impacting Approaches to DEI

Strategies to Shift Perspective on DEI

All too often leaders are resistant to DEI or simply performative in their engagement without a true investment in seeing improvements. Change agents are called on to bring leaders along. How do you provide leaders with opportunities for introspection? It involves unpacking resistance to see what lies beneath.

Developing individually targeted strategies requires meeting each leader where they are on their DEI journey and understanding their belief system as it relates to DEI. For some it might mean starting with evidence-based data, analyzing the positive impact on the business, and adding in perspectives about the ethical imperative. For others, it is using the influence of clients or customers. For still others, this might involve exercising the power of personal stories.

John Kotter and Dan Cohen, in their work on successful change efforts, refer to the "head-heart strategy." While engaging intellectually through rational arguments and data is important, this processing must be supplemented with experiences to see, feel, and react in a noncognitive manner. "People change what they do less because they are given *analysis* that shifts their *thinking* than because they are *shown* a truth that influences their *feelings*."[1]

Behavioral economists have shown us that humans are emotional beings, and that behavior and decisions are largely influenced by emotions—whether a person is aware of it or not.

To lead with purpose and passion, to influence underlying assumptions at the deepest level, leaders need experiences that tug at the heart. Catalyst's research suggests that men who had "experienced the pain of marginalization or exclusion firsthand" were more likely to have a "sense of fair play."[2] Exposing leaders to experiences that help them gain an appreciation of their privilege can be transformative.

Catalyst also observed that a strong sense of fair play was important in recognizing bias. This increases the likelihood of men being champions threefold.[3] "The higher men's awareness of gender bias, the more likely they were to feel that it was important to achieve gender equality."[4] When men identify with discrimination through the experiences of their daughters or wives, as was the case with Rishi and Michel in the previous chapter, they tend to become more committed to efforts to address gender disparities in the workplace.[5] While the introspective work has to be done by the leaders themselves, they can be provided experiences that disrupt and shift their mindset to embrace the value of DEI. Deciding which strategies to use and the sequencing of those strategies requires an understanding of the individual, the organization, and the cultural context in which they are operating. It takes emotional intelligence and skill on the part of the change agent. It often involves sharing painful personal experiences. Leaders must acknowledge the personal toll on the person with the lived experience and take ownership of their own learning.

The public outcry over the fast succession of killings of George Floyd, Breonna Taylor, and Ahmaud Arbery in the US in 2020 was a jolt to some White male executives who still comprise 90 percent of all Fortune 500 CEOs in the US.[6] These deaths were tragic and tide-turning, but a leader's catalyst for change need not rely on such disturbing events.

How else can leaders expose themselves to different experiences in a way that is powerful enough to generate self-reflection and be transformational in their journey? How can leaders be guided through experiences such that they are able to recognize their privilege? And with recognition of their unearned privilege, how can leaders learn to spend that social capital on the inclusion of others?

Head Strategies

The following are some cognitive "head" strategies that can engage leaders to commit to DEI.

Making a Business Case

With the deeply disturbing visual impact of videos of the deaths of innocent Black men in 2020, the dialogue on DEI in the US shifted from the more traditional focus on the business case to one grounded in equity, fairness, and social justice. In fact, it began to seem irrelevant, and in some cases, distasteful, to lead with business as a rationale. These images laid bare the basic moral issue. And to make the business case now required sensitivity not to inadvertently subjugate ethics to profit.

Some people are simply tired of making the business case. "Why do we need to make a case for having more women in our organization? Have we ever been asked to make a business case for men?" one senior American woman bemoaned as her male colleagues, yet again, asked how she knew that greater gender diversity benefitted the organization.

Still, the social justice argument does not resonate in some parts of the world where leadership teams insist on a clear demonstration of the economic value of DEI. In other words, before they invest in DEI, they need to see that it will directly enhance their business outcomes.

Building a compelling rationale for change involves understanding the purpose of the organization, socioeconomic trends in the external landscape, cultural nuances, and talent needs. The impact of a diverse marketplace, the need for innovation, and the external brand all factor into building the best rationale for change. This is covered in more detail in Principle 3, Chapters 5 and 6.

Partnering with Clients

I found that one of the most effective ways to appeal cognitively to leaders was to demonstrate the positive impact DEI could have on client relationships.

One approach I used was to invite like-minded clients to speak to Sodexo executives about the importance of DEI in their own companies. As we introduced the global work on LGBTQ, we first needed buy-in and commitment from Sodexo's predominantly White, straight, male global executive committee, most of whom were resistant to the topic at the time. With Michel Landel's support, we scheduled a session in Paris where we had an executive from a global technology client organization speak to the executive team. We carefully selected a straight White French male who was a sponsor of his company's LGBTQ resource group. The conversation surfaced deep-seated views and helped to begin the perspective-shifting process as the executives identified with the presenter and wanted to align their values to that of a desirable client. It was also effective to have the messages delivered by a peer, another senior executive.

Usually, when we talk about "belonging" in DEI, we are referring to an inclusive workplace where employees feel they can belong. I have also found that organizations feel a powerful pull to belong—particularly to a group of other companies that are considered influential and desirable business partners. If that group is committed to DEI, other organizations are likely to want to join in and to be validated by them. Collectively, leaders can advance their commitment through peer pressure.

As its track record in DEI grew over the years, Sodexo's brand became synonymous with DEI thought leadership, elevating the company's profile. Many Sodexo employees operated at client locations providing meals and caring for the facilities, and as they told clients about Sodexo's global work to advance DEI, those clients increasingly turned to Sodexo as a resource for their own DEI work. As Sodexo leaders became more aware of the benefit to client relationships, the support deepened, allowing the company to invest more in DEI. Organizations that are customer facing can get a similar benefit if their brand is genuinely committed to DEI.

Leveraging External Partners

When organizations get external recognition, they are more likely to follow through on their public commitments with internal actions. When leaders present at conferences, companies sponsor community events such as Pride parades, organizations sign on to joint statements, or influential agencies—such as Catalyst—offer awards, this can further cement an executive team's investment in DEI. Leveraging collaborations with external organizations like the International Labour Organization (ILO) or the UN Global Compact's Women's Empowerment Principles can be an effective strategy to influence leaders. This strategy has worked well in parts of Europe, Asia, and Latin America where such international multilateral organizations have appeal and recognition.

Leaning on Allies

Another motivating strategy is to influence through allies. Frequently the message is heard differently depending on the messenger. White men or members of other dominant groups can be particularly effective at delivering DEI messages as they have more access to those in power. To be effective, change agents need to identify the dominant group in different cultural contexts. It is not always obvious: privilege can be based on race, caste, ethnicity, or religion as we saw in Chapter 2.

This approach served Marcelo Vasquez, former Diversity and Inclusion Director, Sodexo Latin America. He reached out to executive leaders who were key influencers but unlikely allies. He invited an executive from a part of the business that was viewed as an especially *machista* culture with very few women to be the face of a video promoting LGBTQ inclusion. This propelled that leader's commitment to DEI, and the message resonated with the teams, given that this key influencer was delivering it.

While it can be useful to have a member of a dominant group deliver messages in support of DEI, seeking "validation" or endorsement by the dominant group risks perpetuating existing power dynamics. Bringing power brokers along is an effective strategy in most organizations, but it needs to be carefully evaluated and managed by ensuring agency for the marginalized group. In this case, the outcome enabled the LGBTQ employees to form an employee resource group that then worked with the leadership to make the countries in Sodexo Latin America more LGBTQ inclusive.

Engaging the Board of Directors

The board of directors plays a critical role in ensuring that the drumbeat on DEI is sustained. Outside influencers like the investor community are increasingly pressuring boards to diversify their members, disclose their board representation, and report on Sustainable Development Goals or environmental, social, and governance considerations. Gen Z and Millennials seeking purpose-driven companies are adding to those pressures.

Sodexo's board, chaired by Sophie Bellon, is an example of a company whose board drives the commitment to DEI. The Sodexo board had 60 percent women in 2020 and regularly reviews diversity metrics and activity.[7] In fact, Sophie is so personally invested in ensuring the representation of women in senior leadership roles that she co-chaired with me Sodexo's global gender advisory council, SoTogether, for seven years from 2011 to 2018. Her personal engagement, passion, and conviction ensured that the organization stayed focused on DEI in the years that I was at Sodexo.

Heart Strategies

A compelling business reason for leading inclusion culture change is foundational but not adequate. The following are some strategies for influencing leaders emotionally.

Reciprocal Mentoring

Reciprocal mentoring is an excellent way to expose leaders to experiences of those different from themselves. Through this process, leaders mentor protégés on career advancement while learning about their mentees' experiences. Catalyst's research also suggests that, "men who had been mentored by women were more aware of gender bias than men who had not had this experience."[8]

To sensitize its executive team, Coca-Cola Brazil launched a reciprocal mentoring initiative with fifteen Afro-Brazilians as mentors matched with senior leaders. Simone Grossmann, Head of HR for Brazil and the South Cone for The Coca-Cola Company, told me that not only did the engagement advance the careers of Afro-Brazilian employees, but it also served as a learning opportunity for the executives. The leaders "were so shocked because they just didn't know. It revealed to them a new reality because I'm talking about senior leadership that is all White . . . So they were, like, shocked to hear that there were these micro-aggressions that people get in the day to day," she said.[9]

Mia Mends, formerly Chief Administration Officer and CEO, Impact Ventures, Sodexo, said, "I shared my experiences as a Black woman with my mentor, a White French man, and he listened with a newfound understanding of the indignities that I encounter. With the trust we had built and with him as my mentor and sponsor, I have been able to navigate a fulfilling career from a regional sales role to operational roles to Sodexo's C suite."[10]

Personal Stories

In her book, *Data Story*, Nancy Duarte describes an experiment conducted by Chip and Dan Heath in their Stanford class. They tested the impact of facts versus stories. While 5 percent of the students remembered the data, 63 percent recalled the stories.[11] Highlighting peoples' stories increases leaders' awareness of others' experiences and prompts them to emotionally connect.

After the 2013 boycott in response to homophobic comments made by their leader, Barilla set up an external DEI advisory board that included David Mixner, a gay rights advocate and author, "once named by *Newsweek* magazine as the most powerful gay man in America."[12] Mixner refused the invitation four times—reluctant to be associated with the company—before he accepted. When he finally relented, he met the chairman at a New York restaurant and instructed the wait staff to speed up service so he could leave within the hour! He and Barilla ended up spending four hours over lunch during which time Mixner shared his experiences as a gay man: being the target of hate crimes, being estranged from his family, and losing jobs. Moved by Mixner's stories, Guido Barilla launched his company's journey to LGBTQ inclusion. The company ultimately "unveiled a limited edition of its most popular product, Spaghetti 5, in a box illustrated with two women holding hands, a single strand of spaghetti held between their lips."[13] The company launched their LGBTQ employee resource group in Italy and elsewhere, and with the help of the advisory board, they systematically changed their culture to be more diverse, equitable, and inclusive.

Stories combat invisibility in organizations where people feel they must hide certain shades of their identities. Stories invite empathy and shift attitudes. However, in a climate where LGBTQ inclusion is not yet the norm, coming out takes enormous bravery. Sharing such stories in a work environment can carry with it the risk of losing one's livelihood as well as the possibility of alienation and harassment. In some contexts, it is dangerous to be public about your sexual orientation because of the laws in the country.[14]

The burden of telling these stories usually falls on people with lived experiences of discrimination. It can be empowering to speak out, but it can also be exhausting to have to share painful memories again and again in order to educate people in power. DEI change agents need to be aware of the toll it takes. Storytelling initiatives should maximize each story's strategic impact and ensure that any participation is purely voluntary.

Learning at the Edge of Discomfort

When Michel Landel retired in 2018, Denis Machuel, also a White French man, became Global CEO at Sodexo. In one of my early meetings with him, he asked me why I was diluting the global focus on gender by also including other identities like race, which were not relevant globally. I realized that I had to expand his experience in a way that could shift his perspective on race.

I invited him to attend the African American Leadership Forum (AALF), Sodexo's employee resource group, meeting in Texas. He was one of a handful of White men at the meeting and this experience of being an outsider combined with the personal stories of discrimination shared were pivotal to internalizing his understanding of race in the US. The experience created disruption and shifted Denis's perspective on race in the US. As a result, he became increasingly convinced that addressing race globally, with local relevance, was important.

In fact, the session had such an impact that it stuck with him two years later when he sent a powerful personal message to the employees in the US in June of 2020 shortly following the death of George Floyd.

> As a White male, there is much I take for granted, including not having to think about my race. And I know that is not a luxury afforded to all . . . . I was privileged to have shared an intimate moment with Sodexo's African American Leadership Forum. I heard the stories you all shared about the weariness and unrest you feel every time you leave your homes. That touched me deeply and I've never forgotten that your experience is not one that we can fully understand, but it is one we must all acknowledge.[15]

Sponsoring Employee Resource Groups (ERGs)

Exposure to experiences and stories can come from disparate sources, including sponsoring ERGs that have been formed to address challenges and opportunities relevant to a specific identity group. The sponsor often serves as a sounding board and advocate for the ERG. There is value in selecting an executive who has a particular affinity for a group, especially if they are respected within the organization and can share their story on an identity dimension that the organization is particularly resistant to.

For example, in one organization members selected a sponsor for their disabilities ERG who spoke openly and compellingly about mental health issues in his family. His passion came from personal experience with his child and he galvanized the organization that had not yet addressed mental health to launch a multiyear global mental health campaign.

I also have found tremendous value in strategically selecting sponsors who might need to advance their own exposure and understanding of an identity they are particularly resistant to. In one organization that I worked with, an executive perceived as homophobic, was assigned to sponsor the LGBTQ Pride employee resource group. The executive and the Pride leadership were both surprised by this assignment. To the credit of both, they worked at it. When he left the company that executive said, "My biggest growth moment at this company came when I became the sponsor of the Pride group."

Raising Awareness and Knowledge through Learning Experiences

In 2018, Denis Machuel asked me to deliver a session on gender equity to his newly formed executive team in Paris. Denis still talks about how transformative that session was for him! At one point the facilitator asked the six women executives in the room a series of questions including whether they had been harassed, objectified, abused . . . and all six stood up within a nanosecond. Conversely, the men had never had any of these experiences. Denis said that the activity and the ensuing conversations provided a lens into his own privilege and also gave him a glimpse of what women encounter, even those who are senior leaders. It achieved the desired impact of opening and shifting mindsets.

Conclusion

Leaders who have a personal passion for championing DEI and who see the value to business outcomes are critical to leading and sustaining diversity, equity, and inclusion in organizations. When leaders lead DEI with purpose and passion, they embed DEI in the business and culture in a way that benefits marginalized groups. As a result, underrepresented employees have career opportunities, have possibilities to advance, are more engaged, and feel a sense of belonging to the organization.

To embrace that sense of personal passion, leaders often have transformational experiences that shift their world view. Leaders don't always seek out these experiences and frequently they are resistant to the value of DEI. It is, therefore, up to change agents to use a multitude of carefully calibrated strategies to expose leaders to experiences that are disruptive. And leaders need to be guided to take ownership of their learning and recognize the toll it takes on the individuals sharing their lived experiences.

Through the disruptive process, even the most seasoned leader re-emerges with a passion and purpose for driving inclusion throughout the organization. This passion and purpose serves as a motivating driver needed to disrupt the culture and business as usual. Leaders are not expected to be perfect but need to be on a path to leading DEI with conviction. Leaders change to lead change.

At its best, that newfound conviction is propagated in a way that engages the organization, especially middle managers. Ultimately while senior leadership sets the tone and leads from the front, inclusive leadership should be cultivated at all levels of the organization through champions and allies who do the heavy lifting of engaging the organization. If done effectively, all employees understand the rationale for embarking on a DEI cultural evolution that benefits the organization as a whole.

Principle

3

AND IT'S GOOD BUSINESS, TOO

ANY SUCCESSFUL AND SUSTAINABLE TRANSFORMATION effort requires a rationale for change. Without a compelling change narrative, most DEI initiatives are likely to be unsuccessful in the long term. A holistic and persuasive DEI storyline considers the mission and business of the organization, along with regional sociopolitical, legal, and cultural nuances. Drawing on a range of examples, Chapters 5 and 6 demonstrate how convincing cases for social justice can be constructed so that they resonate in different parts of the world while also benefitting the business.

Chapter 5, "Compelling Rationales for Change," explores the evolution of the DEI discipline across global regions. DEI seeks to foster a workplace that provides a sense of belonging and equitable opportunities for all talent as well as advance social justice in the community. But there are different paths to that end. Understanding the evolution of DEI regionally enables us to tailor the appropriate case for change to each region or country where we are working—whether it is a legal case, a business case, a fairness and equity case, or some combination. The chapter describes the development of Sodexo's global rationale for change and then goes on to examine the regional trends and history of DEI in the US, the Middle East, Africa, Asia, and Europe.

Chapter 6, "Creating Competitive Advantage through DEI," argues that to be successful, DEI change efforts cannot be siloed or bolted on. Instead, they must be congruent with the organizational purpose and how business is done. Values build brand, and consumers and employees care about what an organization stands for. The chapter draws on global companies that have successfully embedded DEI in their business model both to be purpose driven and to advance business outcomes.

5

COMPELLING RATIONALES FOR CHANGE

It is not the strongest of the species that survive, nor the most intelligent, but the one most responsive to change.

—CHARLES DARWIN

TRANSFORMATIVE LEADERSHIP IS KEY to embedding DEI within an organization's culture. Equally important is identifying a powerful reason to change. Without a compelling reason for change, any transformational initiative will struggle to be sustained. John Kotter's seminal work on change management revealed that only 30 percent of change efforts succeed in creating and sustaining change over the long term.[1] Other studies have shown very similar results. McKinsey's research of over 3,000 executives found that only one in three transformation attempts succeed.[2] So why is this?

In their article, "The Psychology of Change Management," Lawson and Price suggest that employees will alter their mindsets and enable the change only if they understand the rationale underlying that change.[3] Developing a compelling story to galvanize the organization to embrace DEI is core to success.

A compelling story considers both the organization's key purpose and the geographic context. When organizations incorporate these elements, they are able to transform their DEI strategy from a *transactional business case model to a transformational competitive advantage model.* A transformational model is one in which the rationale for change is fully embraced by all employees. Kotter estimated that 75 percent of a leadership team needs to have bought into the change to enable a sustainable shift.[4] The more holistic the case for change, the more likely it is to be compelling and reach that 75 percent critical mass. Only then can an organization transition DEI from simply being nice to have, to being good for business, to ultimately becoming an integral component of the brand narrative and identity.

Rationales for Change

Over the past seventy years, several persuasive reasons to advance DEI have evolved across different geographies. The DEI business case, or the impact of diversity on an organization's financial performance, has risen to prominence as perhaps the most communicated driver for change over the past thirty years. Given the often-sluggish pace of change, however, perhaps a more holistic, regionally nuanced perspective is required to significantly move the needle. In addition to a business case, national laws compel many organizations to increase their DEI efforts, and a growing number of companies are driving DEI forward because it is simply the right thing to do for social justice, equity, and fairness.

Each of these arguments for addressing diversity, equity, and inclusion presents differently across regions, organizations, and time—and we need to identify which arguments best suit the context. The different rationales are iterative and develop as geographic and organizational events unfold. To be transformational and generate competitive advantage, a change narrative has to draw on all three arguments, be congruent with the business, and resonate with the geographic trends where the business operates (see Figure 3).

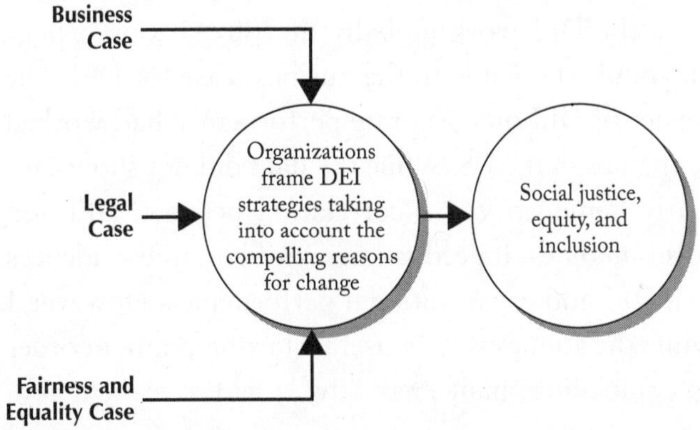

Figure 3: Compelling Rationales for Change

COMMON CHANGE RATIONALES

The Business Case

Empirical and evidence-based return on investment (ROI) that demonstrates that increased diversity can improve profit, revenue, and productivity

The Legal Case

Legislation to eliminate discrimination that ensures organizational compliance and adherence to government mandates

The Fairness and Equality Case

A value-driven rationale founded on the belief that DEI is the right thing to do and that regardless of their identity, everyone should have access to opportunities resulting in a more just, equal, and fair society

Developing a Global Rationale for Change: Advancing Women at Sodexo

When I launched the DEI work globally in 2007, I took a page from the US playbook and led with the business case for DEI. The bottom-line impact of DEI on corporate performance had worked to convince companies in the US. While the data did not show causality, they clearly demonstrated a correlation between DEI and positive business outcomes. Indeed, a library of research evidences the link between DEI and organizational performance. However, I realized that while the studies were a useful starting point, in order to build a truly compelling change narrative, I had to make it core to Sodexo's business and purpose and relevant to the countries and regions where we operated.

Initially, I drew on a wealth of empirical data to make a case for our global gender equity work, starting with specifically increasing women's representation and then shifting to consider the balance in representation between men and women. Looking back now, I can see that this approach was very conventional in how it viewed gender through a binary lens. My own awareness of gender diversity has grown over the years, and at that time, the organization was far from ready to have a conversation about nonbinary identities. Even with the conversation limited to increasing the representation of women, we experienced significant pushback outside the US. Something clearly was not resonating. As most studies at that time were largely based on US data, managers felt their findings did not translate either to the industry or their respective countries.

Leveraging Sodexo Data

To align the rationale for change to Sodexo's business, we conducted a study with Sodexo data. We knew we needed evidence from within the company and from multiple countries in order to generate figures that Sodexo leadership in different countries would find relevant and convincing. The study drew on data from 50,000 Sodexo managers in seventy entities around the world. The intent was to isolate whether gender-balanced entities, defined as entities having 40 to 60 percent women in management, outperformed those entities without gender balance in management. Gender composition was then correlated with Sodexo's key performance indicators (KPIs), including employee engagement, employee retention, client retention, safety, and financial outcomes over a five-year period.[5]

The results indicated that a near-equal balance of men and women in management was critical to observing gains in financial and nonfinancial KPIs (see Figure 4). Once the proportion of men or women exceeded 60 percent, the benefits plateaued, confirming that a mix between 40 and 60 percent is necessary for optimal performance. It confirmed that gender-balanced teams anchored in an inclusive culture made for more sustainable and predictable positive financial and nonfinancial outcomes for Sodexo.[6]

The mere fact that we used Sodexo data was certainly more compelling for Sodexo managers than the generic studies we had been relying on earlier.

Strengthening Client Partnerships for DEI

We had used internal Sodexo data to make a business case for gender equity, but the tipping point occurred when we shared the study externally. The findings drew attention from the media as well as clients. As a result of the study and the global work Sodexo had embarked on, the company soon became regarded as a global thought leader in DEI.

Like-minded clients sought out Sodexo's expertise and mid-level managers took pride in seeing Sodexo positioned as a leader in DEI alongside big-name brands. As managers became aware of the benefits of Sodexo's DEI leadership, it led them to further advance the DEI agenda, which in turn benefitted the business. Through this cycle, DEI was continually reinforced and had become an integral component of Sodexo's brand promise.

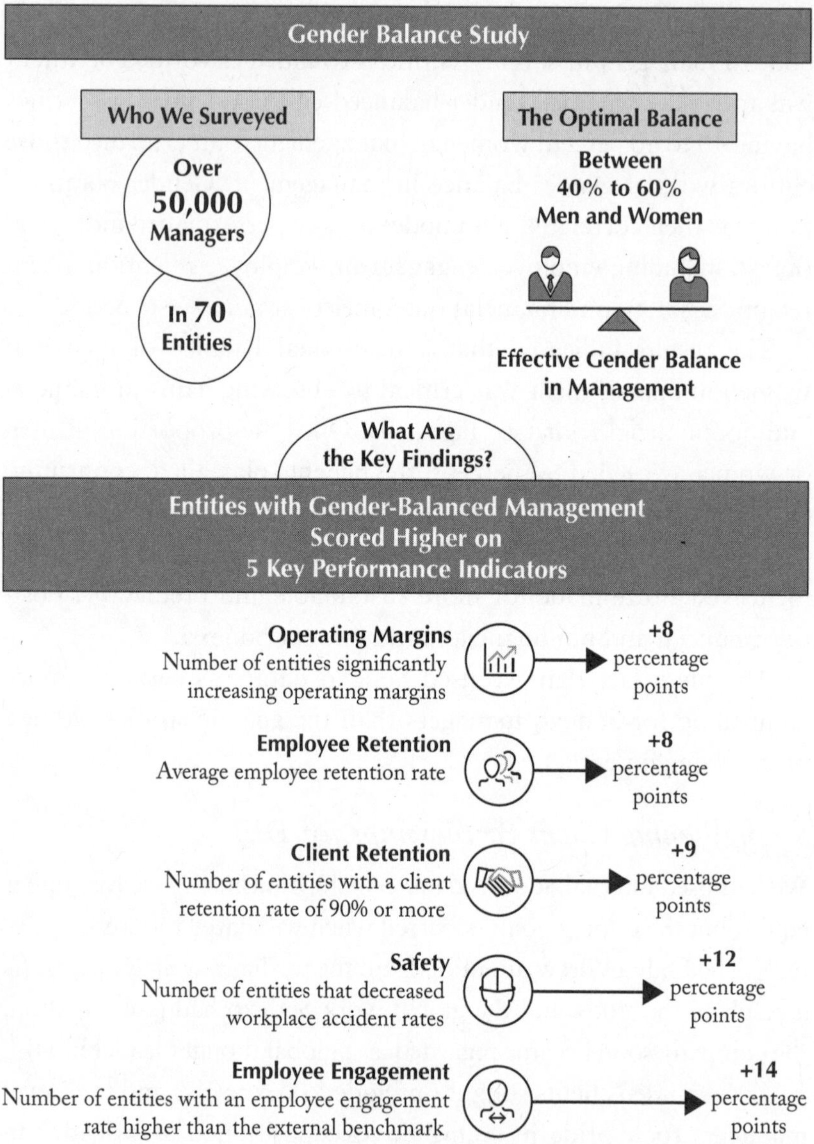

Figure 4: Sodexo's Gender Balance Study. *Source: Sodexo's Gender Balance Study, 2018, https://www.sodexo.com/inspired-thinking/research-and-reports/gender-balance-study-2018.html (Reproduced with permission from Sodexo)*

Building a globally compelling story that would resonate with both managers and employees was important and foundational. However, it had to be linked to Sodexo's purpose of *Improving the Quality of Life* for its workers, clients, customers, and communities. In order to maximize buy-in, we also had to take into account geographic trends. For example, in Asia, we understood that the Sodexo teams were struggling with retaining talent given a severe talent shortage. Building a change rationale that centered on the cost of turnover became the focus in Asia. In Europe, where the laws and compliance often drive change, signing the International Labour Organization (ILO) Global Business and Disability Network Charter in 2016 signaled Sodexo's commitment to people with disabilities (PWD). This public commitment was then reinforced through Sodexo's country leaders agreeing to abide by the ILO Disability Charter: country executive teams pledged to hire PWD and to foster an inclusive culture in which they could engage and succeed.

I found that I could use the Sodexo global gender balance study as an entry point for engaging country leadership. But to be truly transformational and create competitive advantage, it had to incorporate the organizational business and purpose as well as the diversity opportunities specific to their country and region.

Understanding Regional Trends and DEI History in Global Regions

The drivers for DEI—and therefore the rationale for organizations to engage in DEI culture change—vary across regions and evolve over time. How can organizations reframe DEI initiatives to optimize relevance in response to the constantly shifting contexts in which they operate?

An understanding of these trends and the influence of each region's broader macroculture and history is key to identifying the impetus for DEI. Laws have been a key driver for change in Europe, the Middle East, and Africa, while in Latin America and Asia the business case and talent shortage are what have compelled organizations to embrace DEI. I found that the better I was able to understand a region's historical drivers, the more I was able to construct relevant narratives to enhance buy-in within each region. The modern-day DEI journey was born in the United States, so it makes sense to start there.

The United States

DEI in the US arose from the civil rights movement in the 1960s, when equal employment opportunity (EEO) and affirmative action were introduced as policies to adjust for decades of inequities and to create a more level playing field for historically disadvantaged groups.[7] This took into consideration particularly, but not exclusively, sex, race, creed, and national origin.

However, in the 1970s, challenges to affirmative action—which refers to attempts to increase work or educational opportunities for marginalized candidates—began to emerge. People argued that it undermined individual merit, something deeply valued in the US and a core building block of "the American Dream." The resistance and challenge to affirmative action increased through the 1980s, bolstered by the Reagan administration's efforts to reduce federal regulations. It was at this time that DEI advocates recognized that they would have more success by positioning DEI not just as a moral imperative but also as a business cornerstone of any thriving organization. Dr. R. Roosevelt Thomas, Jr., often known as the "father of diversity," further shifted the paradigm from "compliance to a matter of business survival," in light of the increasing numbers of women and people of color entering the workforce and the opportunities it presented.[8] Recognizing that DEI was good for business, organizations took the lead in ensuring that they had an inclusive culture. A good illustration of this is companies' evolving approach to the LGBTQ community.

Companies have been marketing to LGBTQ consumers for over forty years. In 1981 Absolut Vodka started advertising in magazines read by gay men.[9] Since then, LGBTQ consumer power has steadily increased and by 2018 was estimated to be just under $1 trillion in the US.[10] And consumer sentiment favoring LGBTQ-friendly organizations provided an additional impetus for many organizations.

Despite decades of effort by companies to create an inclusive environment free of discrimination for their LGBTQ employees, it was not until 2020 that the Supreme Court protected gay, lesbian, and transgender people from discrimination. Unlike Europe, where governance and laws have been the driving force for corporate change, in the US the commercial world took the lead.

Institutional discrimination was blatantly exposed by the murder of African Americans at the hands of police—something which has been happening for centuries but in recent years has been amplified through social media mobilization. The Black Lives Matter (BLM) movement, which began in 2013, gained momentum and mainstream support in 2020, perhaps finally reaching a tipping point and concentrating public focus on social justice as reason in itself, catapulting the US and other countries toward the fairness and equality case for DEI. The underlying belief was that when organizations lead with purpose and do the right thing, communities and businesses flourish. This, in addition to the fact that we have seen limited progress despite DEI business case evidence, prompted many to question the value and long-term benefits of the monetary-driven business case for DEI. Robin Ely and David Thomas, respected diversity thought leaders, say "the lack of progress suggests top executives don't actually find the business case terribly compelling . . . a simplistic business case isn't persuasive."

They reason that a more holistic view of diversity must be adopted to enable success.[11]

Research at Georgetown University found that "inclusion efforts grounded in antidiscrimination law, or the legal case, are the most likely to curb widely held biases and promote equitable behavior" rather than an emphasis on the business case. This may be because the historical and moral grounding of the law legitimates DEI efforts with more authority, as compared to more transient financial motivations.[12]

That being said, in the US, where imposed compliance is regarded as a cultural anathema, the business case still has value in its potential to garner self-interested buy-in by leadership. But in addition to business interest, a rationale for DEI increasingly must be moored to social justice.

The underlying demographic trends in the US are strengthening the social justice argument. The US has experienced an exponential rise of BIPOC populations, with the Latino population representing the fastest growing minority group in the region.[13] The US is projected to become a majority-minority nation by around 2045.[14] This is indicative of significant demographic changes in both the employee and consumer populations, as well as the potential for more US Americans to become marginalized if they are not integrated into the social and economic fabric.

Could a new business model be emerging in the US that is focused on the ethical imperative to create a more equitable society alongside a drive for profit and financial gain? And will purpose-driven organizations have a leading role to play?

Africa

The Africa and Middle East regions have seen a sharp escalation in awareness of DEI over the last twenty-five years. A burgeoning youth population has been a key factor in both regions. Collectively, the Middle East and Africa have the highest share of youth in the world. By 2025, Africa's youth population (defined by the UN as fifteen to twenty-four years of age) is forecast to make up 40 percent of the world's total.[15] This youth bulge and high levels of unemployment along with high rates of female unemployment prompted governments to act in order to transform a looming economic disaster into a dividend.[16] A 2019 McKinsey study suggested that "accelerating progress toward gender parity could boost African economies by the equivalent of 10 percent of their collective GDP by 2025."[17] This represents a significant business case for driving change in the region. Over twenty countries across the continent have established gender quotas in their legislatures and parliaments.[18] South Africa introduced a National Policy Framework for Women Empowerment and Gender Equality (WEGE), which "strives for 50 per cent female representation on the executive bodies of all organizations."[19]

The extent of gender quotas and legislation across Africa has encouraged organizations to increase women's representation. Indeed, in 2018 the *Financial Times* asserted that Africa had "made the most legislative progress aimed at tackling gender discrimination" of any region in the four years prior.[20] Perhaps as a result, female representation across Africa at the board level is the highest of any region, standing at 25 percent—8 percentage points above the global average.[21] In 2019, Rwanda's legislature was 62 percent women—more than any other country in the world.[22] However, more needs to be done to maintain progress through the pipeline as the representation of women in middle management still lags behind the global average.[23]

Legislation has, to a lesser degree, been utilized to address racial and ethnic imbalances, with a few countries—such as Cameroon, the Democratic Republic of Congo, and Uganda—writing protections for minority groups into their new constitutions.[24] Ethnicity is often included in power sharing agreements against a backdrop of ethnic tensions and a history of colonial interference. Black

Economic Empowerment (BEE) was launched in South Africa in 2005 to redress the inequalities of apartheid. Organizations are awarded BEE points and incentivized by government contracts.[25]

The Middle East

As in sub-Saharan Africa, legislation has been a driving force for change in the Middle East. In this region, a specific local employment supply and demand disconnect has emerged to oblige governments to take action. The disconnect includes inflated employment expectations among new job entrants—particularly in the Gulf states—driven by a public sector that often pays more than the private sector.[26] Furthermore, employer expectations of the skills required for employment have not matched the skill sets of the younger local population.[27] As a result, organizations tend to hire experienced expatriates from outside the region; in 2020 over 35 million foreigners were working across the Middle East.[28] Governments, realizing that continued underemployment of the local youth population would impact future economic growth, have introduced nationalization laws to encourage organizations to hire local nationals.

Remember Alain Morize's campaign to hire more Saudi women at Sodexo? He recognized an opening for that in part because in 2011 the Saudi Arabian government had launched a nationalization program, referred to as Nitaqat. It categorized private sector companies into various color-coded classes based on their number of local hires. If a firm has an excellence green rating, they are fast-tracked through the visa approval process allowing them to hire more expatriates. This benefits businesses as they are able then to hire the most experienced expatriates to support training local staff and it serves as a further incentive for the company to navigate the complicated terrain of better integrating local women into the workforce.[29]

While DEI legislation is instrumental in many regions, there are key differences in what has driven the creation of these laws: in the Middle East and Africa, the primary rationale for change has been the underutilization of youth and women. This created an economic incentive for governments to influence corporate hiring practices, while in the US and in Europe, as we shall see, social justice movements played a larger part in pushing governments to act.

Will legislation be sufficient to compel change in this region and create a more diverse workforce? How will emerging generations' desire for a more equitable and fairer society impact the need to address DEI across the Middle East and Africa?

Asia

While legislation has been a compelling reason for change in parts of Africa and the Middle East, there has been a distinct lack of DEI legislation in most Asian countries. A Mercer report on DEI in Asia Pacific suggests that the focus in the region has historically been on inclusion rather than highlighting differences.[30] Is it possible that legislation based on diversity, which focuses on difference, was viewed at odds with many Asian cultures, which in general tend to value collectivism? That certainly may be the case in some instances; however, there are many disparate Asian cultures and we need to guard against over-generalizing.

In this incredibly diverse region that includes forty-eight countries and over 2,000 languages, some governments have intervened to address inequities.[31] In India, for example, the society is stratified by caste and the government has imposed quotas—50 percent of spaces at many public institutions are reserved for the lowest caste, the Dalits. In Malaysia, where the minority Chinese (23 percent) control the bulk of the economic power, the "New Economic Policy" mandates affirmative action for the majority, indigenous Malays.[32]

Through the 1990s, two regional trends were colliding. First, the economy was strengthening with an average GDP annual growth rate of 7 percent between 1990 and 2010.[33] At the same time, many countries experienced population decline. With a few exceptions, the general trend in the region points to an increasingly aging demographic. Japan's population is shrinking faster than any other country in the world: by 2060, nearly 40 percent of the population will be over sixty-five and it is estimated to fall from 127 million today to 87 million.[34]

These trends have led to severe talent shortages in Asia—the most pronounced of any region. According to Korn Ferry, "Asia-Pacific is expected to face a talent deficit of 47 million skilled workers by 2030, which could result in a potential loss of US $4.238 trillion in annual revenue."[35] Despite the talent shortage, women and the aging population are significantly underemployed. This means that reaching out to women and older generations makes good business sense. Reaching these groups will ease the challenges caused by the talent shortage and fuel economic growth. The talent shortage is the key driver compelling organizations in Asia to address DEI.

The question for Asia moving forward is this: Will a greater number of governments begin to introduce more substantive legislation to further compel organizations to embrace DEI or will the business case be sufficient to drive change?

Europe

In post-World War II Europe, the need to build peaceful relationships with neighboring countries was key given the division that threatened to engulf the continent. The collaboration required between countries working toward a broader, more holistic vision for peace and prosperity has resulted in a macroscopic culture within the continent. The European Union (EU) has enshrined equality in their charter of fundamental rights, including an article specifically prohibiting discrimination on grounds of sex, race, color, ethnic, or social origin.[36] Organizations are obliged to demonstrate their compliance to various enforcement mechanisms.

Laws have shaped and pushed the business sector's stance toward social justice in Europe, but these laws are hard-won results of social movements and grassroots organizing. As we rolled out a global plan at Sodexo for inclusion of people with disabilities (PWD), I was struck by how quickly many of Sodexo's European country teams identified and hired PWD and developed robust initiatives for full integration into a variety of workspaces. I learned later that the first legislation in the world to recognize the rights of PWD was enacted in the UK in 1970.[37] The Chronically Sick and Disabled Persons Act of 1970 was a groundbreaking step on the road to equality and formed a basis for much of the subsequent European legislation for PWD. Many countries in Europe now have quota systems in place to compel organizations to recruit people with disabilities. The quota systems often include severe financial penalties for organizations that do not comply. For example, in Austria, organizations are required "to employ one registered disabled person per 25 employees." Failure to meet the quota results in a compulsory equalization levy of at least 238 euros per month.[38]

In my experience, speaking directly about money in Europe was often perceived as gauche or distasteful as compared to how openly people would talk about the financial payoffs of DEI in North America. The reticence to talk directly about money is borne out in empirical data. When companies were asked by the European Commission to rank the benefits of DEI in order of importance, economic effectiveness was named as one of the areas least affected by DEI. The areas considered the most highly impacted included company reputation and image, and attraction of highly skilled employees, which have a more indirect but still important contribution to profit.[39] This means that selling DEI as a business imperative often falls flat in Europe, or can cause offense.

In recent years, though, the business case is increasingly acknowledged in Europe, in part as a result of the influence of US organizations. In 2005, the European Business Test Panel (EBTP) concluded that DEI has grown in importance for business as well as for fairness and moral reasons.[40]

Will the case for change in Europe continue to gravitate toward the business case, or as social justice movements gain momentum in Europe, will organizations anchor themselves in DEI for moral reasons?

Latin America

Latin America has the highest inequality in wealth distribution of any region.[41] Over the last decade, the continent's high levels of inequality have stymied sustainable growth and social inclusion. Mixed-race and indigenous people experience disproportionate levels of exclusion and marginalization.[42] "The incidence of extreme poverty among indigenous and Afro-descendant individuals is much higher than in the rest of the population, ranging from 1.6 times higher (in Colombia) to 7.9 times higher (in Paraguay)."[43]

As a result of these inequities, governments in the region have established quotas for different marginalized groups including people with disabilities. Fifteen Latin American countries have implemented hiring quotas for PWD.[44] Despite efforts to compel change through quotas, questions remain around their effectiveness. Quotas in themselves are not adequate. They need to be enforced, and this is lacking in much of Latin America as opposed to Europe where penalties ensure compliance. In Peru, a recent study found that, despite the quotas, only "approximately 8% of firms paid for one hour or more of work by a person with a disability."[45] Brazil has fines so the compliance is better, with 39 percent of organizations meeting the 5 percent disability quota mandated by government.[46]

On one of my trips to Santiago, Chile, I visited a training center where women survivors of violence are taught the culinary arts. They then go on to start their own businesses, work for Sodexo, or take other jobs. I had the honor of giving them their graduation certificates at a ceremony where their children beamed and clapped for their mothers. I was flooded with memories of their stories—lived experiences of abuse by partners—and here they were, excitedly anticipating a future of economic independence.

This initiative in Chile was in response to the endemic problem of violence against women in the region. In 2020, over a million protesters took to the streets in Chile on International Women's Day calling for greater equality and an end to gender-based violence.[47] The #MeToo movement, a social movement shining a spotlight on sexual violence and misconduct, and the BLM movement gained momentum in Latin America, raising awareness of the inherent inequality and injustice in the treatment of marginalized people. BLM demonstrations also spread across Colombia in June 2020, incited by the death of a young Afro-Latino man, Anderson Arboleda, at the hands of police.[48] These uprisings highlighted social justice as a compelling case for change across Latin America.

Despite these movements, it is the business case for DEI that has strengthened as a driver for change over the past twenty years. Latin America has one of the widest skills gaps in the world. "Over four in 10 firms in Latin America say they have difficulty finding workers with the right skills."[49] Companies in Argentina, Colombia, and Peru are particularly struggling with 59 percent, 50 percent, and 49 percent of companies respectively citing difficulty finding talent.[50] Women are a significantly underutilized talent pool. "The participation of working age women in the region's labor force is only 52% and continues to lag far behind that of men (77%)."[51]

This underutilized talent pool represents a significant business case for organizations to alleviate the talent shortages in the region. A recent Mercer report suggests that nearly 64 percent of organizations in the region see a clear business imperative for improving gender diversity to address the talent gap.[52]

Although talent is still the compelling business driver for DEI in Latin America, will global social justice movements also prompt organizations to focus on DEI in the region?

Regional Trends: Similarities

While each region is quite different in terms of culture and context, we can draw some broad similarities.

Generational Shift in the Fairness and Equality Case for DEI

Across all regions, we are seeing Millennials (born between 1981 and 1996) and Generation Z (born between 1997 and 2012) pushing for purpose-driven organizations and governments to commit to putting people ahead of profits. Research conducted by Deloitte on the perspectives of more than 27,500 Millennials and Gen Zs, found that "the pandemic has reinforced their desire to drive positive change in their communities."[53]

It is becoming increasingly evident that organizations must step forward and bear responsibility for addressing social concerns. As these emerging generations transition to leadership roles, could the very purpose of organizations shift away from primarily a profit-focused model as a driver for DEI toward a more holistic, purposeful business model that marries profit with social justice?

Business Case and the Talent Shortage

The talent shortage that is evident across most regions is forecasted to increase significantly over the next decade. A study by Korn Ferry finds that by 2030, we will have a global talent shortage of more than 85 million people. "Left unchecked, in 2030 that talent shortage could result in about US $8.5 trillion in unrealized annual revenues." In Asia Pacific, the talent skills shortage as a percentage of the economy is the most pronounced of any region globally with a forecast "labor skills shortage of 47 million and unrealized output of $4.238 trillion" by 2030.[54] This is perhaps the reason why the business case for DEI is particularly pronounced in the Asia Pacific region. The skilled talent gap no doubt represents an extremely significant business case.

Conclusion

The evolving landscape and historical context—economic, social, political—inform each region's impetus for addressing DEI. This sensitivity to regional history provides insight into how to position DEI to achieve change in organizations.

Ask yourself, which of the rationales for change are the most compelling in the geography where you are operating? Are you adapting your DEI strategy to align with these trends? The greater the alignment and connectivity between your DEI strategy and the local context, the greater the resonance and buy-in from your employees. The cases for change are iterative. An awareness of the evolving nature of the case for change is important, as is a willingness to steer a different call to action for DEI should local events unfold.

While understanding the geographic context and case for change is extremely important, equally critical is embedding DEI into the organization's core business. Each organization will build a compelling case for change differently, depending on its purpose.

6

CREATING COMPETITIVE ADVANTAGE THROUGH DEI

Chase the vision, not the money.
The money will end up following you.

—TONY HSIEH, Former CEO of Zappos

WHEN ORGANIZATIONS CAN TAKE INTO ACCOUNT geographic trends and simultaneously embed DEI into their brands and business, they are truly on their way to creating a competitive advantage that not only enhances the business, but also benefits marginalized groups. Getting businesses to a place where their actions and policies truly enhance the lives of disadvantaged employees requires a compelling rationale for change that people at all levels of the company can buy into.

An Inclusive LGBTQ Customer Experience

Same sex marriage is legal in twenty-nine countries, while in seventy countries, same-sex relationships are outlawed and in a dozen countries are punishable by death.[1] Some societies demonstrate growing awareness of transgender and non-binary identities, while in others it remains extraordinarily dangerous to defy conventional binary gender categories. Given this disparity in acceptance across countries, organizations have to tailor their rationale for LGBTQ inclusion.

In 2012, the Managing Director, Head of Global Diversity and Inclusion at Barclays Bank, Mark McLane, was tasked with partnering across the organization to realize the vision of making Barclays the most inclusive bank in the UK. At its core, Barclays is a customer-driven organization. To add value to the business model, DEI would need to strengthen the relationship with existing customers while attracting new ones.

LGBTQ BUSINESS CASE

Benefits to Countries and Cities

The levels of acceptance range from countries such as Nigeria and Iran with LGBTQ-hostile laws in which homosexuality is punishable by death to most Western European countries and North America where same-sex marriage or civil unions are legal. Multiple studies have shown a correlation between LGBTQ inclusion and economic output per person on a national level.[2] Research has shown that when LGBTQ individuals are excluded, it can have economic impacts on organizations such as lost labor time and reduced productivity. The noted economist Lee Badgett estimated that India could be throwing away more than US $30 billion, equivalent to 1.7 percent of their GDP a year by stigmatizing LGBTQ people through its anti-LGBTQ laws and policies.[3]

Increased Consumer Revenue

LGBTQ inclusion results in significant potential consumer revenue for organizations. In 2019, the worldwide buying power of the LGBTQ population was estimated to be US $3.7 trillion.[4]

Consumer sentiment is often a driver of change. LGBTQ consumers and allies hold organizations to account if they perceive they are not being treated fairly. Globally 71 percent of LGBTQ individuals and 82 percent of allies are more likely to purchase a good or service from a company that supports LGBTQ equality.[5]

Employee Retention

Organizations that create a culture enabling employees to be fully out and open about their sexual identity benefit from a retention dividend. Kenji Yoshino, Professor of Constitutional Law at New York University, explored the cost of "covering" an identity at work. The research revealed that when employees felt required to hide a facet of their identity due to pressure from organizational leaders, they would be more likely to leave the organization.[6] Research by Out Now LGBT2020 reveals that an employee is more likely to remain at an organization if they are fully out to co-workers. Their study looked at ten countries to illustrate a company's savings due to retention of LGBTQ staff. An openly out employee is 5 percent more likely to stay with an employer in Brazil, 17 percent in Canada, and 22 percent in France. The report then extrapolated these percentages to estimate the total resulting business savings. In Australia, for example, an employee who is fully out is 11 percent more likely to stay with the organization compared to an individual who is not out to anyone. This 11 percent was converted to a dollar amount to calculate the retention dividend.[7] The business savings for an organization of 100,000 employees was estimated to range from US $603,000 to US $4.5 million. However, if the organization had 250,000 employees, the retention dividend saving was estimated to be between a staggering US $1.5 to US $11.2 million.[8]

Employee Engagement, Commitment, and Creativity

As well as retention, employee engagement and commitment increase in organizations with LGBTQ-inclusive policies. The Center for Talent Innovation found that in organizations with such policies, employees are "significantly more likely to say they are proud to work for their employer (84% versus 68%) and more likely to 'go the extra mile' for company success (84% versus 73%)."[9] Additionally, out LGBTQ employees feel more creative, empowered, and safer.[10]

Given the wealth of data on the business case for LGBTQ, it was a seemingly obvious strategy for Barclays to market to the LGBTQ population. It was particularly compelling in the UK, given the friendly LGBTQ laws and high levels of cultural acceptance. The UK passed the Civil Rights Partnership Act 2004, which allowed same-sex couples to legally enter into binding partnerships, similar to marriage. The subsequent Marriage (Same-Sex Couples) Act 2013 then went further, allowing same-sex couples in England and Wales to marry.

The purchasing power of the LGBTQ community in the UK in 2019 was estimated to be £6 billion a year.[11] Many organizations were already reaching out to this affluent consumer base, and Mark knew Barclays needed to stand out. Something different was needed, something that would truly connect the brand with the LGBTQ market.

In 2012 Barclays aired the first retail banking advertisement in the UK to include a gay couple. The advertisement promoted Barclays personalized ATM cards that were designed to be "less banking and more YOU." The bank also ran the British finance industry's first transgender-awareness event in London in 2013. Both these initiatives built the reputation of the bank as an inclusive brand and laid the foundation for Barclays to strengthen its relationship with LGBTQ consumers.

In 2014, Barclays secured the headline sponsorship of Pride in London and transformed the event into a grander occasion with over 125,000 people visiting over the weekend. They developed a contactless payment band that could be used throughout the event and that doubled as a ticket for the festival. This new technology allowed Pride attendees to donate through the band and "ping a pound for pride." Attendees could also attach their picture to a donation, which would then appear on the big screens in Trafalgar Square, all with Barclays branding. Barclays changed a number of cash machines along London's Pride route into GAYTMs (gay ATMs).[12]

As a result, in 2017 Barclays was showcased as a Star Performer by Stonewall, an LGBTQ rights charity in the UK, and became the bank of choice for the LGBTQ community.[13] The external commitment of Barclays to its LGBTQ customers also positively impacted employees at the bank, as noted by CEO Anthony Jenkins in 2014: "We have definitely had people who have come out in Barclays, who have felt more comfortable bringing their whole self to work because of the commitment we have shown externally."[14]

Barclays kept its commitment to LGBTQ inclusion consistent while adapting its approach to different settings. We looked previously at how Barclays navigated this terrain in Uganda and Singapore. In India, where same-sex marriage was outlawed until 2018, Barclays relied on partnerships with Indian LGBTQ rights organizations and employee network leaders from other countries. This built the confidence of local change agents within the company as they worked toward creating a more inclusive organizational climate for their LGBTQ employees in India.

Barclays never lost sight of its mission but calibrated its approach depending on what it found in each new place. Aligning its rationale for change with its ambition to be the most inclusive brand enabled Barclays to strengthen customer relationships, thereby attracting additional revenue and growth and benefitting its employees by making it safe to be out (see Figure 5).[15]

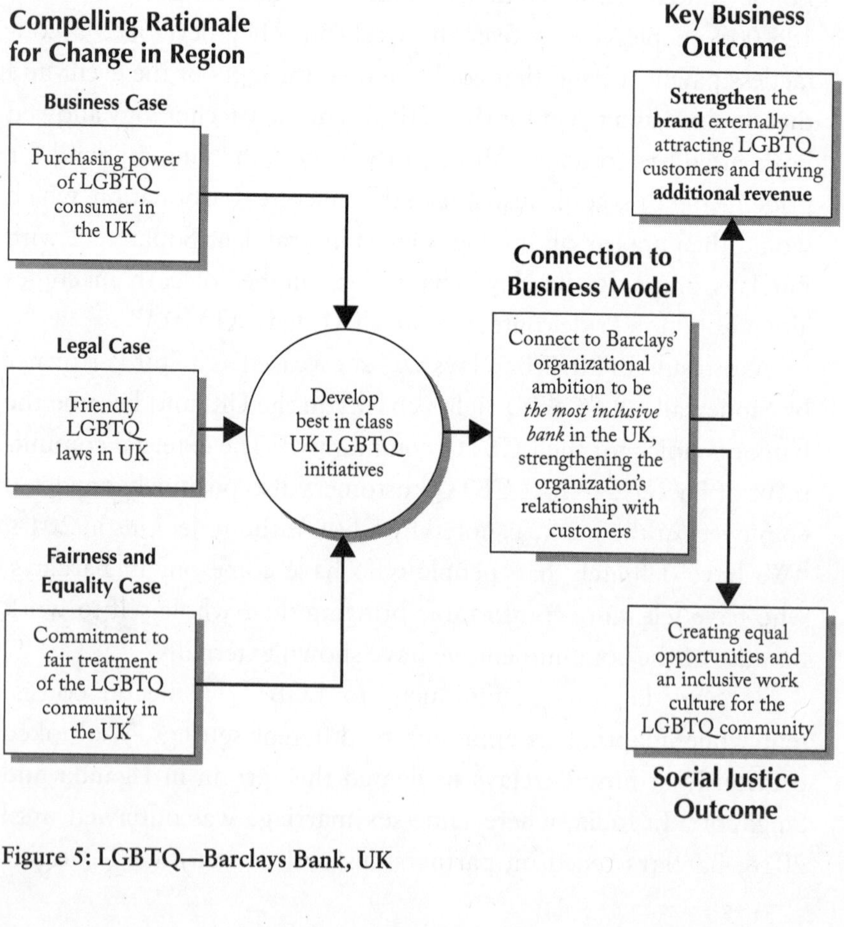

Figure 5: LGBTQ—Barclays Bank, UK

Stability and Independence: Tapping the Potential of the Refugee Community

Developing and implementing DEI strategies focused on ethnicity and race in Europe can be challenging due to the differing definitions and restrictions on data gathering, as we saw in Chapter 2. So how can organizations frame a compelling case for change given local challenges around race? Mass movement of people into Europe provided one entry point.

The ongoing Syrian conflict, along with violence in Iraq, Afghanistan, and other parts of the world, led to a refugee crisis in Europe. According to the Pew Research Center, "a record 1.3 million migrants applied for asylum in the 28 member states of the European Union, Norway and Switzerland in 2015 alone."[16]

This crisis presented an opportunity for organizations to develop a strategy that married both a moral imperative and a business imperative, while providing an entry point to begin the dialogue around ethnicity and race in Europe.

The moral case for hiring refugees is evident. On arrival in their host countries refugees can "experience multiple barriers to integration such as insecure legal status, substandard housing conditions, limited access to education and prejudice."[17] Refugees often experience significant challenges in gaining full-time employment. In Europe, leading with a moral and fairness case by offering employment opportunities can be an extremely compelling driver for addressing DEI.

Deutsche Post DHL Group is the world's leading logistics company operating in over 220 countries in the world. Since 2015, the organization has been supporting aid projects in Europe with a commitment to hire refugees and facilitate integration. Deutsche Post DHL's rationale was advanced by a moral and fairness case with employees advocating for the company to step up to support refugees. To deliver on their commitment, the organization collaborated with external organizations like the Tent Partnership for Refugees, which works with the private sector to support economic independence for refugees.

REFUGEE BUSINESS CASE

Lower Turnover Rates

Refugees are often seeking stability after forced dislocation and have been shown to have higher employment retention and lower turnover rates. The Fiscal Policy Institute and the Tent Partnership for Refugees "found that 73% of U. S. employers interviewed . . . reported a higher retention rate for their refugee employees."[18] These lower levels of employee attrition translate into lower recruitment costs, which are typically one-fifth of an employee's salary—a significant savings for the business.

Filling the Talent Gap

"Many refugees arrive in Europe with a great diversity of skills, experience, and specializations that could make tangible contributions to the EU workforce."[19] Given the talent shortage in Europe with an increasingly aging population, refugees are a skilled talent pool that organizations can draw on.

Increased Loyalty from Younger Generations

Research reveals that clients and customers gravitate to organizations with initiatives that positively impact society. This is particularly true of the Millennial and Gen Z populations. Seventy-six percent of Millennials "consider a company's social and environmental contributions when deciding where to work," and as a result, this generational cohort are more loyal both as workers and consumers to companies with socially responsible business practices.[20] Additionally, employees feel enriched by the opportunity to engage and support their refugee colleagues.

Financial Outcomes

Hiring refugees results in greater racial and ethnic diversity. McKinsey's global "Why Diversity Matters" research finds that "organizations in the top quartile for racial and ethnic diversity are 35% more likely to have financial returns above their respective national industry medians."[21]

Deutsche Post DHL delivered language and professional development classes to over 12,000 refugees in Germany. In Sweden, forklift drivers were in great demand. Through DHL's refugee inclusion program, 9 out of 12 refugees passed a rigorous forklift drivers' test in 2018. As a result, word spread through the refugee community and more refugees applied for these jobs. Not only did the organization's commitment address a talent gap but it also increased employee engagement and pride in their company.

Deutsche Post DHL Group articulated a transformational rationale for change by both addressing a pressing situation of the influx of refugees, while leaning into their unified purpose of *Connecting People, Improving Lives*. The organization tapped into a skilled and motivated talent pool, alleviating challenges caused by the talent shortage while at the same time addressing a humanitarian crisis by providing opportunities to refugees (see Figure 6).[22]

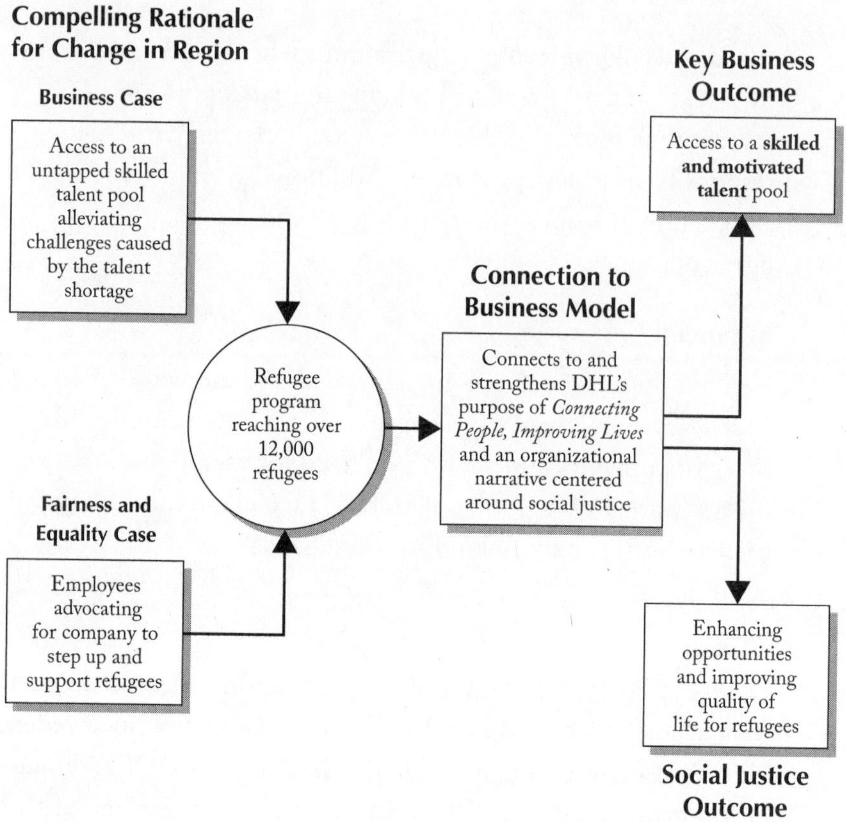

Figure 6: Race and Ethnicity—Deutsche Post DHL Group, Europe

Inviting the Next Generation to Build a Better Work World

As we saw in Chapter 5, the Middle East region has experienced a local employment supply-demand disconnect due to a skills mismatch. This has resulted in underemployment of youth and the recruitment of high numbers of expatriates to meet the unfilled talent needs. Governments implemented localization laws and quotas to require organizations to hire local talent. However, there are significant challenges that organizations must overcome if they are to meet those quotas.

In some countries, local nationals are reluctant to work in the private sector since pay, benefits, and prestige are generally lower than in the public sector, where job security, social status, and flexible working conditions are guaranteed. Despite high unemployment rates, younger people—many of whom are in a financial position to be selective, especially in the wealthy Arab States of the Persian Gulf countries—often do not consider a private sector role, preferring to wait until a public sector opening is available.[23] As a result, the highly educated youth populations have the highest rates of unemployment in the region.[24]

EY, a global, multidisciplinary professional services organization saw this untapped workforce as an opportunity in the Middle East. That, combined with government pressure to recruit locally, provided a compelling reason to reach out to local youth. First, EY framed their entry-level roles as opportunities for local nationals to gain valuable experience that they could leverage to secure a government role in the future. They offered local nationals the opportunity to work on government contracts to gain exposure to the public sector, albeit from within a private sector role. They also provided development programs for local nationals to enhance cross-cultural and leadership skills.

Families of those being interviewed are now invited into the organization to see firsthand the working environment in order to shift negative perceptions of the private sector. These initiatives have increased the number of local nationals working in EY over the last five years with the company meeting and exceeding its quota.

However, it is not only the threat of government penalties that is compelling organizations to hire young local talent. A key outcome of nationalization strategies for organizations is a more locally knowledgeable workforce. Potential local clients in the region routinely ask organizations to share employee nationalization data.

Clients are keen to work with organizations that are recruiting and developing local talent who will be able to relate more effectively with them.

To develop their transformational rationale for change, EY connected the laws in the region to their stated mission of *Building a Better Working World* (see Figure 7). EY exceeded their quota, which resulted in stronger relationships with governments in the region creating the potential for more government contracts. In addition, a more locally knowledgeable workforce resulted in better client partnerships. EY's change narrative both benefitted their business and addressed the social issues of employment for youth in the region.[25]

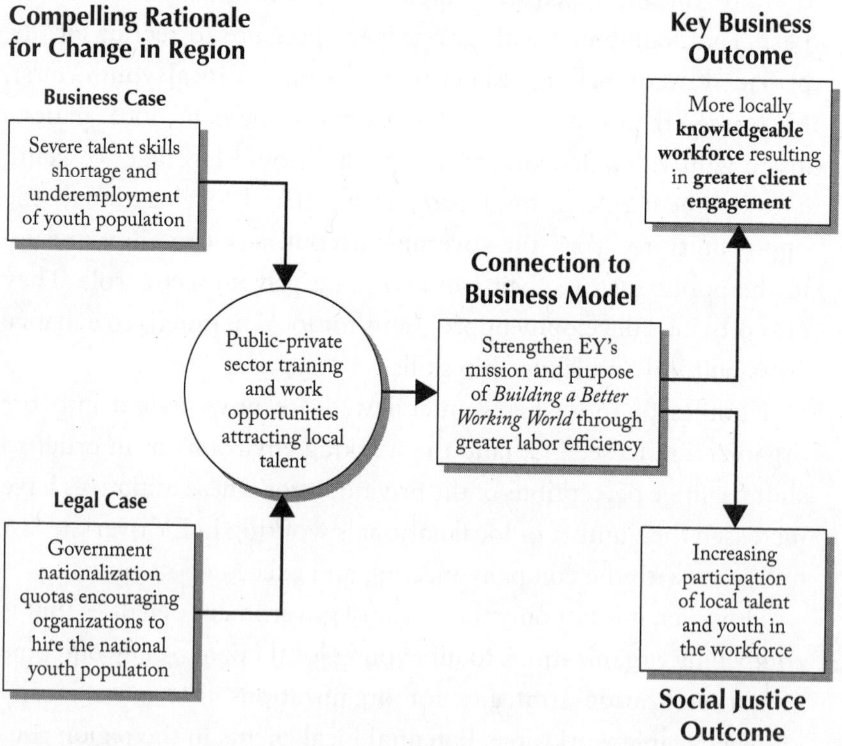

Figure 7: Generations—EY, Middle East

Creativity and Innovation: Improving the Lives of People with Disabilities

Over a billion people worldwide are affected by disabilities and, according to the Harkin Institute, people with disabilities (PWD) face an unemployment rate of 80 percent.[26] Europe has made progress in the economic participation of PWD. The European Disability Forum estimates that in the region just over 50 percent of PWD are employed, which compares favorably with the global picture.[27]

So, what has been the compelling rationale for addressing the inclusion of PWD in Europe? As we saw in Chapter 5, government quotas in conjunction with fines for noncompliance have driven change across Europe. As the population ages, the greater prevalence of disability reinforces the need to include PWD.

PEOPLE WITH DISABILITIES BUSINESS CASE

Employee Impact

Numerous studies going back fifty years, including research by the US Department of Labor and Deakin University in Australia, have found that PWD have high retention and productivity rates and low levels of absenteeism.[28] PWD hired by Marriott Hotel & Resorts through their Pathway to Independence program in the US experienced a 6 percent attrition rate compared to a 52 percent rate for their overall workforce.[29] A lower attrition rate for PWD translates into substantial financial savings. It costs organizations between 16 percent (for lower-skilled positions) and as much as 213 percent (for the highest-level executives) of a person's annual salary to replace them.[30] In addition to retention, PWD often bring a different perspective to the workplace. With high levels of unemployment, hiring PWD not only positively impacts the organization, but it also improves their quality of life.

Consumer Impact

Disability-friendly organizations are more appealing to consumers, with 87 percent of customers in the US saying they would prefer to support businesses employing people with disabilities.[31] An estimated 1.85-billion-strong worldwide, PWD are an emerging market greater than the population of China. "Their friends and family add another 3.4 billion potential consumers who act on their emotional connection to PWD. Together, they control over US $13 trillion in annual disposable income globally."[32] In regions with an aging population, the business case is further strengthened. An older population brings greater numbers of PWD, and as a result, more disposable income. United Nations statistics show that more than 46 percent of people over sixty have a disability compared to a rate of 15 percent for the population as a whole.[33]

In 2017, the Italian pasta company Barilla partnered with Hackability, a nonprofit social and technology research laboratory, to create Hackability@Barilla. Together, they developed an initiative with interdisciplinary teams in which people with disabilities joined forces with Barilla research designers. The team created cooking tools and new packaging to match the requirements of

PWD. The initiative linked directly to Barilla's *Good for You, Good for the Planet* mission. The first Hackability lab was held in Italy, but when Barilla US heard of its success, it started the project there. The innovative spirit born from this collaboration soon triggered a wave of creativity across many countries in the organization.

The partnership with Hackability gave Barilla access to a co-design process in which solutions were designed not "for" but "with" the people who need them. The results have been product designs that are simple yet incredibly effective.

For example, people with sight impairment communicated that package designs were not accessible for them. The packaging for the different types of pasta (except for Spaghetti) was the same. This made it challenging for sight-impaired customers to know what type of pasta they were buying. And this had further practical implications as each pasta shape has a different cooking time. In Italy, it's important to ensure the pasta is al dente. So, understanding both the country context and feedback from people with sight impairments, Barilla is evaluating the option to add braille or a QR code to their pasta packaging to indicate pasta shape and cooking time.

Another Barilla innovation through Hackability was a kitchen tool that allows customers to open pasta sauces using one arm. The lid can be opened with just one rotation of the hand, helping those who may otherwise have difficulty in opening jars.[34]

The drive for PWD inclusion at Barilla hinged on both the aging population trends in Italy as well as a regional employment quotas for PWD. Integrating these realities with their *Good for You, Good for the Planet* mission spurred innovative solutions to customer challenges. This had a positive impact on their revenue and resulted in a competitive advantage for the business, all while also improving the quality of life for employees and consumers with disabilities (see Figure 8).

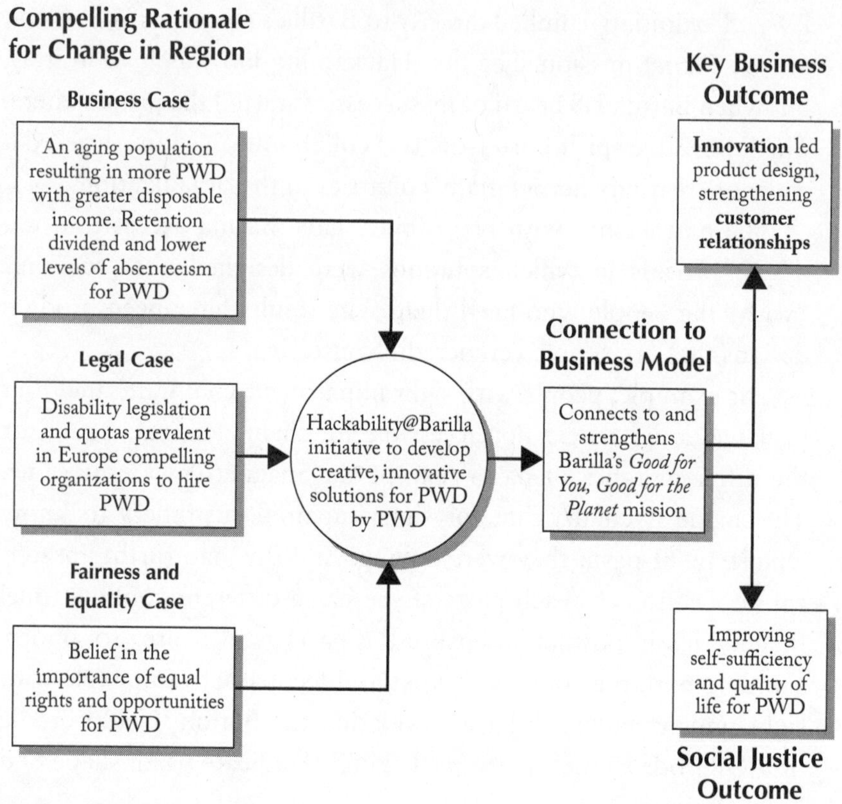
Compelling Rationale for Change in Region
Business Case
An aging population resulting in more PWD with greater disposable income. Retention dividend and lower levels of absenteeism for PWD
Legal Case
Disability legislation and quotas prevalent in Europe compelling organizations to hire PWD
Fairness and Equality Case
Belief in the importance of equal rights and opportunities for PWD
Hackability@Barilla initiative to develop creative, innovative solutions for PWD by PWD
Connection to Business Model
Connects to and strengthens Barilla's Good for You, Good for the Planet mission
Key Business Outcome
Innovation led product design, strengthening customer relationships
Improving self-sufficiency and quality of life for PWD
Social Justice Outcome

Figure 8: Disabilities—Barilla, Italy

A Talent-Based Approach for Addressing the Advancement of Women

Advancement of women often represents the first port of call for organizations on their global DEI journey. The relative ease of measuring progress, as well as the widely promoted business case benefits of a gender-balanced workforce, has compelled many organizations to develop global gender diversity initiatives—although, so far, these have mostly used conventional, binary concepts of gender.

Given the omnipresence of the topic of gender across all regions, it can be tempting to develop a globally universal standardized rationale for gender diversity. However, a transversal approach that contextualizes the rationale for change by considering the geographic specificities and the nature of the business is as important for the advancement of women as any other identity dimension.

In Latin America, for example, a pervasive barrier that hinders the advancement of women is often discrimination at home. While violence against women exists in every culture and region and across all socioeconomic classes, the prevalence of gender-based violence in Latin America has led many countries in the region to legally distinguish femicide from homicide."[35]

In 2016, "A Gendered Analysis of Violent Deaths" reported that fourteen of the twenty-five countries with the highest femicide rates are in Latin America.[36] A report by the World Health Organization in 2013 showed that in "12 Latin American and Caribbean countries studied, between 17% and 53% of women interviewed reported having suffered physical or sexual violence."[37] The global pandemic of 2020 exacerbated the problem, with many countries reporting increases in violence against women. Colombia experienced a 50 percent increase in violence against women in 2020 and femicides rose 65 percent in Venezuela in April 2020. In El Salvador and Honduras, there was a thirty-fold increase in online searches for protection from gender-based violence during this time.[38]

As we saw in Chapter 5, the moral outrage over violence against women led to large protest rallies across the region. From Mexico and Chile to Argentina and Brazil, women took to the streets demanding government action. Governments have begun to take steps to compel change by strengthening legal frameworks and implementing prevention mechanisms. Eighteen countries in the region have passed laws to classify femicide as a crime.

Research shows that those suffering from domestic violence often experience higher levels of job absenteeism, as well as the lesser-known *presentism*, which is being present at work but unproductive and not fully functioning.[39] There are organizational costs associated with absenteeism and presentism in the workplace. Rather than dismissing gender-based violence as a non-work-related personal matter, organizations aspiring to a more diverse workforce must understand the systemic challenges of gender-based violence.

By focusing their strategy on this troubling trend, organizations can begin to create momentum to attract and retain women at all levels. This is particularly important given the talent-skill shortage in the region.

Understanding this context, Sodexo in Latin America considered violence against women as a component of advancing women in the workplace and addressing the talent gap. This drive to bring the best talent into the company was coupled with the organization's mission of *Improving the Quality of Life for All*: its employees, clients, customers, and community. The local team developed a multipronged strategy including awareness building, workplace sexual discrimination training, HR policies to address violence against women, intentional development and promotion of female talent, external partnerships, and communications campaigns. Over 6,000 men and women were trained on the impact of violence and strategies for interrupting the cycle.

By 2018, the representation of women in the overall workforce increased in Sodexo Latin America. Between 2012 and 2018, the percentage of female leaders increased from 22 percent to 44 percent, bringing it within the gender balance range. Employees were more engaged and the engagement of women in management positions increased by 24 percentage points between 2013 and 2018.[40] While we can't prove a direct causal relationship, I am sure that tackling the impact of violence against women, addressing mental health issues, and increasing women's safety contributed significantly to the retention of women at Sodexo.

Rather than take a uniform approach to building a change narrative for DEI, Sodexo incorporated the reality of gender-based violence and the skilled talent gap and focused on the organization's talent needs to make a compelling argument for addressing gender diversity in the region (see Figure 9). The social justice movement, #MeToo, bolstered their efforts.

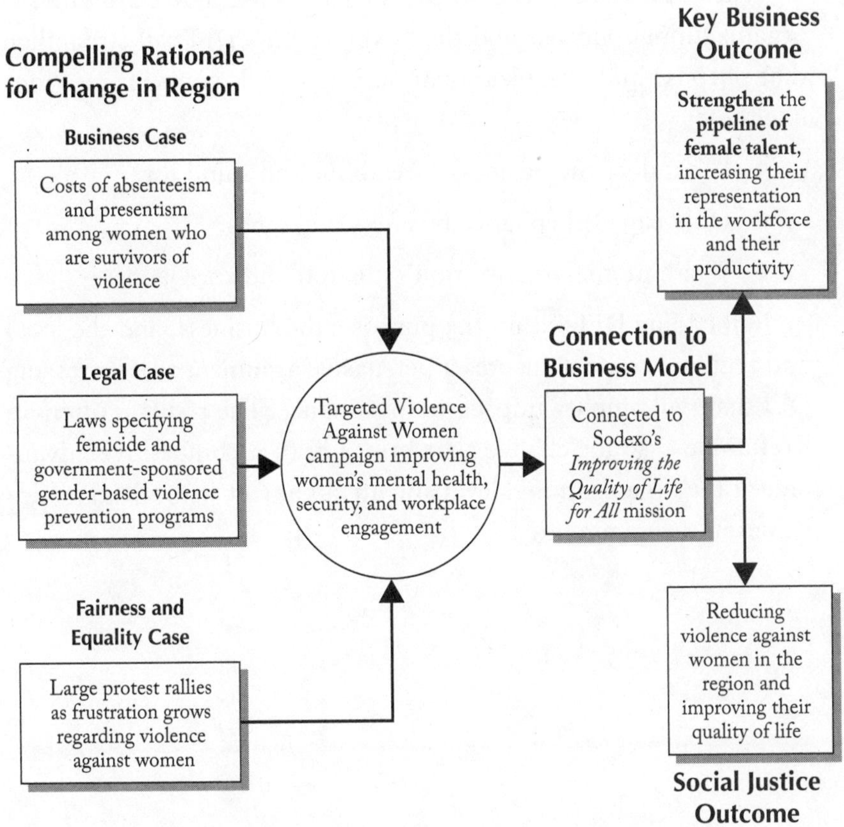

Figure 9: Gender—Sodexo, Latin America

Conclusion

To be successful and to create sustainable competitive advantage, DEI change efforts cannot be siloed or bolted on. Instead, they must be central to what the business is, the mission of the organization, and what they do. Whether it is the customer-focused narrative at Barclays or the social justice business model embedded at the heart of DHL, an understanding of how DEI can strengthen the fundamentals of the organization at the very basic level is critical.

When developing a DEI strategy, it can be useful to start with the organizational purpose and then explore how DEI can strengthen that purpose and organizational narrative. Ask yourself questions like these:

- What does the business care about and stand for?
- How can DEI enhance business outcomes?
- What are the organization's mission and core values?

Embedding DEI within the purpose, the business, and the local and regional context ensures a persuasive argument for addressing DEI that will amplify impact and resonance. The result is often an irrefutable case for change that brings both a competitive advantage at the organizational level and an alignment with social justice values in the community.

Principle

4

GO DEEP, WIDE, AND INSIDE-OUT

ORGANIZATIONS ARE COMPRISED OF INTERCONNECTED systems that work in concert with each other and, as such, DEI needs to be infused into the processes, policies, and structures throughout an organization. The external ecosystem also influences organizational outcomes. Public and private entities need to work in concert with external stakeholders to advance their objectives.

Principle 4 considers the importance of embedding DEI *wide* through thoughtful global governance and strategy frameworks, *deep* through local champions and allies that seed DEI in the organizational culture, and *inside-out* by integrating DEI into internal systems and by engaging the external ecosystem. Drawing on stories from a variety of organizations and countries, Chapters 7 and 8 bring to life successful strategies to go deep, wide, and inside-out.

Chapter 7, "The Scaffolding for Change: Governance and Champions," demonstrates how DEI change needs to be scaled wide through governance structures and strategies that provide a unifying framework for global cohesion, while harnessing the energy and knowledge of local change agents to allow for local implementation and buy-in. It provides lessons learned from global governance structures and considerations in optimizing local diversity champions.

Chapter 8, "Embedding Change: Internal and External Ecosystems," illustrates how DEI can be integrated into systems and processes, with particular attention to the talent lifecycle. Internal systems are interconnected, requiring that DEI be incorporated into the recruiting, development, advancement, engagement, and retention of talent as well as other processes like marketing, supply chain, and business functions. Only with this infusion into all systems can we insert checks and balances so that employees and businesses benefit from a diverse, equitable, and inclusive culture. How DEI is embedded is very local in its implementation. And all this work happens in a broader societal context. Organizations have found that engaging external ecosystems enhances the internal work and builds their commitment to being purpose driven by addressing issues of social justice.

7

THE SCAFFOLDING FOR CHANGE: GOVERNANCE AND CHAMPIONS

If you want to go fast, go alone.
If you want to go far, go together.

—UNKNOWN (often quoted as an African proverb)

GLOBAL DEI TRANSFORMATION needs to be grounded in the local context, led by transformative leaders, and bolstered by a compelling change narrative. For enduring organizational change, systems, structures, and processes must also be revamped to include DEI.

The fourth principle is Go Deep, Wide, and Inside-Out. *Deep* is about seeding DEI within the DNA of the culture by engaging multiple stakeholders at all levels of the organization as champions and allies. *Wide* acknowledges that change must occur across multiple geographies through thoughtful DEI strategies and governance structures that create a coherent, principled through line. *Inside-Out* focuses on embedding DEI into the internal systems and externally in the community to ensure sustainability through leadership transitions. This chapter addresses the governance to scale DEI change wide across geographies and deep through internal change agents and champions.

Wide

Frank Dobbin and Alexandra Kalev, professors at Harvard and Tel Aviv University, respectively, discuss the effectiveness of governance structures—such as diversity task forces—that "help promote social accountability."[1] Ensuring that these governance structures take a wide approach to global DEI provides the essential pathways for knowledge sharing, innovation, economies of scale, growth, and organization-wide storytelling that advances brand, culture, and communities. Transversal DEI strategies and governance structures provide congruence and a global unifying framework along with the flexibility for local adaptation.

The scaffolding for a global transversal DEI strategy considers the workforce, the workplace, the community, and the marketplace. The structure is broad enough to accommodate local adaptation like the prevailing dominant and nondominant groups, regional rationales for change, specific legislation, and cultural and historical patterns.

Considering a transversal wide framework is an important starting point for global DEI because the reach of these strategies and governance structures provides the architecture that activates both the deep efforts (engaging local stakeholders and champions) and enables inside-out approaches that impact organizational systems and processes.

Scaling a Strategy to Advance Women Globally

I have a crystal-clear memory of a meeting in Berlin in 2011. Sodexo's internal gender advisory board, called SoTogether, hosted the meeting. At the time, SoTogether was comprised of senior female leaders who informed the gender strategy for Sodexo.

Twenty-five senior women from across the enterprise sat expectantly in the meeting room, while seven White men, all in what appeared to be identical navy-blue suits and crisp, white shirts and each over six feet tall, walked into the room. This was Sodexo Germany's leadership team.

They looked distinctly uncomfortable, probably never having been in a room with outfits creating a splash of so many colors. And they were expected to present their region's work on DEI, which we knew was nonexistent.

Let's just say that the organization has come very far both in representation of women and in fostering an inclusive culture globally since those early years. And this progress, in large part, can be attributed to SoTogether.

In June 2009, the Sodexo Women's International Forum for Talent (SWIFT), later named SoTogether, was created by CEO Michel Landel "to accelerate the attainment of gender balance within Sodexo through the personal drive, commitment and leadership of its high-level leaders."[2] The primary focus was to advance women in the organization.

Senior female leaders from around the world—though predominantly from Europe—were reluctant participants when we first called them together, hoping to launch SWIFT. This was the all-women meeting that I mention in the introduction that made me realize that even the seemingly straightforward work of advancing women was going to be complicated when rolling it out globally. These executives were uncomfortable that their gender was being called out and disturbed that men in the organization were calling this a "secret meeting" and nothing more than a "shopping retreat." They were adamant that they were in their assignments to these leadership roles based on merit only. "If women work hard there is no reason they can't succeed," they told me.

I was surprised at the early pushback and reluctance to gather in a women-only affinity group. The discomfort, I slowly realized, was less about their own identity as women and more about how they related to the entrenched male-dominant power structures within the organization and the broader society.

It was evident that Sodexo would not gain traction in embedding gender equity unless women leaders were more keenly aware of the barriers their female colleagues faced. The everyday gender bias that they encountered had become so normalized for them that they had internalized it and were unable to see its impact on their own lives and careers. And it was clear that they would more readily embrace gender equity work if men were in on the conversation.

The following year, I organized a session in Paris and also invited Sodexo male managers. In keeping with the strategy to engage clients as a way to reach Sodexo managers, I invited senior women representing some of Sodexo's clients to participate on a panel on gender equity in their respective organizations. The Sodexo participants were extremely engaged, and the women didn't feel spotlighted because men were in the room and because the sessions were on topics also relevant to men, such as work-life effectiveness. They were also able to see that gender wasn't just a Sodexo issue but was a challenge shared with renowned clients. However, some of the most senior women at Sodexo still wanted to distance themselves from the topic, uncertain about how men in power would respond and how it would impact their careers.

It took two years of dialogue to bring these senior women to a point where they acknowledged that other women in the organization could use their support and that it did not have to be as hard for those women as it had been for them.

The resistance changed to support for two reasons. First, in 2013, men were included in SoTogether. A few select male champions were invited to join, and their active engagement and endorsement validated SoTogether as integral to the organization, rather than a special interest group just for women.

When SoTogether was "validated" by the dominant group (men), it gained credibility. I was learning that to counter resistance, I needed to find ways to bring powerholders along. Rather than rally against a male-dominated power structure, it was more effective to use the lever of their influence to upend those power dynamics. The women were relieved at not being singled out. They had spent their careers working to belong and to be accepted by male power structures. This early experience with SoTogether reinforced for me that, clearly, we had to shift the culture to be more inclusive, allowing women to bring their authentic selves to work. I also had to hold on to the vision of these women eventually being comfortable with their gender identity and thriving because of, rather than despite, it.

Sodexo began to frame the goal as achieving a balance between men and women, rather than just focusing on the representation of women. We intuitively knew that gender balance makes a difference for business outcomes but needed to demonstrate the correlations within Sodexo. As mentioned in Chapter 5, Sodexo conducted an evidence-based study that demonstrated the value of gender balance using Sodexo data. Framing it as balance rather than representation appeared less threatening and helped garner support.

Sophie Bellon, board member and later chair of Sodexo's board, became a co-chair of SoTogether, sending a powerful message about the importance of this gender advisory board. With a board member involved, along with two global executive sponsors, SoTogether became a coveted body to belong to. High-potential women from across all business lines considered it an honor to be vetted to join. The vetting included a rigorous 360-degree interview process assembling references from peers, subordinates, and supervisors, and ensured representation across all geographies and business lines.

Men, too, vied to be included in SoTogether. Interestingly, the dynamic had shifted from the group needing male "validation" to being a vehicle for male champions to become visible for their support of DEI. This recognition of male allies served to encourage more men to step up as supporters. This is why, in 2018, SWIFT was renamed SoTogether—as a recognition of the role that male champions also needed to play in advancing the gender strategy.

Remember the meeting in Berlin in 2011 with those seven White men in their navy-blue suits? Well, fast-forward to 2012. The CEO for Germany was replaced by a woman who was part of SoTogether, and her executive team soon was 38 percent women!

Between 2009 and 2019, the representation of women in Sodexo's senior leadership had increased from 16 percent to 34 percent worldwide, thanks to the leadership of SoTogether. The focus, results, and momentum of SoTogether around the world served to further catalyze the organization to expand its investment in other dimensions of DEI.

A Transversal Approach for Global Governance

SoTogether used a transversal governance structure that successfully scaled up Sodexo's strategy to advance women by holding global priorities for the whole organization. It also went deep by catalyzing champions through local gender networks. For SoTogether, an overarching strategy and related metrics and accountability systems provided a global framework, ensuring consistency across all geographies. The global target was 40 percent representation of women in senior management ranks by 2025, a pipeline of women in profit and loss roles, and a culture of inclusion. SoTogether facilitated adoption of the global priorities in part by inspiring local gender networks to implement them with their unique homegrown focus.

The gender ERGs had their own priorities ranging from education on violence against women, to confidence-building development opportunities, to support groups of parents of children with disabilities. The local networks in different countries were brought together regularly—either in person or online—to share best practices, cross-fertilize learning, strengthen connections, and leverage synergies. This created a unified brand, connecting all the gender networks globally while allowing them to focus on local needs.

This transversal structure enabled allies from outside a closed society or a society not as mature on a diversity topic to share stories across boundaries sparking change. To engage leaders globally on the DEI journey, SoTogether met in different countries. The country was selected based either on whether they had some excellent practices to showcase or, conversely, if the country leadership needed to be influenced to support the gender balance strategy. The meetings involved, among other items, a reception where the country management teams, clients, and potentials were invited to an evening of networking and inspirational DEI content with renowned speakers.

The country executive teams, many comprised of all White men, were often put on the spot by being asked to present to SoTogether. They prepared for the meeting by working on a case for why DEI was important and then presented it to an audience of almost entirely senior women, a novel experience for them. Influenced by the SoTogether executives from other countries and seeing clients engaged in DEI, several Sodexo country leaders became passionate advocates, hiring and sponsoring women. As a result, the numbers of women in leadership steadily increased. Burcin Ressamoglu, a female Turkish executive, said, "My involvement in SoTogether improved my perspectives, gave visibility to leadership and opened up opportunities for me to grow across the world. I got inspired to move from leading a smaller business in Turkey to heading Sodexo's large and complex Benefits business in the UK market. I know there are so many opportunities for me at Sodexo!"[3]

Getting the desired impact requires intentionally putting in place a governance structure that has representation from across the organization, enables scale, uses a consistent narrative, and presents a consolidated view while also allowing for local adaptation.

Deep

Regardless of whether the transversal governance structure is a task force, an advisory body, an ERG, or a council, it needs to be able to catalyze DEI allies who can engage the organization in a way that adapts to the local context and penetrates deep within the DNA of the organization. And that can only happen through people.

Local Champions and Allies

When employees at all levels feel empowered, they more readily facilitate the embedding of DEI. Identifying and engaging allies and champions, especially among mid-level managers, who can help integrate the commitment to DEI, accelerates and mainstreams change. These champions provide a feedback loop between the local and global, thereby decreasing resistance that might be provoked by top-down headquarters-driven global efforts. And they are key to effective implementation within the cultural contexts, guiding the pacing and relevance of the efforts.

Champions and allies may come from any level in the organization and from any function, including business leaders who have been tapped to play this role.

Rishi Gour, CEO of Theobroma and former Sodexo India CEO, said, "I was quite clear that as long as it [DEI] was my agenda alone, we are not going to make a lot of progress in a company with 48,000 employees. So somewhere, basically, a whole bunch of people had to own it, not just me. I think at the end of the year, a lot of champions who genuinely believed in diversity and had sort of adopted the agenda, had made it their own. They owned it in their talk, in their team, and they were actually driving it, getting quite passionate."[4]

Aviva Singapore has a title for DEI champions. They refer to them as Chief Engagement Officers—or CEOs! This is quite a recognition of the importance of a DEI champion role. These CEOs can come from any level. They are selected by each business line, and the role is formalized. In recognition of their work as DEI champions, they get a paid day off. Creating a prominent champion role has been a successful strategy in cultivating an inclusive culture and making it more sustainable at Aviva Singapore.[5]

The selection of the champions is important given the critical role they play in engaging the local teams. Champions in any context should be

- Credible and respected locally—this is essential for their messages to have an impact.
- Representative of all levels and roles in the organization
- Passionate about DEI and advancing talent
- Willing to learn and humble enough to admit what they don't know
- Self-aware and working on their own shortcomings
- Committed to the time needed
- Authentic in their commitment
- Allies to marginalized or underrepresented groups
- Willing to speak up when they see inequities or inappropriate behavior

It is important to be sensitive to the potential for burnout in champions who give so much of themselves. It's best to have a broad network so we are not tempted to call on the same people for everything.

The Power of Stories

Inviting empathy, connection, and community is what ultimately leads to real and lasting growth. Diversity champions often use themselves and their own stories as a tool to influence others. I remember the impact of a colleague who quietly and courageously came out to a group of executive leaders who were making hurtful assumptions about the LGBTQ community. It totally shifted the conversation and got unlikely leaders on board. A global online panel with transgender colleagues talking about how caring their Sodexo managers and teams had been in supporting their transitions had people in tears, they were so moved. The willingness of these colleagues to open up dramatically shifted perceptions, creating a more compassionate workplace.

The stories I've heard people share of confronting their own prejudices and unearned privilege have gone a long way to create a climate in which people are honest about their own mistakes and willing to learn. These personal stories are what motivate us to continue the challenging work of DEI and what inspire allies to join the movement to create an inclusion ripple effect.

While there is power in personal stories, we need to be cognizant of the sacrifice and courage it takes to share them. We can create space, but we can never demand that someone share their experience. We can invite personal sharing, but we must not unintentionally pressure people to open up. That should always be an individual choice as it can take a toll on the individual sharing their lived experience. And we need to be mindful that not all cultures are comfortable with public story sharing but may do so in private as Rishi and Michel, two leaders I discussed in Chapter 3, did with me.

What does it look like when DEI champions have an impact?

Passion for DEI: Jennifer's Green Chain

Often a personal connection creates a sense of purpose and passion for DEI that can be infectious and naturally engage others, ultimately creating a groundswell of change.

When Vincent Meehan and his wife went to visit their daughter Jennifer's first grade classroom one day, they found Jennifer, who has Down syndrome, sobbing in the back of the class, saying two words over and over. They looked at her classmates who were making green paper chains and realized that Jennifer was saying "Green chain. Green chain." She wanted a chance to make a chain, but she had been excluded from the activity—an activity she was fully capable of doing.

Now, at age thirty-three, Jennifer works for Sodexo Canada, as does her father. Vincent's experiences raising Jennifer instilled in him a passion for including PWD, and Sodexo Canada's ERG structure was able to offer Vincent a platform to harness that energy to better the organization.

Vincent served as Chair for Sodexo Canada's ADEPT employee network, which stands for All Disabled Employees Possess Talent. ADEPT prioritized pushing for the recruitment of more employees with disabilities. As part of that effort, ADEPT compiled a resource list of ninety-five organizations throughout Canada that specialize in job readiness and recruitment of PWD. Since ADEPT began this work in 2015, over 600 PWD have been hired in Canada, with approximately 100 new people hired each year. Vincent suggested displaying a green paper chain in the office. For every new individual with a disability that joins Sodexo Canada, ADEPT adds a link to Jennifer's Green Chain.

Champions at All Levels

Champions and allies can come from any level in the organization. Engaging at the grass roots ensures that those at entry levels feel included and believe that the organization is "walking the talk." Multiple voices spawn innovation and a more inclusive culture. And people support what they help co-create. Being able to do *with* rather than *to* local employees creates ownership and helps embed the change, creating a domino effect. Sodexo

Canada has a great example of engaging entry-level employees as champions.

Indigenous people make up 4.9 percent of Canada's population. The Indian Act of 1876 aimed to "civilize" Indigenous people through a set of coercive and controlling policies. Under this Act, 150,000 Indigenous children were removed from their families and sent to residential schools. The intent was to isolate them from their cultures and assimilate them into the dominant culture. Research has exposed widespread sexual, physical, and emotional abuse in these schools, and thousands of these children never came home at all: they died or disappeared. Although the schools were closed by the late 1990s, their impact, along with exploitative economic practices, has left a legacy of poverty and intergenerational trauma.[6]

The Native American and Aboriginal Council (NAAC) is an Indigenous ERG at Sodexo Canada, and unlike most other Sodexo ERGs, it includes hourly as well as salaried employees. After they heard about NAAC at a town hall meeting, the hourly employees decided to join NAAC and focus on connecting to their own culture and communities. These were connections that had been broken over time due to the residential school history. To raise awareness of the residential school system, younger employees talked about the impact on their parents and families, and older employees shared their own experiences at the schools.[7]

One of the most successful initiatives of NAAC is also its most simple. They host Sharing Circles once a week. Drawing from an Indigenous cultural practice, people can only talk when an elder passes the stick to them. This helps people listen. "You hear their personal stories, and what people are going through," said Michael Childane, a Sodexo site manager. "Attendance and performance issues began to be more manageable. If there is a personal problem amongst the team that is impacting the operation or if there is an ongoing challenge with an individual, we'll ask someone from the community to facilitate a sharing circle."[8]

In more hierarchical societies with greater power distance, it would not be the norm for the boss to invite the input of their subordinates, and frontline employees might not feel empowered to contribute. When Kristen Anderson was in China leading the Global Innovation and Technology Center for Coca-Cola, she asked her human resources manager for some feedback and cultural coaching. Kristen told me, "The HR manager came to me and said, 'Kristen, you know, it would be better for team-building and inclusion of your staff if you spoke less often and you spoke last.' Because I didn't have a huge cultural understanding of the Chinese, and I didn't realize with the hierarchical culture that if the manager speaks first, you know when the manager says something, no one's going to disagree with them in front of others. I didn't realize that the nodding of heads did not mean I agree with you; it meant I hear you."[9]

External change agents walk a fine line between calibrating their behaviors to the cultural context and considering how to invite and ensure engagement across the spectrum in more hierarchical societies. In the Aviva Singapore example, we saw how assigning a designated role of Chief Engagement Officer was a way of giving credibility and voice to lower-level employees in a hierarchical society, emboldening them to speak up and take initiative.

Visible Allies Speak Up

How do allies lean into speaking up on behalf of marginalized people? Taking a page from the LGBTQ ally approach, Deb Dagit, a US-based disabilities advocate and consultant, created the VOICE program to make PWD allies visible. Deb understood that many people hide their disability for fear of how they might be treated and the impact on their careers. At the same time, people may want to be supportive of coworkers with disabilities but worry about making them uncomfortable and don't know how to start a conversation.

The VOICE program invited allies to display the VOICE symbol to indicate they were open to discussing tough issues related to disabilities and to signal that PWD were valued. These allies had training during which they learned techniques for speaking up when disrespectful comments or jokes were made about people with disabilities.

To be effective, change agents for inclusivity need to take into account the cultural norms. In cultures where the private domain is large, as in France, sexual orientation, for example, is considered a private matter. As a result, according to a 2018 BCG study, 46 percent of LGBTQ employees interviewed in France lie about their sexual orientation to their colleagues.[10] In other cultures, it is more appropriate to be quiet allies as opposed to making the ally position public. Given these norms, how does one effectively push for change? In earlier chapters of this book, I mention several strategies including drawing on senior leaders as allies, sharing examples from other companies, and providing a counter outsider perspective to catalyze change.

Provide Recognition

Given the importance of allies and champions, it is vital to inspire them to continue engaging locally. Barilla declared 2018 "The Year of ERGs," publicly awarding ERGs that had made a contribution, and the CEO made it a practice to always meet with members of local ERGs whenever he visited a branch as a way of keeping his ear to the ground.[11] Kristen Anderson, Barilla's CDO, mentioned that "The CEO always says, 'I want an hour with the ERG on my agenda.' And he meets them—not the head of HR, not the executive sponsor, but the actual leaders and members."[12]

How else can they be recognized? According to Deborah Munster, Executive Vice President at Seramount, a consultancy that provides organizations with integrated tools, benchmarking, and hands-on advisory services, 90 percent of US companies surveyed say that an ERG leadership position is considered during performance reviews and 42 percent of companies factor it into the succession planning process.[13] So being a DEI champion can help career advancement.

Bristol Myers Squibb, a global biopharmaceutical company, announced that it would treat being an ERG leader as a full-time role and pay the position accordingly—a unique recognition of the importance of the role in influencing the culture. Justworks, a US software company, piloted a program compensating their ERG leaders with cash, equity, and career development opportunities. Recognizing DEI champions provides visibility and helps proliferate more such champions.[14]

Conclusion

For successful organizational transformation in DEI, change efforts must be deep and wide. They require a well-conceived and well-implemented governance framework to include a transversal strategy and to scale the inclusion change effort to a global reach (wide). They require champions who bring DEI into the DNA of the organizational culture (deep). They also require metrics to track their success, and this will be discussed in more detail in Chapter 9. However, these alone are not adequate for sustainable change. Lasting change demands transforming an organization's systems (inside-out) by embedding DEI into internal processes and engaging stakeholders in the external ecosystem.

8

EMBEDDING CHANGE: INTERNAL AND EXTERNAL ECOSYSTEMS

To manage a system effectively, you might focus on the interactions of the parts rather than their behavior taken separately.

—RUSSELL L. ACKOFF,
Wharton School, University of Pennsylvania

TO SUSTAIN AN INCLUSIVE CULTURE, it is not enough to implement a wide approach through global governance, and a deep approach with allies and champions. For enduring change, DEI has to inform all systems and processes—internal and external. It cannot be a series of discrete activities operating in isolation, because organizations are comprised of dynamic, interconnected systems internally and inextricably connected to the external environment. The internal and external stakeholders in this ecosystem must be engaged to anchor an inclusive culture deep within the organization and to scale it globally. You need an inside-out approach.

Systems and processes formalize the practice of "paying attention," make visible the values of the organization, and safeguard against inconsistencies.[1] To ensure that bias is eliminated, and diversity is not an afterthought, it needs to be embedded at the onset when processes are designed.

Embedding DEI throughout the System: Born Accessible

Charter Communications, Inc. is a leading broadband connectivity company and cable operator in the US. To address the customer experience, Charter recognized the importance of embedding accessibility at each touch point of the product lifecycle, especially for their aging customers and those with disabilities.

Imagine a technician going into a visually impaired customer's home and leaving their bag of tools on the floor where the customer might trip over them. Or a call center agent asking a blind customer to click on something they cannot see. For a product to be truly accessible for people with disabilities, both the product and all the customer touchpoints have to ensure accessibility, which means that in some cases, processes have to be reimagined. How products are designed, delivered, and supported for customers with disabilities required a new mindset and holistic training for both the Charter Communications, Inc. team members and the customers themselves.

Born Accessible is Charter Communication's initiative to embed accessibility at the onset of the product development process rather than test and remediate later. A twenty-member team, many of whom have disabilities, work side-by-side with developers, user experience designers, testers, and product owners to ensure products launch fully accessible. Peter Brown, Group Vice President, Digital Platforms Agency, spoke to me with passion about how the team helps designers understand how nuances like typography and color contrast can impact disparate disabilities.[2]

Peter said, "We've built accessibility into the foundation of our team culture and processes—this ensures that we have the ability to create a wide range of accessible products and features for every product launch." The result: exceeding compliance standards with a range of assistive technologies including Spectrum Guide, their flagship set-top box video experience that allows customers with a visual disability to easily navigate using text-to-speech to read the TV guide, show titles, times, and descriptions. Charter Communications estimates that 6.7 million subscriber households have someone with a disability using their products.

Initially, Peter focused on the accessible product design but realized that the success of the products was dependent on ensuring that the entire customer journey was attuned to accessibility. He says, "Building the accessible product is just one part. What's more challenging is understanding the impact of accessibility on the whole lifecycle of the product—that's the only way to be truly effective."

Peter and his team went inside-out to ensure accessibility of their products and services for a positive experience for their customers with disabilities.

Integrating DEI in the Talent Lifecycle

It is a myth that if you just hire enough underrepresented talent, over time they will percolate to the top of the organization. Nothing could be further from the truth. It takes intentionality and constant focus. Without that, the World Economic Forum says that it will take women just under one hundred years to reach parity with men.[3] To dismantle the systemic biases that are tenacious barriers to career advancement, we must embed DEI interventions at all points in the talent lifecycle: recruiting, onboarding, engaging, developing, promoting, and retaining employees. This requires collaboration with stakeholders across the organization and externally.

With a holistic approach, it becomes clear that eliminating bias from one part of the talent system is not adequate in itself. Addressing leadership development or mentoring for underrepresented talent may not be enough in themselves to advance talent. But when done in concert with other systemic interventions, like creating a culture of inclusion where the talent feels a sense of belonging and engages enthusiastically, they create a domino effect.

It is challenging to take a systems approach across a large multinational organization, and frequently, the temptation is to roll out a one-size-fits-all model or to leave it to each local entity to do what they want. In a transversal approach, certain policies are globally consistent but executed with deference to local circumstances.

In the following pages, I look at points in the employee lifecycle where DEI interventions are needed and how they look when locally implemented.

Recruiting

While organizations have global targets, the bulk of positions are recruited locally. Understanding local nuances in recruiting and ensuring that bias is eliminated from each step in the process helps advance the goal of hiring the best qualified talent. What constitutes underrepresented talent may differ across countries, as do the best strategies to diversify candidate slates.

Recruiting People with Disabilities: China

In China, PWD are far more impoverished than the general population. The ILO estimated that in 2005 almost 14 million PWD living in rural China were in poverty, and the per capita income of households with PWD was "less than half the average of other households." To combat this, China put in place a number of laws to protect PWD as well as hiring quotas—at least 1.5 percent of public and private workforces must be PWD.[4] This has compelled organizations to ramp up their staffing efforts and, at times, leaves recruiters competing for talent. Considering the full ecosystem is very helpful in recruiting PWDs.

It is not uncommon in China for people with disabilities to live with their parents and siblings. Families are often very protective, and it is not expected that their family member with a disability will work outside the home. The Sodexo China recruiters told me that they make home visits to convince parents that their organization can offer an inclusive, safe environment for their child.

Such an intervention would be unheard of in the United States and many places in Europe. Visiting parents would be viewed as violating privacy, undermining and patronizing to the candidate—even humiliating. But in a Chinese context, this approach was enormously appreciated.

The relationship between the family and the company was extended beyond the hiring phase. For many new employees with disabilities, this was the first time they had left their parents to work, so the recruiters set up a close connection with the family. HR staff occasionally visited the family—especially during festival times. Sometimes they brought gifts, as gift giving is important in China. The resulting connection and trust allowed all parties to be aware of any difficulties that might arise, and to manage them holistically.

This approach to recruitment takes more of an up-front investment. Like any effective locally adapted approach, it relies on relationship building—but this investment pays off many times over with higher retention rates, successful integration into the workplace, and a strengthened reputation for the company within the community.

Involving the Family in Recruiting Women: Turkey

A similar approach to engaging the family is used by recruiters in other parts of the world as well. Istanbul is one of my most favorite cities. As we wove through the traffic in front of the Hagia Sophia and the Blue Mosque, I felt a rush of anticipation for the three days I had in Istanbul. I was meeting the two CEOs for Sodexo Turkey. I was excited about meeting their teams and experiencing the food and culture.

The most meaningful part of my trip came from learning about the initiative to develop women in the culinary arts in Turkey. Female chefs are sorely underrepresented in Turkey and globally they are just 7 percent of all chefs.[5] To combat this, Sodexo Turkey partners with a culinary school exclusively for girls where they provide training and internships and host cooking demonstrations and competitions. Eventually Sodexo employs many of these young women.

But just training girls was not enough. Most of the girls who attend the school do so to learn to cook for their families and husbands when they get married. Damla Yildirim, Sodexo Turkey's human resources director, told me about Ezgi, who was eighteen years old when she graduated from the cooking school. When Sodexo wanted to hire her, Ezgi's family was reluctant to let her work for a French company that they perceived as being too liberal a workplace for their daughter. Damla worked with Ezgi's family and other families with similar reservations, slowly building trust. "Yes, we are a French company, but we are Turkish, and we are behind our women workers," she told them. She built relationships with the teachers, highly respected in Turkish culture, who in turn recommended Sodexo. And she took the few women chefs who worked at Sodexo with her to these meetings with the families to show the possibilities of careers with the company. Now Ezgi works for Sodexo and is excited because she can earn a living and help her family.[6]

The Turkish team told me how they had engaged with the government, the community, Sodexo managers and clients, as well as the families and teachers of these young women to build a pipeline of female talent for culinary roles. Sodexo had a global gender strategy and a company-wide target for representation. Sodexo Turkey adapted the global strategy, implementing it based on the local specificity of culture and the need for female chefs.

Involving the family has been a successful strategy in many countries. In Thailand, for example, recruiters asked men they interviewed if they had wives or daughters who would be interested in part-time or full-time work. In patriarchal cultures where some women may need their spouse's or father's permission to work, the endorsement from the male head of the family can be important. The recruiters realized that they would be able to recruit more women this way; as an added benefit, the men tended to be more comfortable when they knew where their wives would be working and often the couple could commute to and from work together. Seeking permission for adult women to work is unacceptable when viewed through a Western feminist lens. If the recruiters bypassed the men, however, the women might not have been able to work at all and would not gain some economic independence. This reinforces the need to work within a broader ecosystem, incorporating local considerations to meet global objectives in a transversal model.

Job Descriptions

Beyond intentional sourcing of underrepresented talent, organizations also need to ensure that job descriptions and requirements don't adversely impact any population. To encourage more women applicants, Sodexo India scrubbed job descriptions for words that were stereotypically associated with males like *assertive* and *take charge*. In India, it was common to refer to certain roles as *office boys* or *pantry boys*. These words were replaced with words that were gender neutral like *associates*.

In Brazil, to increase the numbers of Afro-Brazilian applicants, many companies are reconsidering the standard job qualifications they use. It's long been a standing practice for most multinational companies to require English fluency, but this systematically excludes a disproportionate number of Afro-Brazilians, because of education disparities. Dow Chemical Company, an American multinational chemical company, eliminated the English requirement. English was something that could be taught on the job. This led to an increase of Afro-Brazilians in entry-level jobs from 30 percent to 50 percent.[7]

Underrepresented Talent Is Locally Expressed

Pragya Singh was elated! She was just married, had graduated, and was headed on a train from Varanasi to Delhi for a job interview. She fell asleep during the train ride and was jolted out of her sleep by unbearable pain. "A jilted man whose marriage proposal my parents had denied threw acid on me," Pragya told me.[8] What followed was a nightmare of weeks in the ICU and multiple surgeries to restore her face. Pragya went on to found Atijeevan Foundation to help women who are victims of acid attacks.[9]

Acid attacks against women are a common occurrence in India. In 2016, the Indian government passed a new disabilities act that included twenty-one types of disability including injuries from acid attacks.[10] Women who suffer acid attacks are disfigured, mostly by men who are seeking revenge because they were rebuffed or over dowry or property conflicts. Working with a nongovernmental organization (NGO), Bank of America has focused on recruiting women who are survivors of acid attacks.[11] They have trained and hired them and encouraged their subcontractors to do the same. In other parts of the world, acid attack survivors might be an unfamiliar category and not be a consideration in a recruiting strategy for people with disabilities.

To embed DEI in the recruiting process, each step needs to ensure that local considerations are being incorporated while also eliminating bias in the process. "Embedding DEI in Recruitment" highlights different aspects of the recruitment process that can be localized and identifies points where bias can be interrupted.

EMBEDDING DEI IN RECRUITMENT

Sourcing Underrepresented Talent

- Go beyond traditional schools to Historically Black Colleges and Universities (HBCUs) or Hispanic Serving Institutions (HSIs) with high enrollment of underrepresented populations in the US or less elite private universities in Brazil or France.
- Build relationships with these schools proactively through presence on campus.
- Mentor young students before they reach university and expose them to careers in your organization.
- Offer internships and scholarships.
- Leverage alumni networks to do outreach.
- Leverage ERGs for referrals and to help with presence at in-person recruiting events.
- Build relationships with families or elders in the community to demonstrate that your organization is a good place for their children/community.
- Partner with nonprofit and community-based organizations.
- Involve recruiters and ERGs in community-based activities to build trust in your organization's brand.
- Keep in "soft" touch with the high-quality declined candidates.

- Ensure that all open positions are posted and communicated.
- Review all job descriptions for nondiscriminatory language.

Selection Process

- Review selection criteria to ensure that they are essential for the job.
- Ensure a diverse interview panel.
- Provide pre-interview preparation skills and coaching to potential candidates.
- Focus on onboarding by providing a sense of belonging through the ERGs.

Targets

- Provide bonuses for referring underrepresented populations.
- Provide recruiters with targets and incentives for sourcing underrepresented candidates.
- Set clear and relevant hiring targets and hold managers accountable.

Internal Talent

- Identify an internal diverse candidate pool that can be tapped to apply for openings.
- Stay in touch with women who have temporarily off-ramped their careers.

Monitoring

- Review all applicants to ensure diversity in the candidate slate.
- Monitor adverse impacts at each stage of the recruiting process.
- Provide checks and balances to ensure fairness in the selection process by reviewing the candidate slates including candidates forwarded to the hiring manager and selection made.

Training

- Provide training on unconscious bias to recruiters and hiring managers.

Branding

- Build diversity messaging into the corporate brand.
- Identify external branding opportunities to reach diverse candidates.
- Use targeted and culturally appropriate advertising.
- Leverage your ERGs, diverse employees, and allies as ambassadors and buddies in external community events.

Talent Development

Simone P. Grossmann of The Coca-Cola Company told me that they, like several other companies in Brazil—such as Bayer and Magazine Luiza—have instituted a small internship initiative exclusively for

Black Brazilians. Beyond any specific program, they are deliberate about how they retain and develop Black talent—supporting them in their roles, dealing with problems proactively, and moving people to new positions if necessary to ensure that each person is set up for success. As a result, many interns have been permanently hired.[12]

Intentionality in developing the careers of underrepresented talent is critical to ensuring equity in advancement opportunities. This can take many forms including exposure to high-profile assignments, coaching on career paths, mentoring, and sponsorship. Analyzing data to examine the blockages in advancing talent, along with an assessment of the criteria for promotions, ensuring unbiased performance appraisals, and calibrating succession planning discussions to ensure that targeted populations are well represented, all further anchor DEI in the talent lifecycle.

Embracing Diverse Leadership Models

If organizations are serious, they must also examine the leadership models that have traditionally been premised on male behaviors. Are conventional Western male leadership qualities the only competencies relevant in today's complex global economy? Are our narrow concepts of leadership biasing our promotion decision-making?

A McKinsey study found that leadership behaviors females tend to lean into (such as participative decision-making) are more effective today and into the future.[13] They are behaviors that are needed to engage globally, compete for talent, and respond to changing expectations.

Cultures differ in the behaviors and competencies leaders need to display. In some cultures, leaders are expected to demonstrate consensus decision-making, and in others, leaders are most respected when they make unilateral decisions and take responsibility. Our idea of leadership needs to be disrupted by moving away from narrow Western male models to incorporate multiple leadership competencies. (See "Embedding DEI in Talent Development and Advancement.")

EMBEDDING DEI IN TALENT DEVELOPMENT AND ADVANCEMENT

Leverage Data

- Analyze length of stay in position.
- Analyze rate at which underrepresented, high-potential talent is promoted.
- Analyze overall rate of promotion for women and other underrepresented groups compared to their overall representation.
- Analyze succession planning data and ask yourself: Who is in the successor pool? What percent are underrepresented talent? Do the key positions have successors that also belong to underrepresented groups?

Development

- Provide opportunities for development including high-profile assignments, mentoring, sponsorship, and leadership development.
- Provide exposure to senior leadership.
- Intentionally manage and support career paths.
- Encourage underrepresented talent to take on profit and loss roles as a pathway to senior leadership.

Advancement

- Calibrate performance reviews and analyze data by diversity identity to check for bias.
- Intentionally identify underrepresented high-potential talent as successors in talent reviews and provide them with development plans.

Targets

- Provide leaders targets for diversity in successor pools and/or for promotion of women and other underrepresented groups.

Engagement of Talent

There is a plethora of factors that provide a sense of belonging and engagement for diverse employee groups. These can include an inclusive culture, purpose-driven work, pay, advancement opportunities, benefits, job titles, and the values of the organization, among other things. To understand what engages disparate employee groups, we need to analyze data as well as seek feedback, so that we can tailor strategies to enhance employees' sense of belonging.

Engagement survey data is often used to gauge inclusion and can indicate an employee's desire to stay with an organization and the extent to which they feel they belong. However, responses to engagement surveys are culturally bound. I was very surprised by the huge disparities in engagement scores between countries. In Asia the scores were very high. Some of it could of course be explained by the caliber of leadership. But overall, I found that in hierarchical and indirect cultures where it is not comfortable to challenge or provide feedback to the supervisor or to cause "loss of face," the scores tended to be higher. By contrast, in France the scores were extremely low. In my conversations I learned that in France where the education system encourages "first building one side of the argument, then the opposite side of the argument, before coming to a conclusion,"[14] scores tend to be lower. Strategies to address inclusion should factor in cultural approaches to providing feedback by comparing organizations in the same country rather than only comparing scores across countries globally.

Even within the same country, scores differ based on how employees from various identity groups experience the workplace. For example, if Millennial women have lower scores than their male counterparts, it presents an opportunity to unpack the data and examine the underlying cause.

In many parts of the world, ERGs provide a sense of belonging and can be even more effective when integrated into the onboarding phase of the talent lifecycle. Ken Barrett, Global Chief Diversity Officer at General Motors (GM), told me that in the US, they assign ambassadors from their Latino/a ERG to answer questions from primarily Latino/a candidates who have received employment offers. The ambassador engages with the candidate once the offer is extended and welcomes them into the GM community. As a result, GM's recruitment of Latina/o hires increased threefold.[15] In cultures where there is less of a comfort with community around group identity, this might seem unusual, as we have seen earlier in this book. In the US, however, ERGs are often an anchor for employee engagement and retention.

Similar to recruitment, leaning on employees' families can be an engagement and retention strategy. In China, the one-child policy from 1980 to 2016 and rapid economic growth have resulted in a severe talent shortage. Jingqing Xia, CP Kelco's Global HR Business Partner Commercial and HR Lead for Asia Pacific, told me that employees are "quick to fire their company and their boss" as they job hop for increased pay and title and are impatient for acceleration in both.[16] Multinationals are competing for talent with local Chinese companies that are very desirable. With this backdrop, companies are implementing innovative strategies to engage and retain talent.

The hot pot chain in Shanghai, Haidilao, sends a portion of each employee's bonus directly to the employee's parents. And parents are invited to attend employee award ceremonies in an expenses-paid trip. The parents are exposed to the company in the hopes that they will influence their children to stay.[17] This might be unacceptable in other cultures where a young adult's earned bonus, privacy, and right to make decisions for themselves is sacrosanct. However, in the China cultural context, this was a very clever engagement and retention strategy.

Talent Retention

Inserting DEI in the retention process includes examining the turnover data, conducting exit and stay interviews to determine why people are leaving and what makes them stay, and assessing benefits and pay.

Addressing pay equity is foundational to retention of diverse talent. We still have a long way to go to achieve pay equity! According to the World Economic Forum's 2020 report, women earn 31.4 percent less than men globally.[18] Some countries are attempting long-overdue bold strategies and enforcing laws toward reaching pay equality. For example, the UK changed the Equality Act in April 2017, making it mandatory for companies with more than 250 employees to report their gender pay gap figures. There is now pressure to enact similar legislation for race and ethnicity. In 2018, France began requiring companies to disclose their gender pay gap data and to develop action plans to narrow the gap. Companies were given three years to improve things. If they don't report, or the gap has not narrowed, they risk fines of up to 1 percent of their total payroll. Germany also requires companies with over 500 employees to publish any pay disparities and their plans to mitigate them. In addition to that, the German Wage Transparency Act allows employees of large companies to ask what their coworkers make: they can now access the average salary of the opposite gender within their same grade. Other countries like Iceland,

Denmark, and Canada also enforce laws to reduce the gender pay gap.[19]

Organizations should broaden their commitment to analyze gender pay data with an intersectional lens. In 2021, women in the US earn $0.82 for every dollar earned by men.[20] However, African American women earn $0.63 for every dollar earned by White male executives.[21] More women than men have exited the workforce since the start of the pandemic, and in the US, participation of women in the workforce has dropped to 57 percent, the level it was in 1988.[22] Organizations need to be intentional about reintegrating women into the workforce and ensuring they are not penalized through pay.

Benefits can be designed to consider a range of family structures. For example, in Kenya where employed people are often responsible for the care of extended family including nieces and nephews and elderly aunts and uncles, organizations need to consider how to acknowledge that the conventional Western notion of a household may not be the most appropriate organizing mechanism.

Companies can do their own analysis to ensure they are mitigating any disparities for women and other underrepresented populations regardless of country laws. For example, family-friendly maternity benefits can appear on the surface to promote women's careers, but can sometimes have unanticipated consequences, furthering the gender pay gap. In my visit to Germany during the SoTogether meeting, I had expected to find an open and progressive stance toward advancing women's careers. Instead, I encountered obstacles I never anticipated. Germany, along with much of Europe, has family leave policies that parents in the United States would envy. In Germany, parents can take up to thirty-six months off and still protect their jobs, with up to fourteen months of 65 percent of their last net income paid by the government.[23]

These seemingly pro-women benefits in fact might be impeding women's career advancement—or at least social attitudes about these benefits are problematic. First, women claim parental allowances far more than men. On average, women apply for basic parental allowance for 11.7 months compared to 2.7 months for men.[24] Secondly, when mothers do come back to work 66.2 percent of them were working part time as compared to 6.4 percent of fathers.[25] And the majority of Germans view part-time jobs as "career killers."[26]

The culture tends to encourage women to be the primary caregivers and a strong bias against early childcare adds pressure on mothers to stay home with their children. Women taking more than a year of maternity leave, however, earn 7 percent less than other women when they are back in the workplace.[27] This reminded me that policy changes cannot work in isolation—these benefits need to be coupled with incentives for men to take parental leave and with initiatives that shift attitudes about flexible working and caregiving.

See "Embedding DEI in Employee Engagement and Retention."

EMBEDDING DEI IN EMPLOYEE ENGAGEMENT AND RETENTION

Leverage Your Data

- Analyze engagement surveys disaggregated by identity demographics.
- Analyze attrition data disaggregated by identity demographics.

Gather Employee Feedback

- Conduct stay interviews to determine what encourages underrepresented talent to stay.

- Conduct exit interviews to understand why underrepresented talent is leaving.
- Get feedback on whether benefits are meeting needs of all employees.

Provide a Sense of Belonging

- Ensure that benefits are addressing the well-being of all employees.
- Leverage ERGs to create a sense of community and belonging to the organization.
- Engage employees in community volunteer activities that resonate personally.
- Ensure that equitable flexible work arrangements are offered where possible.

Pay Equity

- Conduct regular pay equity analysis disaggregated by level, function, and identity demographics.
- Address inequities in pay.
- Conduct regular analysis of pay increases and bonuses across the enterprise to ensure no adverse impact.
- Transparently publish salary ranges for each position.
- End the practice of salary negotiation that may disadvantage some underrepresented talent and women.
- End the practice of asking for last salary, which perpetuates the pay gap.

Unconscious Bias

As part of a global company's mentoring initiative, a male European leader was paired with a more junior woman who managed a high-security prison. She had a collaborative, low-key leadership style that surprised him. After a year, he supported her promotion and told me that before this mentoring experience, if he had been presented with a choice between a male and a female to manage a prison, he would have chosen the male without a second thought. Given the dangerous environment, he thought an assertive style was needed. After having met his mentee, he realized there was more than one way to lead. From then on, he committed to do his best not to prejudge candidates based on gender.

Unconscious bias is still pervasive. It can lead people to make choices based on beliefs they may not even be aware of but that adversely impact one group and favor another. Even when DEI is inserted at every point in the talent process, it is not uncommon for managers' unconscious biases to impact talent decisions. In many parts of the world, marital status, number of children, and a photograph all form a part of the resume. This exacerbates bias in the selection process against mothers or candidates from certain ethnic or racial groups. Names can also trigger bias if they signal a particular religious or ethnic identity.

Many companies train recruiters and hiring managers to recognize their own unconscious bias and how it may be impacting their interviews and decisions. While training is not a panacea and is not successful in isolation, if it is combined with changing systems and policies, it can help interrupt bias in the talent lifecycle.[28]

Integrating DEI beyond Human Resources

DEI is a business driver and needs to be integrated in processes beyond talent such as multicultural marketing and the supply chain.

Given the diversity of many organizations' customer base and their corresponding purchasing power, companies have segmented the market and developed goods, services, and advertising campaigns for specific demographic groups. Procter & Gamble (P&G), an American multinational company, is known for its compelling commercials about race in the US. In India, P&G decided to address gender roles through its #ShareTheLoad campaign advertising the laundry detergent Ariel. The commercial features an aging father watching his young professional daughter coming home from work, still fielding calls from the office, preparing dinner, and doing laundry all while her husband relaxes on the sofa watching TV. We hear him reading a letter to his daughter as a voiceover. "Now you manage your own house. And your office. I am so proud. And I am so sorry. Sorry that you have to do this all on your own." He goes on to take responsibility for the example he set, and in the end, he goes home to his own wife and begins to do the laundry.[29]

Having an older man carry the message plays into the respect for age and the father role in India. It elevates the brand among young women without alienating other customers. It makes it an attractive company for female talent and those with like values, thereby reinforcing the talent loop. It is a reminder of the interconnected nature of this work, with each initiative adding together to become greater than the sum of their parts.

Including women and underrepresented groups in the supply chain is another way to build economic opportunity for those businesses. It also provides a broader range of offerings for organizations. Some organizations not only identify and source from diverse vendors, but also build mentoring and coaching into these business partnerships to build suppliers' capacity to take on bigger contracts.

Increasingly DEI and corporate responsibility (CR) are aligned in many parts of the world. Both disciplines speak to common stakeholders but address them with different messaging.[30] When corporate responsibility is enriched by a DEI lens, it can bolster the purpose and impact of CR initiatives addressing the community, environment, or supply chain.

The External Ecosystem

I had not had a weekend off in several months and was not happy about traveling to Chicago on a Friday afternoon to participate in a community event being held on Saturday. But what I experienced left me uplifted—I could not have thought of a better way to spend a Saturday morning! Busloads of Latina mothers and their children from the surrounding community attended a cooking demonstration hosted by Sodexo chefs at a university client in Chicago. Sodexo provided food and facilities management services at the university, and this was an initiative that grew out of a partnership between Sodexo and the Mexican American Legal Defense and Educational Fund (MALDEF), a leading Hispanic civil rights organization in the US.

The mothers and children were riveted by the explanations of portion size and calorie content and enjoyed the food tastings. They learned how to cook healthy gazpacho soup, quesadillas, and tamales and left with bags of fresh produce and recipe books. Next, they moved on to an interview with Sodexo and the university recruiters while their children got a tour of the university where the session was being hosted.

This external engagement built a bridge between the social impact and the business in a practical way. While Sodexo was enriching the quality of life in the Hispanic community, they were also accessing potential hires. And they were elevating the brand of their university client who used it as an opportunity to expose potential students and hires to their institution. A win-win all around!

Internal systems are impacted by the external ecosystem as employees live in a broader nexus that includes their families and the community. Many of the examples we saw in this chapter draw on this external ecosystem. Thriving communities enable thriving businesses in a virtuous cycle by providing skilled talent, diverse suppliers, and economic opportunities that, in turn, result in stable communities. Research by the global consulting company McKinsey found a "strong link between gender equality in society, attitudes and beliefs about the role of women, and gender equality in work. The latter is not achievable without the former two elements."[31] Recognizing the connection, external stakeholder groups—advocacy organizations, clients, customers, vendors—are becoming increasingly vocal and organizations need to partner with them to ensure success.

In the Sodexo-MALDEF partnership, the success hinged on identifying the external and internal stakeholders and collaborating with them—engaging the Sodexo chefs, partnering with Sodexo business leaders so they saw the benefit to the business, involving Sodexo recruiters, and engaging clients in a way that benefitted them. And the Sodexo chefs and employees who had also volunteered to give up their Saturday were motivated and energized; this experience was affirming and uplifting for them! One Latina employee said, "I wish I had this when I was growing up."

Conclusion

When we move our DEI initiatives from the inside out and embed our change initiative in the internal and external ecosystem, it builds our brand and our reputation with external stakeholders while reinforcing to our employees that our commitment is consistent and comes from an authentic desire to build a better world. In return, our external partnerships sustain our inner work as a company—providing both concrete resources and expertise, but also motivation and inspiration to continue to do the often-arduous work of creating more diverse, equitable, and inclusive organizations.

The framework of a transversal strategy and governance structure are critical to scale DEI transformation *wide* and provide consistency. Local allies and champions help to embed the change *deep* within the organization locally. Addressing the systems and processes makes possible the sustainability of our efforts. All too often organizational commitment to DEI is contingent on a leader's conviction. Transforming systems and processes to integrate DEI ensures that it is embedded *inside-out* and is continued across leadership transitions. Collecting data on the impact of our initiatives and holding leaders accountable provides a further guarantee that DEI endures.

Principle

5

KNOW WHAT MATTERS AND COUNT IT

METRICS PROVIDE A GLOBAL FRAMEWORK and a cohesive narrative. They communicate both an organization's intent and its commitment. They spotlight problem areas and possible solutions. They align productive focus on business processes that can lead to systemic change. They enable and promote accountability.

Metrics are instruments for change, but they are most effective when they are aligned with the local context and managers are held accountable for achieving them. When metrics and accountability work in concert with leadership commitment, a powerful change narrative, and embedding DEI into the processes and DNA of organizations, the change effort is likely to be far-reaching and sustained.

Chapter 9, "Metrics and Accountability," considers different approaches to metrics and accountability, including what data can be captured legally in the local context, approaches to quotas or targets, and how to hold teams accountable. It emphasizes the importance of including both lead and lag measures in developing a suite of metrics that advance change deep within the organization. Setting DEI key performance indicators and holding teams accountable frequently elicits resistance. The chapter examines the root causes of that resistance and offers ways to counter it.

The chapter also captures some important considerations for well-calibrated metrics from data structure and parsing that data to stakeholder involvement and addressing the needs of the business.

9

METRICS AND ACCOUNTABILITY

The fact that we needed diversity metrics was almost a non-discussion. So, I am intrigued sometimes when people get into a very emotional discussion on why do we need metrics? Well, is it important or not? Isn't it part of your strategy? Wonderful! Then how are you going to measure it? We are a process and metrics driven company. So, for us, the discussion was: of course, we're going to measure it.

—TIGER TYAGARAJAN, CEO Genpact

HOW DO YOU KNOW YOUR ORGANIZATION is more inclusive, diverse, and equitable? How do you know your efforts are effective? Through measurement. "What gets measured gets done," may seem trite, but it also speaks to another core purpose of metrics: promoting progress. Metrics shine a spotlight on what matters. They power change and advance new ways of operating. Measures are instruments of transformation.

Metrics and targets provide a framework at the enterprise level that can then be contextualized to the local culture and business.

The key performance indicators (KPIs) selected to measure success depend on local laws, historical context, and an organization's maturity in DEI.

Think about metrics in terms of lag measures (sometimes referred to as lag indicators) and lead measures (lead indicators). *Lag measures* are the specific outcomes you want to achieve, such as the number of underrepresented staff in management positions. They are retrospective assessments of whether you have reached your targets.

Lead measures, on the other hand, look at activities and behaviors that you want to encourage and, if done consistently, will result in the desired outcomes. Lead measures are powerful tools—allowing for more nimble and responsive adjustments. By measuring inclusive actions and behaviors, you build in day-to-day accountability, rather than simply setting targets and hoping for the best. This ties representation outcomes to inclusive actions, and measures both. To only measure the representation lag outcomes is insufficient. You must also measure and quantify the inclusive actions necessary to achieve those outcomes. (See the appendix for sample lead and lag measures.)

Metrics only work if there is clarity of ownership and responsibility. To ensure that results are attained in alignment with business goals, leaders at all levels need to be held accountable for lead and lag measures. This accountability can take multiple forms as incentives or disincentives to either reward progress or penalize discrimination—but it demands a cogent and cohesive framework.

DEI Scorecards Have an Impact at Sodexo USA

In late 2003, I presented a DEI talent and accountability framework to the Sodexo North American executive team. At the time we needed to make significant progress in the representation of women and people of color in leadership—especially African American leadership—as the lawsuit had highlighted for us. I walked into the meeting well-versed in the data and confident. I had the CEO's backing—he had decided he would hold his team accountable for progress in DEI and link it to financial incentives. I was not prepared for the collective resistance that I encountered in the room that day! The executives saw the talent representation targets as quotas and they resisted the link to incentives.

At its inception, the Sodexo Diversity and Inclusion Index (SDII) tracked only lag measures: the recruitment, retention, and promotion of women and people of color. Based on a point scoring system, it allocated 300 points each to recruiting and retention and 400 points to promotion, as this was the area that needed the most attention.

Ten to twenty-five percent of the total bonus pool was allocated to the DEI scorecard for managers.[1] The bonus was available regardless of the financial performance of the company in a given year. This signaled to employees the importance of sustaining an ongoing commitment to DEI for the long term (see Figure 10).

With compensation tied to the scorecard, it drew attention and significant pushback. Through conversations with other colleagues, we learned that lag measures alone, or a sole focus on increasing underrepresented talent, was confused with quotas. As we saw in earlier chapters, quotas are used in many parts of the world, but in the US there has always been a particularly strong—almost visceral—opposition to quotas. "The American Dream" builds a myth that anyone can succeed no matter their identity. Quotas are too limiting and too prescribed in a culture that values individual freedom so highly. Feedback suggested that we would see more widespread buy-in and less resistance if managers were also rewarded for changing their behaviors and actions to be more inclusive.

In response to the feedback, we added lead measures consisting of inclusive behaviors and actions to the scorecard. To reflect this

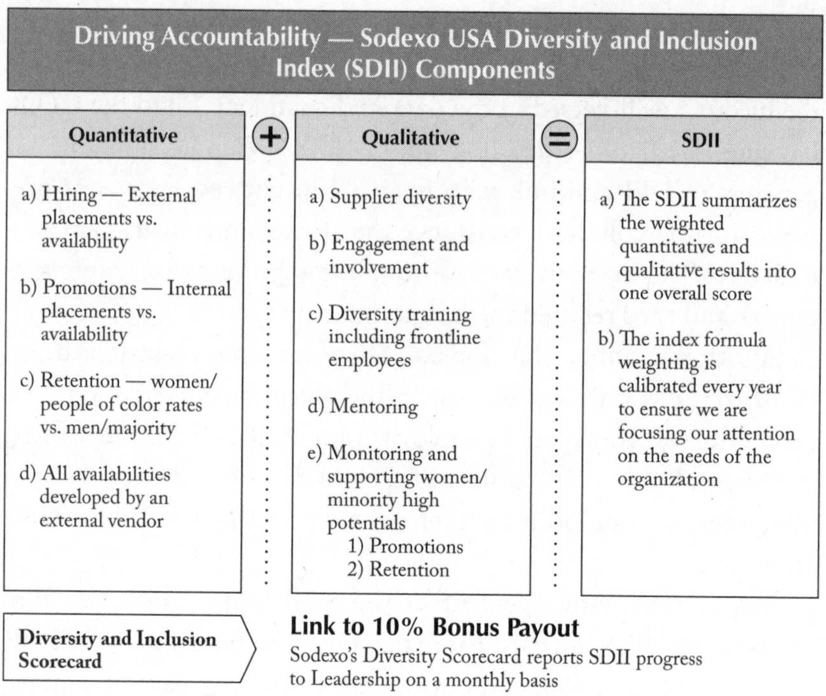

Driving Accountability — Sodexo USA Diversity and Inclusion Index (SDII) Components
Quantitative
a) Hiring — External placements vs. availability
b) Promotions — Internal placements vs. availability
c) Retention — women/ people of color rates vs. men/majority
d) All availabilities developed by an external vendor
Qualitative
a) Supplier diversity
b) Engagement and involvement
c) Diversity training including frontline employees
d) Mentoring
e) Monitoring and supporting women/ minority high potentials
1) Promotions
2) Retention
SDII
a) The SDII summarizes the weighted quantitative and qualitative results into one overall score
b) The index formula weighting is calibrated every year to ensure we are focusing our attention on the needs of the organization
Diversity and Inclusion Scorecard
Link to 10% Bonus Payout
Sodexo's Diversity Scorecard reports SDII progress to Leadership on a monthly basis

Figure 10: The Sodexo Diversity and Inclusion Index (SDII) (Reproduced with permission from Sodexo)

change, the point scoring was recalibrated, allocating 400 points to inclusive behaviors and 200 points each to the lag measures of recruiting, retention, and promotion of talent. With the addition of the lead measures, the scorecard eventually gained widespread acceptance by the executives who had been resistant, became integrated into the performance management process, and was cascaded to all bonus-eligible managers throughout the company.

Workforce Diversity: Lag Measures

Sodexo designed lag measures to track hires, promotions, and retention of talent. We based the hiring thresholds on those identified as available to do the jobs using US census data. Promotion thresholds were established using the population internally eligible for promotions.

To ensure integrity and the most accurate data, we had an outside vendor annually recalculate talent availability in the external labor market. Using these numbers provided legitimacy to the lag measures as it was based on internal and external talent pools available to do the jobs. Additionally, given a litigious US environment, this approach was considered legally more defensible from possible lawsuits alleging reverse discrimination by the White male population.

We analyzed the data separately for women and for individual racial groups: Asian, African American, Hispanic, and Native American, as each of these groups has a different experience in the workplace. Each year we analyzed the data and we recalibrated our focus based on the roles or levels where we saw leaks in the talent pipeline. (See Figure 11 for a prototype of a lag indicator DEI scorecard.)

Inclusive Behaviors and Actions: Lead Measures

We started getting more widespread buy-in when we added inclusive behaviors and actions that focused attention on the underlying processes that drive outcomes and anchor a sustained inclusive culture.

Some of the inclusive behaviors and actions included *pipeline development*—external sourcing of diverse talent and internal talent development such as mentoring and sponsorship; *inclusive leadership*—hosting DEI learning activities for teams, and sponsorship of employee resource groups; and *external engagement*—speaking on DEI outside the company, involvement with diverse communities, and leveraging DEI with clients. Leaders were required to develop their own inclusive leadership action plans with activities for each of these areas. Internal DEI coaches were assigned to assist them. Giving managers credit for demonstrating behaviors that collectively influenced the outcomes helped garner more widespread acceptance (see the appendix for more details on sample lead measures).

			Target or Above: 80%				Approaching Target: 75%–79%				Area of Concern = 0–74%			
Minority Score:			Jan	Feb	March	April	May	June	July	Aug	Sept	Oct	Nov	Dec
	Availability	**Hires Year to Date:**												
African-American		Hires to Date												
		% of Total Hires												
		Performance												
Asian-Pacific Islander		Hires to Date												
		% of Total Hires												
		Performance												
Native-American Two+ Races		Hires to Date												
		% of Total Hires												
		Performance												
Hispanic		Hires to Date												
		% of Total Hires												
		Performance												
Total Minority		Hires to Date												
		% of Total Hires												
		Performance												
Caucasian		Hires to Date												
		% of Total Hires												
		Performance												
Gender Score:	**0**		Jan	Feb	March	April	May	June	July	Aug	Sept	Oct	Nov	Dec
	Availability	**Hires Year to Date:**												
Male		Hires to Date												
		% of Total Hires												
		Performance												
Female		Hires to Date												
		% of Total Hires												
		Performance												
Performance for each period is measured against availability														

Figure 11: Prototype of a US DEI Scorecard: Lag Indicators (Reproduced with Permission from Sodexo)

Results and Reflections

The measurement system focused on trouble spots, articulated the desired outcomes, and highlighted what needed to be done to achieve those outcomes. Once we got the balance right between lead and lag measures and had socialized it, it operated as more than just a system to track results. Its very existence was a lead measure to help us achieve those results. The measurement system served to highlight the areas that needed attention.

Metrics supported Sodexo's sustained double-digit increases in representation of people of color in leadership. Over five years, we saw impressive gains in female representation: a 10 percent increase at entry and manager level; 20 percent at the senior executive level; and a two-fold increase in the company's executive ranks.[2] Engagement for women and people of color grew exponentially with DEI being one of the two key drivers of engagement for six years in a row. This success was a result of a measurement system linked to accountability as well as consistently and intentionally integrating DEI throughout the talent lifecycle and embedding DEI in the culture by creating a groundswell of champions at all levels.

The SDII was considered an innovative practice and was profiled extensively in external publications, presentations, and conferences. This further reinforced Sodexo's brand as a thought leader in DEI. Sodexo was able to share these best practices with like-minded clients and potential clients, demonstrating that DEI could add competitive value and positively impact business outcomes.

To counter the initial resistance, our messaging repeatedly emphasized that these were not quotas: we hire the best qualified but are intentional about sourcing. We shared data on the numbers of open positions and the percentages filled by women and people of color. Once we introduced inclusive actions, we focused attention on these lead metrics.

If I had to do it over again, I would have included the lead measures—the inclusive behaviors, actions, and processes—along with the lag measures at the inception. Rather than implement the incentive link soon after the launch, I would have spent some time building understanding and acceptance before introducing it. We did this when we launched the global scorecard. Today the scorecard is widely accepted as a way of life at Sodexo.

Global Metrics: Global DEI Scorecard at Sodexo

Given the variations in laws and limitations around personnel data collection, Sodexo only captured gender and age data globally. The global scorecard (see Figure 12) had an aspirational target for the representation of women. Starting from a baseline of 17 percent women in senior leadership roles in 2009, it established an initial target of 25 percent women in senior leadership roles globally by 2015, and subsequently a target of 40 percent by 2025.

The 40 percent target was founded on the evidence-based research Sodexo conducted using internal data showing that entities with 40 to 60 percent women outperformed those with less than 40 percent women. Given the practice of quotas for women on boards globally, we found more of an appetite for aspirational targets outside the US.

To ensure progress, interim annual targets were calculated through scenario modeling taking into account business growth, turnover, promotions, and hires. These annual targets were modeled for each business line and geography, ensuring that they were realistic and based on the current level of representation of women. The modeling demonstrated that the targets were attainable.

To secure buy-in, we solicited stakeholder feedback including HR and operations leaders, and we referenced the gender balance study. Just like in the US, we saw resistance to linking incentives to the DEI metrics. Having learned from our experience, though, we phased the incentive in gradually, starting with initially paying to reward any progress over baseline. Lead indicators of inclusive behaviors and actions formed part of the process. The 40 percent target was widely communicated internally and externally as a longer-term goal. It was not until 2016 that each year's incremental targets were linked to 10 percent of the senior leadership bonus.

Gender Scorecard Template

Summary Current Situation

Women Representation	Senior Leaders	Middle Management	Supervisors
Current #			
Current %			
Target			

Gender Representation

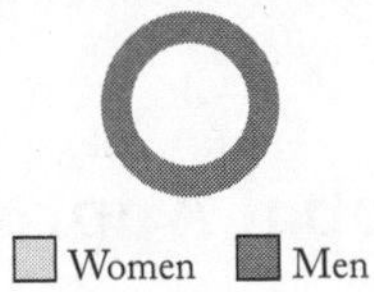

Business Line

Women Representation						
#						
%						
#						
%						

Target for Leaders

Fiscal Year (FY) —women	Year	Year	Target
Baseline #			
Baseline %			
Estimated net increase #			
Year End %			

Engagement by Gender and by Management Categories (Sample Number)

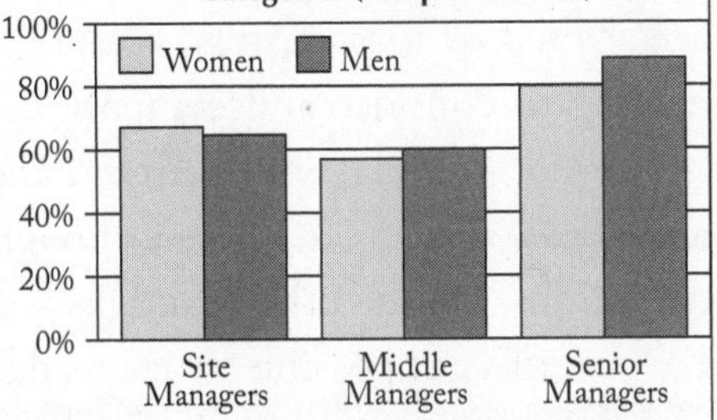

Actions

Action Plan	• Requires gender-balanced slates for all open positions • Sponsors high-potential women • Cascades gender targets and holds teams accountable * Requires gender balance in successor pool for key positions

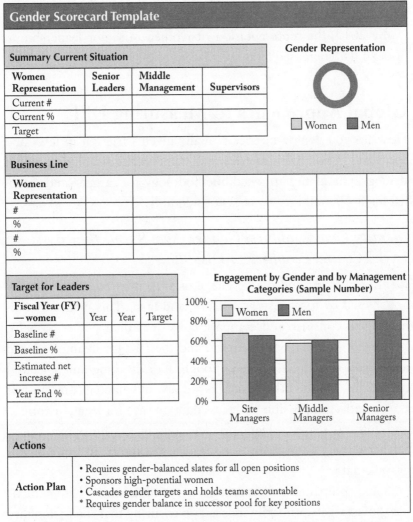

Figure 12: Prototype of a Global Scorecard (Reproduced with Permission from Sodexo)

While senior executives were the first to be answerable to set targets, the accountability and rewards were cascaded deeper into the organization based on the local context. In India, where women's participation was low overall in the formal labor force, targets permeated all levels of the organization, including entry-level positions. In other parts of the world, the focus was on particular functions, such as women in operations or profit-and-loss roles, where women were underrepresented.

By 2019, the representation of women in senior leadership at Sodexo had increased from 17 percent to 34 percent.

Global Approaches to Measuring DEI

How do you deploy metrics globally given variation in laws and contexts? How DEI metrics are approached—including what demographic data is tracked, methodology for targets, and establishing accountability—varies considerably.

Identity Demographics: Gender, Age, Race/Ethnicity, LGBTQ, and People with Disabilities

Identity markers and the language used to refer to group identity are shaped by local history, culture, and laws. This makes it challenging to consider and compare consistent data points globally. In the US, Canada, South Africa, and the UK, for example, racial and ethnic data are gathered, though with differing language and definitions. On the other hand, as we saw in Chapter 2, in most of Europe, it is not possible to access data on race for legal, historical, and cultural reasons. Data privacy laws in the European Union further restrict an organization's ability to capture accurate demographic data.

Some companies collect metrics on nationalities. These companies have targets primarily focused on ensuring that the nationality of their leadership reflects their growth markets. Wema Hoover, formerly at Sanofi, told me, "We are very Western focused [but] some of our largest markets are outside the West. We wanted to make sure our talent represented these growth markets."[3]

Mark McLane, Head of Diversity, Inclusion, and Wellbeing at M&G PLC, a British investment manager in the UK, told me that they had a target of 20 percent diverse ethnicity in senior leadership by 2025. In some parts of the world, like the UK and the US, they could identify employees by race or ethnicity. Where this was not possible, they used nationality as a proxy. Mark had challenging conversations with leaders to help them understand the intent—that it was not just about diverse nationality but also about nondominant race and ethnicity within that nationality. He said,

> I recall that one leader wanted to count someone from South Africa who had moved to the UK as part of the aspirational target. I had a conversation with the leader and we talked about that individual being a White male and not adding to the racial diversity of the team. Or a White Italian colleague in the senior leadership team in Luxemburg may add to nationality diversity, but that's not in keeping with the intent. We talked about and are clear on the intent and what we are trying to accomplish.[4]

Some companies also attempt to capture data on people with disabilities. Currently 103 countries have disability quotas.[5] Where quotas exist, organizations are obliged to track hires of people with disabilities or risk paying a penalty. Definitions of disability also differ, making it difficult to analyze and compare data across regions. Some countries use very narrow and medically certified classifications while others rely solely on employee self-disclosure.

In regard to LGBTQ data, the laws in seventy countries criminalize same-sex couples, so asking employees to self-identify in these contexts is not prudent.[6] Instead, companies focus metrics more on lead measures like nondiscrimination policies, equal benefits for same and opposite sex couples, medical coverage for gender transitioning, and employee resource groups.

Organizations in some countries do include sexual orientation and disability as voluntary self-identification demographic questions, which then allow them to analyze the workplace experiences of their LGBTQ employees and those with a disability. IBM, for instance, collected self-identification data in thirty-three countries after a rigorous assessment of the data protection laws and discrimination legislation. In 2016, 86 percent of IBM's employees were administered self-identification surveys that included LGBTQ and disabilities.[7]

Increasingly, some employees are identifying their gender as nonbinary rather than male or female. Organizations are adding comment boxes in data collection forms to allow nonbinary employees to identify themselves.[8] However most organizations use binary gender representation as their lag measurement globally.

Given this context, the only data that can consistently be captured across the globe are age and gender. Depending on the context, age data is used differently ranging from targeting Millennial and Generation Z talent in Asia to the retention and engagement of the Baby Boomer population in Europe.

When data is collected in a culturally sensitive manner—within the framework of the laws, accounting for history and societal practices, and with involvement of local stakeholders—it offsets concerns that DEI is imposed from the organization's headquarters or is a US export.

Resistance

Despite widespread acceptance of the business benefits of DEI, there remains considerable resistance to the idea of metrics and accountability.

Much of the resistance is due to the confusion between targets and quotas and the differing approaches to each of these.

At their essence, *quotas* are mandated outcomes that are fixed and must be achieved. They are often established by an external regulatory body. In many parts of the world, governments set quotas for women on company boards.[9] Many countries in Europe have them: Spain, France, Belgium, Norway, Germany, and the Netherlands all have mandated quotas for women on boards. As a result, women represent 33 percent of board positions in the EU.[10]

Targets, on the other hand, are "aspirational goals and are more flexible than fixed."[11] These are set by organizations. They are ambitious and often based on "market availability, in-house talent pools, market best practices or—at times—government bodies' recommendations."[12] The UK has taken a different approach to many of its EU neighbors, recommending a target of 25 percent women on boards.[13] Procter & Gamble, a US-headquartered multinational consumer goods company, has a 50 percent aspirational target for women globally, based on their consumer population.[14]

The varying approaches to targets and quotas have triggered a range of responses. In the US, the term *affirmative action* refers to policies and practices that aim to increase the representation of underrepresented groups based on their gender, race, creed, or nationality in areas in which they were excluded in the past, such as education and employment.[15] These are not quotas: they do not include a fixed number of positions that must be filled by a particular group. However, they are often mistaken as such.

The conflation of DEI metrics and quotas gives rise to much anxiety and emotion. The unsubstantiated argument often is that having targets implies lowering the bar and means hiring "less qualified" individuals. The belief that diverse hires are likely to be "less qualified" is often an indicator of bias that keeps disparities in place. In fact, broadening the talent pool from which we can recruit often results in raising the bar, because it increases the numbers of people being considered and therefore heightens the competition. In response to the suggestion that increasing gender representation will lead to unqualified managers and board members, Noreen Doyle, Vice-Chair of Credit Suisse and Chair of the British Bankers' Association, said, "We'll be considered equal when equally incompetent women get the same opportunity as incompetent men."[16]

It is easy to talk about a commitment to DEI, but when it comes to metrics linked to incentives, it becomes very personal and can be threatening.

Considerations for Identifying Appropriate Metrics

While different approaches to metrics and accountability are shaped by the history, culture, and laws around the world, some common considerations can ensure that the metrics selected are meaningful and meet the business needs of the organization. Begin by asking these questions:

Is the data structured to provide clear line-of-sight on leaks in the talent pipeline?

- While the representation of women may appear robust overall, it could mask the lack of women in operational roles or in positions with profit and loss responsibility—positions critical to the advancement of women into senior leadership.
- If several business lines are grouped together, the shortage of women or other underrepresented groups may be overlooked in certain functions. For example, a lack of women in the technology or sales business lines may be compensated for by more women in roles like human resources and communications.

- Similarly, if representation is not analyzed by level, you could miss trouble spots in the advancement of talent from one level to the next

Where race and ethnicity are tracked, is the data parsed individually by each identity?

- We know that the experiences of racial and ethnic groups differ and that their representation and advancement experiences are varied.
- In grouping the data, the overrepresentation of one race or ethnicity can mask the underrepresentation of other identity groups.

Are your calculations deliberate and comprehensive?

- Talent data needs to be thoughtfully considered. If retention and turnover are being measured, consider whether voluntary only or involuntary terminations should be included.
- Determine whether retention targets will be assessed by incremental progress, or will women be benchmarked against men, and minorities against non-minorities?
- Who gets credit for the promotion: the manager who develops the individuals or the receiving manager or both? These decisions have consequences in whether talent is shared!
- If you are using progress over a baseline for representation, how do you address a low baseline? What is the right progress annually?

Are you including data other than talent?

- Some companies track the numbers and cost of lawsuits.
- Organizations have used the cost of turnover and absenteeism as metrics.

- Frequently supplier diversity is captured through the number of diverse suppliers, the spend, and the percentage increase year over year.
- Market share in and revenues from ethnic communities are also measured.

How are you incorporating iterative evaluations and fine-tuning your strategy?

- Some organizations include pulse surveys or employee engagement surveys as a proxy for measuring an inclusive culture. These gauge employee perceptions of their sense of belonging.
- Are you clearly linking the lag and lead metrics so that teams know how their actions can impact the outcomes?
- Are you analyzing the metrics to identify the root cause, recalibrating analysis of the metrics to address new choke points, and implementing initiatives in response?

Keeping the Metrics Relevant: Key Strategies to Remember

Metrics are living, breathing, and ever evolving. We need to constantly be revisiting them to ensure their relevance.

Keep raising the bar to meet the changing business environment. Organizations' needs are not static and therefore DEI metrics need to be continually recalibrated to "raise the bar" as objectives are met. In the US, for example, once we uncovered that diverse talent representation in two areas—senior leadership and profit and loss—were particular pain points, we redesigned the scorecard to focus attention on these two tiers.

Facilitate stakeholder involvement. Consulting all the key stakeholders—including human resources, legal, supply chain, operational leaders, and others—helps get buy-in and ensures local relevance and alignment. While this takes time, it is an opportunity for the DEI teams to partner across the enterprise and to give stakeholders credit. It is also an opportunity to ensure that leaders understand the DEI narrative so they can help to cascade accountability. Metrics can start to feel like a top-down imposition from headquarters. So engaging stakeholders in co-creating what they are going to track is particularly important to ensuring a sense of ownership, not only of the metrics but also the entire DEI effort.

Make your metrics simple for meaningful adoption. In order to be effective, metrics should be simple so that they are easily understandable by the end user. When Sodexo initially designed the lead metrics, we included a long list of activities. Given that the scorecard was based on a point scoring system and the inclusive behaviors were allocated 400 points, each individual action was diluted, making it complex to explain and burdensome to achieve. To make it simpler, we ultimately landed on a critical few lead-indicator behaviors that were instrumental in influencing the outcomes.

Make your targets aspirational but achievable. Balancing short-term and long-term goals while showing incremental progress ensures a view of the future while making the targets less overwhelming and more accessible. Modeling scenarios and predictive analytics are useful to show how the objectives can be attained. These tools factor in a variety of assumptions around recruiting, promotion, turnover, and business growth to demonstrate the feasibility.

Continually communicate and educate about the meaning of your metrics. It is critical that senior leaders set the tone by signaling the importance of DEI metrics and reviewing them on a regular basis, just as they would with other metrics. Clear, concise, regular communication that simplifies a complex process of measurement and accountability is key to the success of the DEI metrics. While it is important to communicate the data, it is also helpful to explain the thinking behind the selection of the data. The why goes a long way in getting people aligned. The narrative of what is being solved for—and how they can help with the solution—provides the context and empowers managers. Regardless of the process, it is critical that the results be shared transparently.

Evaluate DEI initiatives. Apart from tracking workforce diversity and inclusion behaviors, it is important to measure the effectiveness of DEI initiatives themselves to determine their contribution to the realization of DEI goals. It can be extremely empowering and inspiring, for example, for managers to see concrete evidence that the time they spent on mentoring is paying off as promotions increase. All too often, DEI initiatives are not evaluated for their impact on the overall DEI objectives. Sodexo conducted an Employee Business Resource Group (EBRG) commitment survey to assess the effectiveness of the EBRGs in advancing the DEI strategy. The findings showed tangible and intangible gains validating that these groups were contributing in a substantive way to the inclusive culture, including engagement and retention as well as visibility and exposure to senior leaders. This reinforced the company's investment in the ERGs. Based on the evidence of their impact, initiatives should be recalibrated to maximize effectiveness (see Figure 13).

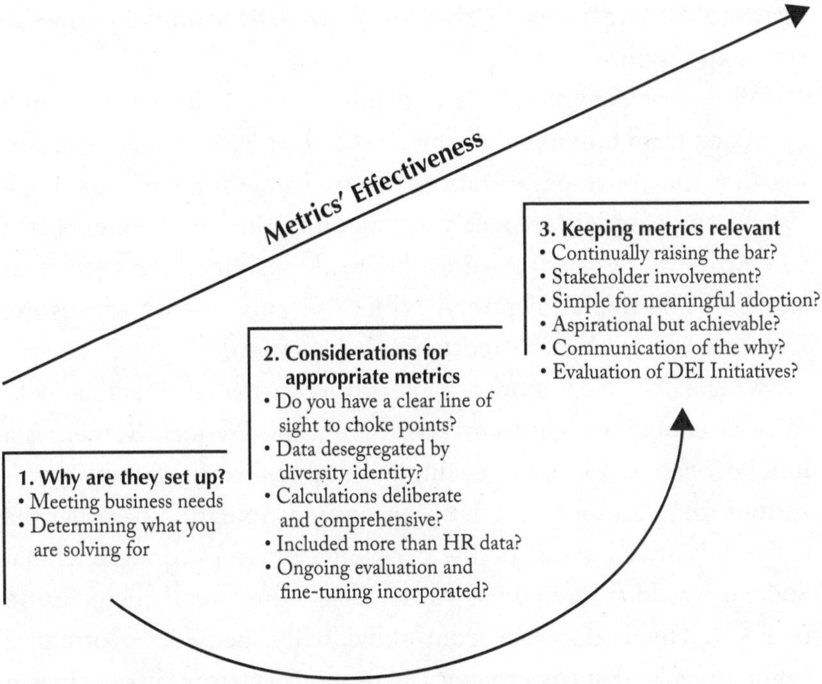

Figure 13: Considerations for Identifying Appropriate Metrics

Cascading Accountability

Metrics are only part of the equation. They only matter if there is accountability. Rishi Gour, CEO of Theobroma India, said,

> When I was at Sodexo, we allocated 10 percent of the variable compensation to our gender target. And when we missed it, no one debated. They said, "We will do better next time and we will get the 10 percent." I remember that year we made the maximum progress. We progressed by 2.7 percent, which is quite massive given the size of the Indian team of 48,000 people.[17]

Accountability is both structured and received differently depending on the culture. In India, given the hierarchical culture, the teams accepted when they missed their objective. Instead of resisting the target setting, they strove to deliver on their supervisor's expectations.

Who is held accountable and how? Companies vary in their approach from holding just senior executives accountable to ensuring that the entire organization is responsible for DEI outcomes. When senior leaders are solely accountable, they are then expected to cascade the objectives—together with accountability—to their teams. While this allows for flexibility in how the objectives are structured, it can lead to spotty implementation.

When DEI is a component of performance management, it needs to carry enough weight to make it significant. Frequently, there is a link between performance evaluation and bonus pay. Some organizations make attaining the DEI objective a stipulation to either the entire incentive payout or the people incentive payout. In China, Sodexo would financially reward whole teams for their inclusion of PWD. This is different from individually focused performance evaluations, and speaks to cultural differences around collectivism and the positive impact of peer pressure.

Incentives are not always in the form of financial compensation. In some organizations, DEI performance indicators are considered a pre-condition for a promotion but not directly linked to a monetary reward. This is often the case in nonprofit organizations.

Tracking data also tells you when a manager or a department is veering off course and suggests actions for addressing bias (conscious or unconscious) that is uncovered by analysis of the metrics. The very fact of tracking and communicating the data can set up some healthy competition and can shame the laggards into action. "When the site manager saw his or her scorecard going red because of the lack of representation of women, they paid attention. People like to achieve targets," Rishi said to me. Depending on how they are positioned, targets can be motivating rather than daunting or causing resistance!

Conclusion

Metrics matter. They communicate both an organization's intent and its commitment internally and externally. When thoughtfully selected, they also help to illuminate critical problem areas and facilitate the resourcing and development of strategic solutions. DEI metrics are equally instruments for assessment and catalysts for progress that can motivate and inspire. They can likewise provide a highly effective framework for accountability, when pairing lead and lag measures. All of this works together.

Finally, a one-size-fits-all approach to DEI metrics will almost certainly come up short. A great deal must be considered to develop appropriate KPIs, from data structure and parsing that data, to stakeholder involvement and addressing the needs of the business. Above all, consideration must be sensitive to the local context. Only then can we find true meaning in the results and the outcomes we seek.

CONCLUSION:
Elevating Diversity, Equity, and Inclusion for the Long Haul

. . . there is always light,
if only we're brave enough to see it.
If only we're brave enough to be it.

—AMANDA GORMAN, "The Hill We Climb"
written and recited for the US Presidential Inauguration,
January 2021

GLOBAL DIVERSITY, EQUITY, AND INCLUSION culture change is complex and challenging work that requires a holistic, systemic approach. It takes a principled outlook and a global and growth mindset.

The five principles explored in this book serve as a guide to embed DEI systemically in the ethos of organizations.

Make It Local ensures that DEI change efforts are contextualized by addressing power dynamics, the fluidity of identity, and local laws and history. While it is important to adjust to the local culture, outside change agents need to be bold and push to address inequities in partnership with local change agents.

Leaders Change to Lead Change speaks to the importance of leadership commitment to DEI and their willingness to work on deep personal transformation to be able to lead with purpose and passion. Not all leaders seek out these experiences and some are even resistant, so change agents need to develop cognitive and emotive strategies to guide leaders. *And It's Good Business, Too,* requires organizations to develop compelling rationales for change that are calibrated to the local nuances and organizational purpose and business. The change narrative is about advancing social justice *and* benefitting the business.

Go Deep, Wide, and Inside-Out is critical to ensure that a global governance model and strategy provides an encompassing framework, while allowing space for local champions and allies to seed DEI deep within the organization. It is going inside-out that ensures that DEI is embedded holistically in the internal systems and extends to external stakeholders. And importantly, relevant metrics and holding people accountable in *Know What Matters and Count It* further ensures DEI is embedded and sustainable.

The principles provide a framework, but the real work is in changing mindsets. DEI culture change evokes emotional responses, as deeply held beliefs—that are often unconscious—are challenged. Being a DEI change agent requires passion that is driven by personally held values, a commitment to social justice, a desire to contribute, and the courage to push. It requires that change agents are highly resilient and ever creative in the face of resistance—that they hold onto their vision despite experiencing disheartening slippage. Leaders must support change agents and acknowledge the fortitude and grit required to get individuals in organizations to see the value in addressing DEI.

I've encountered many barriers during the course of my work. I overcame some, but also realized that I could not surmount every obstacle. I had to keep my eye on the goal, so I did not miss the forest for the trees, as the saying goes. While I was able to engage leaders to be active players in the DEI change narrative, there were some leaders I was unable to influence. And that was okay. As the culture became more inclusive, it swept them along or left them behind.

Sustaining Diversity, Equity, and Inclusion

Progress has been slow. Despite the best-laid efforts, organizations are flailing in their attempts to sustain DEI. This often happens because organizations have simply not been ambitious enough. Or they approach the work as a checklist of discrete linear initiatives rather than infuse it into everything the organization does. Much of the global DEI research generally focuses on initiatives that work or strategies that have fallen short. But global DEI work is complex and addresses deep-seated beliefs requiring more than a series of initiatives and strategies.

In my experience, even when organizations make the investment to address the five principles holistically, they can slide back when their commitment to DEI declines—often with a leadership change or economic challenges. Other competing business priorities become a convenient excuse to dilute the focus. As we have explored, though, DEI can be the very thing that lifts an organization out of its challenges. A study by the Boston Consulting Group (BCG) found that "from 2007 to 2009, the S&P 500 index declined by more than 35%, but the stocks of inclusive companies actually increased by 14%."[1]

Organizations sometimes choose to focus on one main diversity priority, such as gender, as it is globally measurable. Given limited budgets and resources this might seem like the practical approach. While it might serve as a starting point, there is a risk in not fostering a diverse, equitable, and inclusive culture holistically and not taking into consideration local priorities. Coca-Cola settled a race-discrimination class action lawsuit in the US in 2000 for $192.5 million. In a December 2020 article, the *Wall Street Journal* reported that by 2010, Coke's efforts appeared successful with 15 percent of executive roles in the US held by Black employees, up from 1.5 percent in 1998. In 2020, representation of Black executives had regressed to 8 percent. Why were the accomplishments not sustainable? Coca-Cola shifted their focus to another area needing attention—gender, globally—and took their eye off African American progress in the US.[2]

Not only does this example illustrate the need to stay focused on an inclusive culture for all identity dimensions, but it also demonstrates that local priorities, in this case the criticality of race in the US, have to be factored into a transversal global strategy.

When leaders believe that DEI is sufficiently infused in the culture, they argue that it's time to merge DEI with a broader talent agenda without calling it out. However, the external ecosystem, with its incomplete social justice journey, is still operating against these efforts and stakeholders are proliferating in an interconnected world. So, organizations must remain intentional and focused on DEI and elevate it for the long haul or risk losing hard-won ground.

All too often, leaders view DEI as a series of incremental initiatives that are dispensable during crises. This was true in 2020 during the Covid-19 pandemic and the economic downturn when organizations downsized their DEI budgets—only to realize that they now had to deal with the disparate impact of the pandemic on women and marginalized communities. And then within a few months, the systemic racism further magnified by the murder of George Floyd in the US accelerated the Black Lives Matter movement as it swept across the globe requiring organizations to double down on their focus on DEI. It couldn't and wouldn't wait for the pandemic crisis to be resolved.

As the Black Lives Matter movement went viral, corporate leaders made new commitments and promises to redouble their efforts to address DEI. In the US, Fortune 1000 companies committed US $66 billion to address racial inequities.[3] Will these very vocal responses result in meaningful and sustained change or are they simply reactive and performative in order to benefit the brand but with little substance behind them? It is time for organizations to deliver!

A Burning Platform: Organizational Pivots

The Covid-19 pandemic exposed and amplified healthcare disparities for marginalized communities resulting in higher death rates. A global study conducted by McKinsey & Company concluded that, "In every country [in the study], members of diverse populations reported additional challenges and felt them more acutely than their nondiverse counterparts" including women, the LGBTQ population, and ethnic minority populations.[4] The pandemic and the Black Lives Matter movement exposed and magnified longstanding inequities rooted in a history of systemic discrimination. They laid bare the deep divides and what is broken in our society—and they exposed what is possible!

We learned that organizations can pivot, as they did in response to the pandemic, in a way that was unimaginable. They accomplished what was previously thought unattainable. From healthcare organizations pivoting overnight to set up the technology and infrastructure for telehealth; to an American multinational consumer electronics retailer that had spent months testing curbside pick-up in a handful of stores rolling it out to all their stores in just two days; to a retail conglomerate in the Middle East retraining 1,000 people in two days from working in movie theaters to grocery retailing.[5]

Perhaps the clearest example was the speed at which organizations embraced a remote working model in countries and industries where it was previously considered anathema. Employees and employers were abruptly forced into remote work with no prior warning or well-planned change initiative rollout. What was once considered impossible was suddenly possible, creating new ways of working and interacting. BCG's research revealed that, "Although the COVID-19 pandemic has led to economic, health, and social devastation, it has also created an unprecedented opportunity: to run the world's biggest-ever workplace experiment."[6] Employees said they were more productive and expected the flexibility and remote work to continue. This crisis presented an opportunity to reinvent how work is done.

Widespread remote working presented both opportunities and challenges for diversity. On the plus side, organizations could recruit talent from Nairobi to Naples and from Melbourne to Morocco without having to relocate employees. And employees could be more productive with individual flexibility and without time spent on commutes. This particularly increased accessibility for some people with disabilities allowing them to access online meetings where they couldn't previously attend in person.

On the downside, virtual meetings exposed disparities in living situations and also exacerbated the digital divide with varying access to the Internet. If technology is not accessible, it disadvantages people with disabilities. And frontline workers, usually less privileged and frequently from marginalized populations, did not have the luxury of working from home. Remote work created mental health issues disproportionately impacting disadvantaged communities. Organizations had to figure out how to make it work, including exploring hybrid models where some employees came to work, and others worked remotely.

Regardless of how organizations addressed remote work, we know that it can be done. Organizations unfroze traditional ways of working and explored new ways of doing business. In the article, "The CEO Moment: Leadership for a New Era," the authors suggest that "There is an opportunity to reset how work gets done in ways that make it multiple times more efficient and effective—free of the burden of historical norms."[7]

Contrast this to the response to systemic racism magnified by the murders of African Americans at the hands of police in the US in 2020 and protests the world over. There was no meaningful pivot addressing DEI. True—companies donated to social justice causes, committed to increase their board diversity, and made a flurry of appointments of individuals with DEI responsibility. Glassdoor, a recruiting website, said that in 2020 job postings for DEI roles online increased 30 percent in the US. In the UK, Germany, and France, they increased 106 percent, 79 percent, and 53 percent respectively from the prior year.[8] However, DEI professionals shared with me that many of these roles have insignificant budgets and no support teams. Some are figureheads with limited influence. These are an important but far from adequate start.

We can galvanize the energy from a reactive response to situations that exposed the depth and brutal impact of inequities. Yes, these moments can be used to leap forward in DEI pursuits. However, to ensure that these beneficial actions aren't just performative, disruption of the status quo needs to become a normalized conversation in organizations. Giving money and adding DEI positions is the easiest thing to do. The danger is that that can feel like enough. It isn't. The hard part for today's leaders is to acknowledge and change the very rules that have privileged their own success over others'. That takes a commitment to a compelling vision, and it takes sacrifice to uphold the values at the heart of this work—even when it's not breaking news. We need a sense of urgency to go from situational action to sustainable progress in addressing social justice in our communities and diversity, equity, and inclusion in our organizations.

So, what do organizations need to do to unfreeze how they approach and operationalize DEI and dramatically change mindsets and behaviors? We need the public and private sectors to fundamentally reset their approach to DEI. We must be bold and ambitious! Radical change is possible, as we witnessed. And we have a burning social justice platform to raise the heat on it.

We Must Be Ambitious!

Historically, crises have dramatically changed societal models. After World War II, mothers redefined their role as they started joining the workforce. Organizations took bold action and pivoted their operating models as a matter of survival in response to Covid-19. We now know that what was impossible is possible.

How can organizations seize this opportunity to reset their behaviors and mindsets to address DEI boldly and ambitiously within their organizations? How can we work internally and externally to create a new, more equitable social order? How can we allow this turning point in history to broaden our vision?

At the individual level, it is time to not only embed DEI into the very way we do things, but also to open ourselves to new ways of understanding identity and inequality. Given the increasing recognition of the intersectionality of our identities, is it time to add social class to our DEI discourse? Socioeconomic background is a determinant in career progression, but it has long been unacknowledged in the DEI field[9]—addressed mainly through charity rather than true partnership. Unilever, the British multinational consumer goods company, announced in early 2021 that they would be addressing the "persistent and worsening issue of social inequality" by committing that all those in their supply chain would "earn at least a living wage or income by 2030."[10]

At an organizational level, leaders need to examine how their institutional cultures and processes have reinforced systems that disadvantage some and favor others. They must act audaciously to eliminate these harmful practices and to level the playing field for all talent. It takes courage for leaders to disrupt those same systems that have supported their own success. And it takes empathy. What makes oppressive systems tenacious is that many leaders do not realize or acknowledge what got them to their positions.

Organizations are inextricably linked to broader society and many stakeholders—from customers to employees—are calling for them to take daring and unequivocal stands on injustice in their communities. In 2016, the state of North Carolina in the US passed House Bill 2 (HB2), also known as the bathroom bill, "which required transgender people to use bathrooms in state-run buildings that correspond to the sex on their birth certificate rather than their gender identity."[11] Organizational boycotts cost the state hundreds of millions of dollars causing the state to rescind the bill. Such audacious positions by organizations to address societal injustice can and do influence outcomes!

Now is the time to make bold moves and reinvent a new normal for DEI.

Now is the time to address DEI beyond the walls of organizations—to *make it local* by pushing for change globally while understanding the context and positively impacting local communities.

Now is the time for leaders to be ambitious and ready to harness their privilege to benefit others as they do their own internal work by *changing to lead change.*

Now is the time to take a stand for social justice everywhere, because it is the right thing to do—addressing inequities benefits everyone *and it's good business, too.*

Now is the time to reset mental models and change behaviors and systems to fundamentally shift how we approach DEI *deep, wide, and inside-out.*

And now is the time to set lofty goals for organizations and for a new social order because we *know what matters and count it.*

DEI work happens at the intersection of the personal and the systemic, and it is work that is ongoing. Leaders and change agents have to keep pursuing their own change as they work to change organizations to be more diverse, equitable, and inclusive.

This is an inflection point. The next DEI chapter is yet to be written by leaders like you. It's a moment—an opening—of timely opportunity. For society to become equitable, organizations must make it their business. I have never been more excited and hopeful for the future and the role that organizations and the people in them can play in advancing a more equitable, just, and sustainable society for future generations.

LEADING GLOBAL DIVERSITY, EQUITY, AND INCLUSION
Discussion Guide

THE FIVE PRINCIPLES IN THIS BOOK were designed to provide insights to guide you as you transform your organizations to be more diverse, equitable, and inclusive. In addition to the principles, change agents must have a deep awareness of themselves as instruments of change, and with that awareness they must be cognizant of how their identity and orientation impact the process.

These discussion prompts are meant to both deepen your understanding of the principles and steer you as you go about the hard and gratifying work of implementing them.

Principle 1—Make It Local

For each context, ask yourself

1. Who are the dominant and subordinate groups and what is their history? How does this play out in your organization? How and where do decisions get made? Who are the key influencers?
2. How is identity expressed locally? Is it expressed based on race, ethnicity, class, color, religion, or something else?

What identities are taboo to discuss? What identities do people collect around? How are you perceived?

3. Who are the local change agents? What are their goals and strategies? What are the obstacles and entry points to partnering with local change agents? What are the risks (legal, political, social, financial) to local change agents in taking on this work?
4. How is race talked about? Based on that knowledge, what is the best way to frame your work and what is the most appropriate language to use?
5. What are the specific obstacles to inclusion? What are the best entry points for a conversation on race or other sensitive dimensions of diversity?

Principle 2—Leaders Change to Lead Change

For each leader you hope to influence, ask yourself

1. What is the leader's perspective on addressing diversity and social justice and their source of resistance to it? Where do they fall on the Continuum of Common Beliefs and Mindsets described in Chapter 4?
2. How can the leader and the organization benefit from an inclusion culture change?
3. What strategies can you use to disrupt the leader's worldview and shift their perspective on DEI? Are head or heart strategies most relevant?
4. How are your strategies grounded in the leader's cultural context?
5. How will you know if the leader has been motivated to lead DEI authentically with purpose and passion? How is

the shift in the leader's perspective on DEI expressed and to what extent is that expression influenced by their cultural context?

Principle 3—And It's Good Business, Too

For each location where your organization operates, ask yourself

1. What is the rationale for embarking on DEI change?
2. How are you aligning your DEI strategy with that rationale for change? Are you drawing on the legal, moral, and business drivers in each geography?
3. How are you embedding the rationale for addressing DEI into the core of your organization's business, mission, and brand and connecting it to how business is done?
4. How are you communicating the reason behind your DEI change efforts to your employees to maximize resonance and buy-in?
5. What are the business *and* social justice outcomes of your DEI strategy?

Principle 4—Go Deep, Wide, and Inside-Out

When designing your global strategy, ask yourself

1. What global governance structure do you have that is representative of all lines of business and geographies? Are roles and objectives clearly assigned? To what extent do your policies, targets, and governing mechanisms provide latitude for local champions of DEI? How are local champions selected and recognized?

2. What groups are underrepresented in your organization? With that knowledge, what are the barriers to their advancement and how do you plan to address them?
3. How are you embedding DEI at every point of the talent lifecycle to eliminate bias—in recruiting, advancement, engagement, and retention? How are you ensuring that your strategies are locally relevant?
4. What leadership qualities are valued in your organization? To what extent are you reexamining your leadership models to make sure that they recognize disparate leadership styles?
5. How are you partnering with external stakeholders to improve the quality of life in communities?

Principle 5—Know What Matters and Count It

When setting up your measurement system, ask yourself

1. How are you measuring the success of your DEI change efforts?
2. To what extent have you analyzed your talent data to assess blockages in the talent pipeline?
3. How are you getting input and buy-in for your measurement system from across the organization?
4. What lead and lag indicators are you including in your measurement? Have you included measures that are beyond talent, and what are they?
5. How are you holding managers accountable for the outcomes?

APPENDIX: Sample Lead and Lag Measures

This table suggests lead and lag measures you can consider as you develop a measurement system for DEI. The list is not comprehensive and should be calibrated to local cultural needs as well as to your organization.

Lag Measures: Outcome Metrics	Lag Measures KPI*[1]	
REPRESENTATION		
Underrepresented population by business line, level, function, and role benchmarked against majority as well as against population available to do the jobs	Increased representation of underrepresented groups	
RECRUITING		
Underrepresented population recruited by business line, level, function, and role benchmarked against population available externally to do the jobs External recruits from underrepresented groups benchmarked against majority recruits	Increased recruiting of underrepresented groups	

	Lead Measures and Actions	Lead Measures KPI
	Analyze data to assess pain points. Address gaps in specific roles and levels through external recruiting, promotion, and retention strategies.	
	Diversify sourcing channels. Develop early relationships with schools and brand recognition in underrepresented communities. Ensure diverse interview panels. Provide referral incentives to employees. Provide oversight to review hiring decisions. Train recruiters and hiring managers on unconscious bias. Analyze adverse impacts to see at what point in the recruiting process bias prevents progress for underrepresented populations. Evaluate job descriptions to eliminate biased language. Provide targets for recruiters and hold them accountable with incentives. Provide internships and scholarships to underrepresented populations. **Track and Analyze Recruitment Data** Benchmark hires against applicant pool. Benchmark hires against candidates interviewed. Compare recruitment offers vs. acceptances. Track employee referral rates. Track diversity of candidate pool forwarded to hiring manager.	Increased diversity in applicants Increased brand recognition in underrepresented communities Increased diversity of interns Increased numbers of interns from underrepresented groups converted to permanent hires Increased referrals for hires from underrepresented populations Increased diversity of candidate slate presented to hiring manager

Lag Measures: Outcome Metrics	Lag Measures KPI*[1]	
PROMOTION		
Promotion of underrepresented population by business line, level, function, and role benchmarked against promotions in the majority population and overall promotions Promotions benchmarked against internal pipeline of eligible population	Increased promotions of underrepresented groups	

Lead Measures and Actions	Lead Measures KPI
Development Ensure participation by underrepresented groups in • Sponsorship and mentorship programs • High-profile projects • Global assignments • Fast-track programs • Career planning • Job rotation and lateral moves • Leadership development • Visible task forces • Exposure to high-profile clients **Track and Analyze Development Data** Track lateral moves for underrepresented populations. Consider the number of underrepresented talent mentored and sponsored. Analyze the participation of underrepresented populations in development opportunities. **Performance Management** Provide timely and clear feedback. Invest in development plans to address gaps for underrepresented populations. Administer 360 performance evaluations (a process for getting feedback from an employee's subordinate, superiors, peers, and self) and develop plans for development opportunities. Analyze and benchmark performance ratings of underrepresented talent to majority talent and design interventions to address any gaps.	Increased percentages of underrepresented talent in development opportunities Shorter times in position for target populations Improved performance ratings for target population Increased percentage of target population identified as high potential Increased percentage of target population identified as successors

Lag Measures: Outcome Metrics	Lag Measures KPI*[1]	
PROMOTION		
ATTRITION/RETENTION		
Voluntary and involuntary separations for underrepresented populations Underrepresented population retention rate benchmarked against majority population Underrepresented population turnover benchmarked against their representation	Reduced turnover of target population Reduced cost of turnover	

	Lead Measures and Actions	Lead Measures KPI
	High-Potential Talent Identify high-potential underrepresented talent participating in development initiatives. Analyze percentage of target population identified as high potential compared to their representation and the majority population. Track percentage of high-potential underrepresented talent that are promoted. **Succession Planning** Integrate DEI lens into all succession planning discussions. Track the percentage of target populations that are identified as successors, especially for key positions. Track the percentage of target population identified as successors who are promoted compared to majority population. **Unconscious Bias Training** Provide managers with unconscious bias training so bias does not impact promotion decisions.	
	Conduct exit interviews and analyze reasons for leaving. Conduct stay interviews. Address inclusive culture and amplify belonging through initiatives like employee resource groups, etc. Sponsor and mentor high-potential underrepresented talent. Provide career planning for underrepresented talent. **Track and Analyze Turnover Data** Compare the retention of high-potential underrepresented talent against majority. Track regrettable losses for underrepresented populations.	Reduced turnover of high potential underrepresented populations Reduced regrettable losses for underrepresented populations

Lag Measures: Outcome Metrics	Lag Measures KPI*[1]	
ENGAGEMENT		
Disaggregate engagement by demographics benchmarked against external comparable data.	Increased engagement of target populations Increased engagement in overall population	
PAY EQUITY		
Compare pay for individuals in similar positions. Compare average pay overall for underrepresented population to average pay for majority populations.	Pay equity	

	Lead Measures and Actions	Lead Measures KPI
	Address specific gaps in engagement scores through policies and benefits that address the needs of target populations (parental leave, elder care broadly defined, child care). Communicate 401(k) and other benefits and encourage participation by underrepresented populations. Sponsor ERG activities. Advocate for and cascade benefits of flexible work arrangements. Implement training, ombudsperson, external complaints hot line, and other initiatives to prevent discrimination. **Track and Analyze Engagement Data** Track: • Participation in benefits and 401(k) • Increased participation in ERGs • Increased participation in flexible work arrangements • Discrimination lawsuits Analyze disaggregated engagement data by demographic identity. Take an intersectional lens to disaggregating and analyzing engagement data; i.e., women by age cohorts and by race as experiences and challenges differ. Compare underrepresented populations' responses to questions on perception of fairness, advancement, work culture with majority populations.	Increased satisfaction for target population in engagement survey/pulse survey Decreased volume of lawsuits Decreased lawsuits settled for cause Decreased cost per settlement
	Conduct pay equity analysis and develop plan to address gaps. Ensure that underrepresented populations are provided with career planning so not clustered in lower-paying roles. Monitor bonuses and merit increases for bias.	Equity in bonuses and merit increases

Lag Measures: Outcome Metrics	Lag Measures KPI*[1]	
SUPPLIER DIVERSITY		
	Increased percent of total procurement spend with diverse suppliers	
COMMUNITY ENGAGEMENT		
	Improved quality of life of marginalized communities (jobs provided, improved healthcare outcomes, etc.)	
MARKETING		
	Increased revenue from marketing to diverse populations Increased market share in these communities	

	Lead Measures and Actions	Lead Measures KPI
	Source diverse suppliers. Mentor diverse suppliers. Educate organization about benefits of supporting and purchasing from diverse suppliers.	Increased numbers of diverse suppliers year over year.
	Develop initiatives that positively improve the lives of marginalized communities. Enhance the organization's brand in target communities. Build trusting relationships in target communities.	Quality of brand impressions Risk avoidance for the organization due to stronger relationships Numbers of people impacted Amount of money spent Volunteer hours
	Develop strategies for marketing to under-represented populations. Recruit individuals to mirror target populations. Develop cultural competence in teams to leverage target markets. Target culturally competent advertising to diverse markets.	Relationships built with diverse markets Brand impressions in diverse markets Increased net promoter score

NOTES

Preface

1 Lynn M. Shore, Amy E. Randel, Beth G. Chung, Michelle A. Dean, Karen Holcombe Ehrhart, and Gangaram Singh, "Inclusion and Diversity in Work Groups: A Review and Model for Future Research," *Journal of Management* 37, no. 4 (July 2011): 1262–89. *https://doi.org/10.1177/0149206310385943*; Andrés T. Tapia, *The Inclusion Paradox: The Obama Era and the Transformation of Global Diversity* (Hewitt Associates, 2009); Jeanine Prime and Elizabeth R. Salib, "Inclusive Leadership: The View from Six Countries," Catalyst: Workplaces That Work for Women, May 7, 2014, *https://www.catalyst.org/research/inclusive-leadership-the-view-from-six-countries-methodology/.*

2 Eric Zorn, "Column: Should 'White' Be Capitalized? It Feels Wrong, but It's the Way to Go," *Chicago Tribune*, July 9, 2020, *chicagotribune.com/columns/eric-zorn/ct-column-capitalize-white-black-language-race-zorn-20200709-e42fag6ivbazdblizpopsp4p2a-story.html.*

Introduction

1 Although some people use the term *LatinX*, the Hispanic Association on Corporate Responsibility (HACR) advises against it as it can cause offense. While it is an increasingly common term used by non-Latinos to refer to Latinos, according to HACR, less than 3 percent of Latinos refer to themselves as LatinX. HACR suggests using Hispanic or Latino/a. President and CEO of HACR, email exchange with author, January 8, 2021. See also Luis Noe-Bustamante, Lauren Mora, and Mark Hugo Lopez, "About One-in-Four U.S. Hispanics Have Heard of Latinx, but Just 3% Use It," Pew Research Center, August 11, 2020, *https://www.pewresearch.org/hispanic/2020/08/11/about-one-in-four-u-s-hispanics-have-heard-of-latinx-but-just-3-use-it/.*

2 Maryam Jameel and Joe Yerardi, "Workplace Discrimination Is Illegal. But Our Data Shows It's Still a Huge Problem," *Vox*, February 28, 2019, *https://www.vox.com/policy-and-politics/2019/2/28/18241973/workplace-discrimination-cpi-investigation-eeoc.*

3 Kenneth Johnson, Chair, Legal Advisor to the African American Leadership Forum, Assistant General Counsel, Sodexo; interview with author, November 10, 2020.

4 Allen Smith, "EEOC Explains How to Report Nonbinary Individuals on EEO-1 Form," SHRM, August 27, 2019, *https://www.shrm.org/resourcesandtools/legal-and-compliance/employment-law/pages/eeoc-nonbinary-individuals-comments-eeo-1-form.aspx*.

5 Wema Hoover, former Global Head of Inclusion, Diversity, and Culture, Sanofi, interview with author, September 7, 2020.

Chapter 1

1 Natasha Winkler-Titus, President, Society for Industrial and Organizational Psychology, interview with author, October 8, 2020.

2 Mustafa Özbilgin, Ahu Tatli, and Karsten Jonsen, *Global Diversity Management: An Evidence-Based Approach* (London: Palgrave Macmillan, 2008), 256.

3 Pride is a name used by LGBTQ movements in many countries.

4 Subarna Malakar, former Vice President Global Diversity, Ahold Delhaize, interview with author, November 7, 2020.

5 *Britannica Online*, s.v. "Cultural Imperialism," accessed May 26, 2020, *https://www.britannica.com/topic/cultural-imperialism*.

6 Thomas Buckley, "Barilla Pasta's Turnaround from Homophobia to National Pride," *Bloomberg Business*, May 7, 2019, *https://www.bloomberg.com/news/features/2019-05-07/barilla-pasta-s-turnaround-from-homophobia-to-national-pride*.

7 Kristen Anderson, Global Chief Diversity Officer, Barilla, interview with author, August 28 and September 16, 2020.

8 Paul Ingram, "The Forgotten Dimension of Diversity," *Harvard Business Review*, January–February 2021, *https://hbr.org/2021/01/the-forgotten-dimension-of-diversity*.

9 Evangelina Holvino, "'Tired of Choosing': Working with the Simultaneity of Race, Gender, and Class in Organizations," *CGO Insights* #24 (Simmons University: Center for Gender in Organizations, March 2006), 1, *https://www.simmons.edu/sites/default/files/2019-03/Insights%2024.pdf*.

10 Andrés Tapia and Mary-Frances Winters, "Who Am I, Who Are We—Really? The Multiple Identities of Individuals, Organizations, and Nations—And Why This Challenges Key Fundamentals of Current Models of Diversity Work," Diversity and Inclusion Insights Paper, *Diversity Best Practices*, April 2011, *https://www.diversitybestpractices.com/insights-report-who-am-i-who-are-we-really*.

11 Nitasha Tiku, "India's Engineers Have Thrived in Silicon Valley. So Has Its Caste System," *The Washington Post*, October 27, 2020, *https://www.washingtonpost.com/technology/2020/10/27/indian-caste-bias-silicon-valley/*.

12 Lawrencia Quarshie, Manager Global Mobility, Boehringer Ingelheim, interview with author, August 20, 2020 and March 24, 2021.

13 Alain Morize, Senior Vice President, Energy and Resources, US, Sodexo, interview with author, June 3, 2020.

14 World Economic Forum, *Global Gender Gap Report 2020*, accessed November 15, 2020, *http://www3.weforum.org/docs/WEF_GGGR_2020.pdf*.

15 Human Rights Watch, "Boxed In: Women and Saudi Arabia's Male Guardianship System," Human Rights Watch, July 16, 2016, *https://www.hrw.org/report/2016/07/16/boxed/women-and-saudi-arabias-male-guardianship-system*.

16 Feminist Majority Foundation, "Saudi Women Prepare to Vote for the First Time," Feminist Majority Foundation, August 26, 2015, *https://feminist.org/news/saudi-women-prepare-to-vote-for-the-first-time/*.

17 Malak Al-Shehri and Nasir M., "The Feminist Movement in Saudi Arabia," *Viewpoint Magazine*, August 6, 2019, 1–17, *https://viewpointmag.com/2019/08/06/the-feminist-movement-in-saudi-arabia/*.

18 Martin Chulov, "Saudi Arabia to Allow Women to Obtain Driving Licenses," *The Guardian*, September 26, 2017, *https://www.theguardian.com/world/2017/sep/26/saudi-arabias-king-issues-order-allowing-women-to-drive*; Tamara Qiblawi, "Divorced Saudi Women Win Right to Get Custody of Children," CNN, March 12, 2018, *https://edition.cnn.com/2018/03/12/middleeast/saudi-arabia-custody-law-intl/index.html*; Aya Batrawy, "Saudi Arabia Allows Women to Travel without Male Consent," ABC News, August 2, 2019, *https://abcnews.go.com/International/wireStory/saudi-women-travel-male-consent-64722730*.

19 Sarah Hassan, "Saudi Women Join the Workforce as Country Reforms," CNN: Inside the Middle East, February 7, 2018, *https://edition.cnn.com/2018/02/06/middleeast/saudi-women-in-the-workforce/index.html*.

20 UNESCO Institute for Statistics, accessed February 7, 2021, *http://uis.unesco.org/en/country/sa*.

21 Hristina Byrnes, "13 Countries Where Being Gay Is Legally Punishable by Death," USA Today, June 19, 2019, *https://eu.usatoday.com/story/money/2019/06/14/countries-where-being-gay-is-legally-punishable-by-death/39574685/*.

22 David Glasgow and Kenji Yoshino, "Opening Up the World: How Multinational Organizations Can Ascend the Maturity Curve on LGBT+ Rights," Center for Diversity, Inclusion, and Belonging, NYU School of Law, accessed June 8, 2021, *https://www.law.nyu.edu/sites/default/files/OpeningUpTheWorld_report_FINAL_508.pdf*.

23 Anuradha Purbey, People Director for Europe and Asia, Aviva, interview with author on July 8, 2020.

24 Mark McLane, Head of Diversity, Inclusion and Wellbeing, M&G PLC, interview with author on July 21, 2020.

25 BBC, "Uganda Court Annuls Anti-Homosexuality Law," BBC News, August 1, 2014, *https://www.bbc.co.uk/news/world-africa-28605400*; Emmanuel Leroux-Nega (AFP), "Uganda Court Scraps New Anti-Gay Law," *Digital Journal*, August 1, 2014, *http://www.digitaljournal.com/news/world/uganda-constitutional-court-annuls-new-anti-gay-law/article/394083*.

Chapter 2

1 *Britannica Online*, s.v. "Race," accessed August 10, 2020, *https://www.britannica.com/topic/race-human*.

2 Guardian staff, "Australia Protests: Thousands Take Part in Black Lives Matter and Pro-refugee Events amid Covid-19 Warnings," *The Guardian*, June 13, 2020, *https://www.theguardian.com/world/2020/jun/13/australia-protests-thousands-take-part-in-black-lives-matter-and-pro-refugee-events-amid-health-warnings*.

3 Marion Ferreira, Controller, NKG Stockler LTDA, Brazil, interview with author, August 7, 2020; Lilian Rauld Campos, Head of Diversity and Inclusion, On-site, Sodexo Brazil, interviewed with author, July 31, 2020.

4 Cole Stangler, "France's Black Lives Matter Movement," *Tribune*, June 21, 2020, *https://tribunemag.co.uk/2020/06/frances-black-lives-matter-movement/*.

5 Billy Perrigo and Melissa Godin, "Racism Is Surging in Germany. Tens of Thousands Are Taking to the Streets to Call for Justice," *Time*, June 11, 2020, *https://time.com/5851165/germany-anti-racism-protests/*.

6 Estelle Ndjandjo, "Senegalese Artists Take a Stand for Black Lives Matter Movement," *Voice of America*, June 15, 2020, *https://www.voanews.com/episode/senegalese-artists-take-stand-black-lives-matter-movement-4324531*.

7 Pete Pattisson, "Migrant Workers in Qatar Face 'Structural Racism' Says UN Report," *The Guardian*, July 15, 2020, *https://www.theguardian.com/global-development/2020/jul/15/migrant-workers-in-qatar-face-structural-racism-says-un-report*.

8 Tanya Katerí Hernández, *Racial Subordination in Latin America: The Role of the State, Customary Law, and the New Civil Rights Response* (New York: Cambridge University Press, 2013), 19–46.

9 Aperian Global, "How Can Organizations in Asia Address Equity and Inclusion Issues?," webinar from Aperian Global, October 22, 2020, *https://www.aperianglobal.com/wp-content/uploads/2020/10/Race-and-Ethnicity-Webinar-22Oct2020.pdf*.

10 Monica Robayo-Abril and Natalia Millan, *Breaking the Cycle of Roma Exclusion in the Western Balkans* (Washington DC: World Bank, 2019), *https://openknowledge.worldbank.org/handle/10986/31393*.

11 Kaitlyn Greenidge, "Why Black People Discriminate among Ourselves: The Toxic Legacy of Colorism," *The Guardian*, April 9, 2019,

https://www.theguardian.com/lifeandstyle/2019/apr/09/colorism-racism-why-black-people-discriminate-among-ourselves.

12 Maliha Rehman, "Getting Rich from the Skin Lightening Trade," *The Business of Fashion*, September 27, 2017, *https://www.businessoffashion.com/articles/beauty/profiting-from-the-skin-lightening-trade.*

13 M. Ridder, "Forecasted Market Value Skin Lightening Products Worldwide from 2017 to 2027," Statista, November 23, 2020, *https://www.statista.com/statistics/863876/global-forecasted-market-value-of-skin-lightening-products/.*

14 Lawrencia Quarshie, Manager Global Mobility, Boehringer Ingelheim, interview with author, March 24, 2021.

15 Mark McLane, Head of Diversity, Inclusion and Wellbeing, M&G PLC, interview with author, July 21, 2020.

16 Excerpted with permission from Laura Shipler Chico, Sodexo, *Addressing Culture and Origins across the Globe: Lessons from Australia, Brazil, Canada, the United Kingdom and the United States* (Sodexo, 2019), 3, *https://www.fi.sodexo.com/files/live/sites/com-us/files/about-us/AddressingCultureOriginsAcrossGlobe.pdf.*

17 Sodexo, *Addressing Culture and Origins Across the Globe*, 4.

18 *Britannica Online*, s.v. "Rwanda," accessed May 31, 2021, *https://www.britannica.com/place/Rwanda*; *Britannica Online*, s.v. "Burundi," accessed May 31, 2021, *https://www.britannica.com/place/Burundi.*

19 Peter Uvin, "Ethnicity and Power in Burundi and Rwanda: Different Paths to Mass Violence," *Comparative Politics* 31, no. 3 (April 1999): 253–271, *https://www.jstor.org/stable/422339?read-now=1&refreqid=excelsior%3A514f121f3278b41663936b258f8745f9&seq=13#page_scan_tab_contents.*

20 Stef Vandeginste, "Ethnic Quotas and Foreign NGOs in Burundi: Shrinking Civic Space Framed as Affirmative Action," *African Spectrum* 54, 3 (October 30, 2019), 181–200, *https://journals.sagepub.com/doi/full/10.1177/0002039719881460.*

21 Vince Chadwick and Christin Roby, "Turmoil for International Aid Groups in Burundi over Ethnic Quotas," Devex, January 21, 2019, *https://www.devex.com/news/turmoil-for-international-aid-groups-in-burundi-over-ethnic-quotas-94125.*

22 Chadwick and Roby, "Turmoil for International Aid Groups."

23 Nitasha Tiku, "India's Engineers Have Thrived in Silicon Valley. So Has Its Caste System," *The Washington Post*, October 27, 2020, *https://www.washingtonpost.com/technology/2020/10/27/indian-caste-bias-silicon-valley/.*

24 Connexion journalist, "Assembly Removes Word 'Race' from French Constitution," *The Connexion*, July 13, 2018, *https://www.connexionfrance.com/French-news/france-assembly-votes-to-remove-race-French-constitution.*

25 Erik Bleich, "Race Policy in France," Brookings, May 1, 2001, *https://www.brookings.edu/articles/race-policy-in-france/*.

26 Ngofeen Mputubwele, interview by Gregory Warner, "We Don't Say That," *Rough Translation Podcast*, NPR, May 1, 2019, *https://www.npr.org/transcripts/718729150*. "We Don't Say That" cites the following as its sources: Crystal Marie Fleming, author of *Resurrecting Slavery: Racial Legacies and White Supremacy in France*; Amandine Gay, the director of the documentary *Ouvrir La Voix*, or *Speak Up; Noire N'est Pas Mon Métier* by Nadège Beausson-Diagne et al.

27 Mputubwele, *Rough Translation Podcast.*

28 Molly Moore, "French Discrimination Suit Calls Égalité into Question," *The Washington Post*, January 15, 2006, *https://www.washingtonpost.com/wp-dyn/content/article/2006/01/14/AR2006011401103.html*.

29 Staffing Industry Analysts, "Belgium/France—Adecco Receives Fine for Racism," SIA, June 6, 2011, *https://www2.staffingindustry.com/eng/Editorial/Daily-News/Belgium-France-Adecco-receives-fine-for-racism-18688*.

30 Bruce Roche, Adecco, Director of Social and Environmental Responsibility, Adecco France, interview with author, September 23, 2020.

31 Lilla Farkas, *Analysis and Comparative Review of Equality Data Collection Practices in the European Union; Data Collection in the Field of Ethnicity* (Luxembourg: European Commission, 2017), 14.

32 Reza Hariri, Secretary General, Club 21e Siecle, and Vice President, Digital Transformation, Renault Group, and Batoul Hassoun, Board Member—Strategy and Transformation, Club 21e Siecle, interview with author, February 10, 2021.

33 Farkas, *Comparative Review of Equality Data Collection*, 13.

34 Farkas, *Comparative Review of Equality Data Collection*, 10.

35 Hernández, *Racial Subordination in Latin America*, 26–31.

36 Hernández, *Racial Subordination in Latin America*, 34–38.

37 F. James Davis, *Who Is Black? One Nation's Definition* (University Park, PA: Pennsylvania State University Press, 1991). Excerpt reprinted on *https://www.pbs.org/wgbh/pages/frontline/shows/jefferson/mixed/onedrop.html*.

38 Hernández, *Racial Subordination in Latin America*, 38–46.

39 Associated Press, "136 Variations of Brazilian Skin Colors," Associated Press, July 8, 2014, *https://apnews.com/article/692538d8883a4d20842425d1d265b862*.

40 Grant Suneson and Samuel Stebbins, "These 15 Countries Have the Widest Gaps between Rich and Poor," *USA Today*, May 28, 2019, *https://www.usatoday.com/story/money/2019/05/28/countries-with-the-widest-gaps-between-rich-and-poor/39510157/*.

41 Hernández, *Racial Subordination in Latin America*, 47.

42 Hernández, *Racial Subordination in Latin America*, 85; Soledad Dominguez, "Self-Made, Successful and Black: Lessons from a Brazilian Executive," *Americas Quarterly*, February 19, 2020, *https://www.americasquarterly.org/article/self-made-successful-and-black-lessons-from-a-brazilian-executive/*.

43 Bruna Galvoa, Natura & Co, Brazil, Learning and Development Specialist, interview with the author, November 30, 2020.

Chapter 3

1 Robin J. Ely, David A. Thomas, "Getting Serious about Diversity: Enough Already with the Business Case," *Harvard Business Review*, November–December 2020, *https://hbr.org/2020/11/getting-serious-about-diversity-enough-already-with-the-business-case*.

2 Jeanine Prime and Corinne A. Moss-Racusin, "Engaging Men in Gender Initiatives: What Change Agents Need to Know," *Catalyst* (May 4, 2009): 11, *https://catalyst.org/research/engaging-men-in-gender-initiatives-what-change-agents-need-to-know/*.

3 Andrés Tapia and Alina Polonskaia, *The 5 Principles of Inclusive Leaders: Unleashing the Power of All of Us* (Oakland, CA: Berrett-Koehler Publishers, 2020), 4.

4 Joanna Barsh, "Change Point: How Business Leaders Can Save the American Dream—And America" (unpublished manuscript, September 9, 2020), Microsoft Word file.

5 Keysa Minnifield, Former VP Human Resources, Sodexo and member of the African American Leadership Forum Leadership Team, interview with the author, November 16, 2020.

6 Richard (Dick) Macedonia, former CEO Sodexo North America, interview with the author, December 21, 2020.

7 Kenneth Johnson, Assistant General Counsel, Sodexo and AALF Leadership Team, Sodexo, interview with the author, November 10, 2020.

8 Macedonia, interview with author.

9 Minnifield, interview with author.

10 David A. Thomas and Stephanie J. Creary, "Shifting the Diversity Climate: The Sodexo Solution," *Harvard Business School Case 412-020* (July 2011): 6, *https://www.hbs.edu/faculty/Pages/item.aspx?num=40727*.

11 Fons Trompenaars and Charles Hampden-Turner, *Riding the Waves of Culture: Understanding Cultural Diversity in Business*, 2nd ed. (London: Nicholas Brealey Publishing, 2002), 83.

12 Augusto Muench, Boehringer Ingelheim, Country Managing Director for Mexico, Central America, and the Caribbean, interview with the author, July 13, 2020.

13 Erin Meyer, *The Culture Map, Breaking through the Invisible Boundaries of Global Business*, ill. ed. (New York: PublicAffairs, 2014), 125.

14 Meyer, *The Culture Map*, 39.

15 Rishi Gour, CEO, Theobroma, former CEO Sodexo India, interview with author, June 30, 2020.

16 Gour, interview with author.

17 Michel Landel, Former Global CEO, Sodexo and Board Member, Danone, interview with the author, June 8, 2020.

18 Vijay Sharma, Regional Director and Head of Food Service Platforms, Asia-Pacific, Sodexo, and former member of the leadership team for Sodexo's Pan-Asian Network Group, conversation and email exchange with the author, April 12, 2021.

19 Wema Hoover, former Global Head of Diversity, Inclusion and Culture, Sanofi, interviewed by the author September 7, 2020.

Chapter 4

1 John P. Kotter and Dan S. Cohen, *The Heart of Change: Real-Life Stories of How People Change Their Organizations*, 1st ed. (Boston: Harvard Business Review Press, 2012), 1.

2 Catalyst, "Engaging Men in Gender Initiatives: What Change Agents Need to Know," *Catalyst* (May 4, 2009), 11, *https://www.catalyst.org/research/engaging-men-in-gender-initiatives-what-change-agents-need-to-know/*.

3 Catalyst, "Engaging Men in Gender Initiatives," 11.

4 Catalyst, "Engaging Men in Gender Initiatives," 11.

5 W2O Consulting & Training, "9 Key Tips to Engage Senior Leaders in Gender Diversity," W2O Consulting & Training, accessed November 16, 2020, *https://www.w2oconsultingandtraining.co.uk/gender-balance/9-key-tips-to-engage-senior-leaders-in-gender-diversity/*.

6 Richie Zweigenhaft, "Fortune 500 CEOs, 2000–2020: Still Male, Still White," The Society Pages, October 28, 2020, *https://thesocietypages.org/specials/fortune-500-ceos-2000-2020-still-male-still-white/*.

7 Sodexo, "Caring about Quality of Life: Fiscal 2020 Universal Registration Document," Sodexo, August 31, 2020, *https://www.sodexo.com/files/live/sites/com-global/files/02%20PDF/Finance/Sodexo-Universal-Registration-Document-FY2020.pdf*.

8 Catalyst, "Engaging Men in Gender Initiatives," 7.

9 Simone Grossmann, Head of HR for Brazil and the South Cone, The Coca-Cola Company, interview with the author, October 23, 2020.

10 Mia Mends, Global Chief Diversity and Inclusion Officer and CEO, Impact Ventures; interview with author, July 7, 2020, and email exchange, April 18, 2020.

11 Nancy Duarte, *Data Story: Explain Data and Inspire Action through Story* (Oakton: Ideapress Publishing, 2019), 5.

12 Thomas Buckley, "Barilla Pasta's Turnaround from Homophobia to National Pride," *Bloomberg Businessweek*, May 7, 2019, *https://www.bloomberg.com/news/features/2019-05-07/barilla-pasta-s-turnaround-from-homophobia-to-national-pride.*

13 Buckley, "Barilla Pasta's Turnaround."

14 Daniel Avery, "71 Countries Where Homosexuality Is Illegal: Acceptance of the LGBT Community Continues to Spread around the World, but Homosexuality Is Still Illegal in Many Parts of the World," *Newsweek*, April 4, 2019, *https://www.newsweek.com/73-countries-where-its-illegal-be-gay-1385974.*

15 Denis Machuel, email message on inclusion to Sodexo employees, June 2, 2020.

Chapter 5

1 Carolyn Dewar and Scott Keller, "The Irrational Side of Change Management," McKinsey & Company, April 1, 2009, *https://www.mckinsey.com/business-functions/organization/our-insights/the-irrational-side-of-change management.*

2 Dewar and Keller, "Irrational Side of Change Management."

3 Emily Lawson and Colin Price, "The Psychology of Change Management," *The McKinsey Quarterly*, June 1, 2003, *https://www.mckinsey.com/business-functions/organization/our-insights/the-psychology-of-change-management.*

4 John P. Kotter, *Leading Change* (Boston: Harvard Business School Press, 1996), 48.

5 Sodexo, "Gender Balance Study 2018," Sodexo.com, February 28, 2019, *https://www.sodexo.com/inspired-thinking/research-and-reports/gender-balance-study-2018.html.*

6 Sodexo, "Gender Balance Study 2018."

7 Will Kenton, "Affirmative Action," Investopedia, February 10, 2021, *https://www.investopedia.com/terms/a/affirmative-action.asp.*

8 Rohini Anand and Mary-Frances Winters, "A Retrospective View of Corporate Diversity Training from 1964 to the Present," *Academy of Management Learning and Education* 7, no. 3 (2008): 356–72.

9 Jim Edwards, "30 Years of Absolut Ads Targeting the Gay Community," CBS News, October 29, 2011, *https://www.cbsnews.com/news/30-years-of-absolut-ads-targeting-the-gay-community/.*

10 John Schneider and David Auten, "The $1 Trillion Marketing Executives Are Ignoring," *Forbes*, 2018, *https://www.forbes.com/sites/debtfreeguys/2018/08/14/the-1-trillion-marketing-executives-are-ignoring/?sh=5dd15e7fa97f.*

11 Robin J. Ely and David A. Thomas, "Getting Serious about Diversity: Enough Already with the Business Case," *Harvard Business Review*, November–December 2020, *https://hbr.org/2020/11/getting-serious-about-diversity-enough-already-with-the-business-case*.

12 Jamillah Bowman Williams, "Breaking Down Bias: Legal Mandates vs. Corporate Interests," Georgetown Law Faculty Publications and Other Works, March 22, 2017, *https://scholarship.law.georgetown.edu/facpub/1961/*.

13 D'Vera Cohn and Anthony Cilluffo, "6 Demographic Trends Shaping the U.S. and the World in 2019," Pew Research Center, April 11, 2019, *https://www.pewresearch.org/fact-tank/2019/04/11/6-demographic-trends-shaping-the-u-s-and-the-world-in-2019/*.

14 William. H. Frey, "The US Will Become 'Minority White' in 2045, Census Projects," Brookings, March 14, 2018, *https://www.brookings.edu/blog/the-avenue/2018/03/14/the-us-will-become-minority-white-in-2045-census-projects/*.

15 Damian Hattingh, Acha Leke, and Bill Russo, "Lions (Still) on the Move: Growth in Africa's Consumer Sector," McKinsey & Company, October 2, 2017, *https://www.mckinsey.com/industries/consumer-packaged-goods/our-insights/lions-still-on-the-move-growth-in-africas-consumer-sector*.

16 Nader Kabbani, "Youth Employment in the Middle East and North Africa: Revisiting and Reframing the Challenge," Brookings, February 26, 2019, *https://www.brookings.edu/research/youth-employment-in-the-middle-east-and-north-africa-revisiting-and-reframing-the-challenge/*.

17 Lohini Moodley, Mayowa Kuyoro, Tania Holt, Acha Leke, Anu Madgavkar, Mekala Krishnan, and Folakemi Akintayo, "The Power of Parity: Advancing Women's Equality in Africa," McKinsey & Company, November 24, 2019, *https://www.mckinsey.com/featured-insights/gender-equality/the-power-of-parity-advancing-womens-equality-in-africa*.

18 International Idea Institute for Democracy and Electoral Assistance, "The Implementation of Quotas: African Experiences," September 1, 2004, *https://www.idea.int/publications/catalogue/implementation-quotas-african-experiences*.

19 Janine Hills, "Addressing Gender Quotas in South Africa: Women Employment and Gender Equality Legislation," *Deakin Law Review* 20, no. 1 (2015), *https://ojs.deakin.edu.au/index.php/dlr/article/view/498*.

20 Valentina Romei, "Africa Has Made Most Legislative Progress for Women," *The Financial Times*, December 10, 2018, *https://www.ft.com/content/7cdd7612-fa01-11e8-af46-2022a0b02a6c*.

21 Moodley et al., "The Power of Parity."

22 Kennedy Elliott, "Rwanda's Legislature Is Majority Female. Here's How It Happened," *National Geographic*, October 15, 2019, *https://*

www.nationalgeographic.com/culture/graphics/graphic-shows-women-representation-in-government-around-the-world-feature.

23 Moodley et al., "The Power of Parity."

24 Jeremie Gilbert, "Constitutionalism, Ethnicity and Minority Rights in Africa: A Legal Appraisal from the Great Lakes Region," *International Journal of Constitutional Law* 11, no. 2 (April 2013), 414–437, *https://doi.org/10.1093/icon/mot002.*

25 Amber Kardamilakis, "Broad-Based Black Economic Empowerment—Basic Principles," *Norton Rose Fulbright*, July 2018, 4 *https://www.nortonrosefulbright.com/en-za/knowledge/publications/fe87cd48/broad-based-black-economic-empowerment--basic-principles.*

26 World Bank, *Middle East and North Africa Public Employment and Governance in MENA* (Washington, DC: World Bank, May 2016), 4, *http://documents1.worldbank.org/curated/en/339381472236811833/pdf/ACS18501-WP-OUO-9-Final-Output-Document-has-been-approved-P147520.pdf.*

27 Sheerin Vesin, "3 Insights into Closing the Life Skills Gap in MENA," International Youth Foundation, January 25, 2018, *https://www.iyfnet.org/blog/3-insights-closing-life-skills-gap-mena.*

28 Pedro Goncalves, "GCC to Suffer 10% Drop in Population under Expat Exodus," International Investment, September 25, 2020, *https://www.internationalinvestment.net/news/4020733/gcc-suffer-drop-population-expat-exodus.*

29 Neha Bhatia, "Saudi's Revised Nitaqat to Take Effect in September 2017," *Construction Week*, August 24, 2017, *https://www.constructionweekonline.com/article-46034-saudis-revised-nitaqat-to-take-effect-in-september-2017.*

30 Mercer, "Diversity & Inclusion: An Asia Pacific Perspective," Mercer, 2014, accessed November 13, 2020, *https://docplayer.net/25371558-Diversity-inclusion-an-asia-pacific-perspective-executive-summary.html.*

31 Victor Kiprop, "Major Languages Spoken in Asia," WorldAtlas, December 18, 2020, *https://www.worldatlas.com/articles/major-languages-spoken-in-asia.html*; Worldometer, "Countries in Asia," accessed May 19, 2021, *https://www.worldometers.info/geography/how-many-countries-in-asia/.*

32 Ernest Gundling, "Race, Ethnicity, and Social Justice," *Aperian Global*, September 2020, 11, *https://www.aperianglobal.com/wp-content/uploads/2020/09/Featured-Insight-Race-Ethnicity-and-Social-Justice-A-Global-Perspectivev1September2020.pdf.*

33 Tatsuyuki Ota, "Economic Growth, Income Inequality and Environment: Assessing the Applicability of the Kuznets Hypotheses to Asia," *Palgrave Communications* 3, 17069 (July 25, 2017), *https://doi.org/10.1057/palcomms.2017.69.*

34 BBC, "Japan Population to Shrink by One-Third by 2060," BBC News, January 30, 2012, *https://www.bbc.co.uk/news/world-asia-16787538*.

35 Korn Ferry, "Potential Talent Deficit of 47 Million Workers in APAC Could Threaten Business Growth," Korn Ferry Focus, 2017, accessed October 21, 2020, *https://focus.kornferry.com/leadership-and-talent/potential-talent-deficit-of-47-million-workers-in-the-apac-could-threaten-business-growth/*.

36 EU, "Article 21 - Non-Discrimination," EU Charter of Fundamental Rights, accessed December 30, 2020, *https://fra.europa.eu/en/eu-charter/article/21-non-discrimination*.

37 Lord Corbett of Castle Vale, "Chronically Sick and Disabled Persons Act 1970: 40th Anniversary—Debate," TheyWorkForYou, June 17, 2010, *https://www.theyworkforyou.com/lords/?id=2010-06-17a.1123.4*.

38 Julian Cuppage, "The World and Disability: Quotas or No Quotas?," IGlobal Law, December 11, 2013, *https://www.igloballaw.com/the-world-and-disability-quotas-or-no-quotas/*.

39 European Commission, "The Business Case for Diversity: Good Practices in the Workplace," European Commission, December 2, 2005, *https://op.europa.eu/en/publication-detail/-/publication/57e667e2-d349-433b-b21d-1c67fd10ebb1*.

40 EBTP, "Diversity Management in 2008: Research with the European Business Test Panel," EBTP, 2008, 4, accessed November 18, 2020.

41 Alicia Ibarra Barcena and Winnie Byanyima, "Latin America Is the World's Most Unequal Region. Here's How to Fix It," World Economic Forum, January 17, 2016, *https://www.weforum.org/agenda/2016/01/inequality-is-getting-worse-in-latin-america-here-s-how-to-fix-it/*.

42 Dominguez Soledad, "Self-Made, Successful and Black: Lessons from a Brazilian Executive," *Americas Quarterly*, February 19, 2020, *https://www.americasquarterly.org/article/self-made-successful-and-black-lessons-from-a-brazilian-executive/*.

43 Antonio Giuffrida, "Racial and Ethnic Disparities in Latin America and the Caribbean: A Literature Review," *Diversity in Health and Care* 7 (April 1, 2010): 122, *https://diversityhealthcare.imedpub.com/racial-and-ethnic-disparities-in-latin-america-and-the-caribbean-a-literature-review.pdf*.

44 Inter-American Development Bank, "Inclusion of People with Disabilities in Latin America and the Caribbean," 2019, 20, *https://publications.iadb.org/publications/english/document/We_the_People_Inclusion_of_People_with_Disabilities_in_Latin_America_and_the_Caribbean_en.pdf*.

45 Inter-American Development Bank, "Inclusion of People with Disabilities," 20.

46 Staffing América Latina, "Unemployment among Disabled People in Latin America," Staffing América Latina, March 14, 2020, *https://staffingamericalatina.com/en/el-desempleo-entre-las-personas-con-discapacidad-en-america-latina/*.

47 Sandra Cuffe, "Feminist Groups Hold Mass Women's Day March across Chile," *Al Jazeera*, March 8, 2020, *https://www.aljazeera.com/news/2020/3/8/feminist-groups-hold-mass-womens-day-marches-across-chile.*

48 Ashley Westerman, Ryan Benk, and David Greene, "In 2020, Protests Spread across the Globe with a Similar Message: Black Lives Matter," NPR, December 30, 2020, *https://www.npr.org/2020/12/30/950053607/in-2020-protests-spread-across-the-globe-with-a-similar-message-black-lives-matt.*

49 Monica Flores and Angel Melguizo, "Latin America Has the Biggest Skills Gap in the World. Here's How to Bridge It," World Economic Forum, March 13, 2018, *https://www.weforum.org/agenda/2018/03/latin-america-has-the-biggest-skills-gap-in-the-world-here-s-how-to-bridge-it/.*

50 Flores and Melguizo, "Latin America Has Biggest Skills Gap."

51 Aniela Unguresan, Magali Saúl, and Lauren Murphy, "The Power of Gender Equality in the Workplace," IDB Invest, March 2020, *https://we-fi.org/wp-content/uploads/2020/03/thepowerofgender0318.pdf.*

52 Mercer, *When Women Thrive, Businesses Thrive: Challenges and Opportunities in Latin America* (Mercer, November 2017), 7, *https://edge-cert.org/wp-content/uploads/2017/11/Mercer-WWT-LatAm-Report.pdf.*

53 Deloitte, "The Deloitte Global Millennial Survey 2020: Millennials and Gen Zs Hold the Key to Creating a 'Better Normal,'" Deloitte, accessed October 26,2020, *https://www2.deloitte.com/global/en/pages/about-deloitte/articles/millennialsurvey.html.*

54 Korn Ferry, "The Global Talent Crunch," Korn Ferry, February 2015, *https://focus.kornferry.com/wp-content/uploads/2015/02/The-Global-Talent-Crunch.pdf.*

Chapter 6

1 Rosie Perper, "The 29 Countries around the World Where Same Sex Marriage Is Legal," *Business Insider*, May 28, 2020, *https://www.businessinsider.com/where-is-same-sex-marriage-legal-world-2017-11?r=US&IR=T.*

2 Lee Badgett, Kees Waaldijk, and Yana van der Meulen Rodgers, "The Relationship between LGBT Inclusion and Economic Development: Macro-Level Evidence," *World Development* 120 (August 1, 2019): 1–14, *https://doi.org/10.1016/j.worlddev.2019.03.011.*

3 Lee Badgett, "Economic Cost of Homophobia," The World Bank, February 2014, *https://www.worldbank.org/content/dam/Worldbank/document/SAR/economic-costs-homophobia-lgbt-exlusion-india.pdf.*

4 Nick Wolney, "The LGBTQ+ Community Has $3.7 Trillion in Purchasing Power; Here's How We Want You to Sell to Us," *Entrepreneur*, June 10, 2019, *https://www.entrepreneur.com/article/334983.*

5 Sylvia Anne Hewlett and Kenji Yoshino, "LGBT-Inclusive Companies Are Better at 3 Big Things," *Harvard Business Review*, February 2, 2016, *https://hbr.org/2016/02/lgbt-inclusive-companies-are-better-at-3-big-things*.

6 Kenji Yoshino and Christie Smith, "Fear of Being Different Stifles Talent," *Harvard Business Review*, March 2014, *https://hbr.org/2014/03/fear-of-being-different-stifles-talent*.

7 Ian Johnson and Darren Cooper, "LGBT Diversity: Show Me the Business Case," Gay Market News: Out Now, February 11, 2015, 29, *http://www.gaymarketnews.com/2015/02/lgbt-diversity-show-me-business-case.html*.

8 Johnson and Cooper, "LGBT Diversity," 29.

9 Hewlett and Yoshino, "LGBT-Inclusive Companies Are Better."

10 Pierre Dupreel, Gabrielle Novacek, Jeff Lindquist, Nathan Micon, Simon Pellas, and Glennda Testone, "A New LGBT Workforce Has Arrived—Inclusive Cultures Must Follow," Boston Consulting Group, June 23, 2020, *https://www.bcg.com/publications/2020/inclusive-cultures-must-follow-new-lgbtq-workforce*.

11 SpringFair, "The LGBT Market: How Much Is the Pink Pound Worth?" *SpringFair*, June 26, 2019, *https://www.springfair.com/news/lgbt-market-how-much-is-the-pink-pound-worth*.

12 Scott Thompson, "Barclays Gives ATMs Pride in London Makeover," FSTech, May 19, 2014, *https://www.fstech.co.uk/fst/Pride_in_London_Barclays_Pingit.php*.

13 British LGBT Awards, "Case Study: Barclays—British LGBT Awards," May 18, 2017, *https://www.britishlgbtawards.com/case-study-barclays/*.

14 James Ashton, "Same-Sex and the City: Barclays CEO Antony Jenkins on Why the Bank Is the Headline Sponsor of Pride in London," *London Evening Standard*, June 19, 2014, *https://www.standard.co.uk/lifestyle/london-life/samesex-and-the-city-barclays-ceo-antony-jenkins-on-why-the-bank-is-the-headline-sponsor-of-pride-in-london-9548210.html*.

15 Mark McLane, Head of Diversity, Inclusion and Wellbeing, M&G PLC; Former Head of Diversity, Inclusion and Culture at Barclays Bank, interview with the author, July 21, 2020.

16 Pew Research Center, "Number of Refugees to Europe Surges to Record 1.3 Million in 2015," Pew Research Center, August 2, 2016, *https://www.pewresearch.org/global/2016/08/02/number-of-refugees-to-europe-surges-to-record-1-3-million-in-2015/*.

17 Alice Beste, "The Contributions of Refugees: Lifting Barriers to Inclusion," United Nations University, Institute on Globalization, Culture and Mobility, August, 28, 2015, *https://gcm.unu.edu/publications/articles/the-contributions-of-refugees-lifting-barriers-to-inclusion.html*.

18 Tent, "UK Employers' Guide to Hiring Refugees," Tent: Breaking Barriers, November 2018, *https://www.tent.org/wp-content/uploads/2018/11/Tent_Guidebook_UK_singlepages.pdf*.

19 Beste, "The Contributions of Refugees."

20 Cone, A Porter Novelli Company, "Three-Quarters of Millennials Would Take a Pay Cut to Work for a Socially Responsible Company, according to the Research from Cone Communications," Cone, A Porter Novelli Company, November 2, 2016, *https://www.conecomm.com/news-blog/2016-cone-communications-millennial-employee-engagement-study-press-release*.

21 Vivian Hunt, Dennis Layton, and Sara Prince, "Why Diversity Matters," McKinsey, January 1, 2015, *https://www.mckinsey.com/business-functions/organization/our-insights/why-diversity-matters*.

22 Annette Mock, Deutsche Post DHL Group, interview with author, August 26, 2020.

23 Lida Bteddini, "Governance and Public Sector Employment in the Middle East and North Africa," Worldbank, September 25, 2012, *https://blogs.worldbank.org/arabvoices/governance-and-public-sector-employment-middle-east-and-north-africa*.

24 Shanta Devarajan, "The Paradox of Higher Education in MENA," World Bank Blogs, June 30, 2016, *https://blogs.worldbank.org/arabvoices/paradox-higher-education-mena*.

25 Irada Aghamaliyeva, MENA Diversity and Inclusiveness Leader, MENA talent team, EY; interview with the author, September 14,2020.

26 Return on Disability, "Insights: Return on Disability Research," 2014, accessed November 7, 2020, *https://www.rod-group.com/insights*; Thorkil Sonne, "Why People with Disabilities Are Your Company's Untapped Resource," World Economic Forum, January 10, 2019, *https://www.weforum.org/agenda/2019/01/disabilities-autism-in-employment-thorkil-sonne/*.

27 European Commission, "People with Disabilities—Fighting Poverty and Social Isolation," European Commission: Employment, Social Affairs and Inclusion, 2010, accessed November 6, 2020, *https://ec.europa.eu/employment_social/2010againstpoverty/about/topicofmonth_disability_en.htm*.

28 Nancy Geenen, "Employing Individuals with Disabilities May Solve Your Talent Crisis," *Entrepreneur*, November 2, 2018, *https://www.entrepreneur.com/article/321984*; Joseph Graffam, Kaye Smith, Alison Shinkfield, and Udo Polzin, "Employer Benefits and Costs of Employing a Person with a Disability," Deakin University, *Journal of Vocational Rehabilitation* 17, 4 (2002): 251-263, *http://dro.deakin.edu.au/view/DU:30001618*.

29 Hannah Weiss, "How Hiring People with Disabilities Can Help Your Bottom Line," Workology, April 14, 2015, *https://workology.com/how-hiring-people-with-disabilities-can-increase-your-bottom-line/*.

30 Heather Boucher and Sarah Jane Glynn, "There Are Significant Business Costs to Replacing Employees," Center for American Progress (November 16, 2012), 2, *https://www.americanprogress.org/wp-content/uploads/2012/11/CostofTurnover.pdf*.

31 Featured Partner of DiversityInc, "Myth-Busting: Hiring Workers with Disabilities," DiversityInc, February 24, 2010, *https://www.diversityinc.com/myth-busting-hiring-workers-with-disabilities/*.

32 Return on Disability, "Return on Disability Research."

33 United Nations, "Ageing and Disability," United Nations: Department of Economic and Social Affairs, Disability, accessed November 9, 2020, *https://www.un.org/development/desa/disabilities/disability-and-ageing.html*.

34 Kristen Anderson, Global Chief Diversity Officer, Barilla, interview with the author, August 28 and September 16, 2020.

35 Isabel Kennon and Grace Valdevitt, "Women Protest for Their Lives: Fighting Femicide in Latin America," Atlantic Council, February 24, 2020, *https://www.atlanticcouncil.org/blogs/new-atlanticist/women-protest-for-their-lives-fighting-femicide-in-latin-america/*.

36 Mireille Widmer and Irene Pavesi, "Gendered Analysis of Violent Deaths," Small Arms Survey, November 1, 2016, *http://www.smallarmssurvey.org/fileadmin/docs/H-Research_Notes/SAS-Research-Note-63.pdf*.

37 World Health Organization, "New Report Documents Extent of Violence against Women in 12 Countries in the Americas," World Health Organization, 2013, accessed November 6, 2020.

38 Christine Murray, "Rising Violence against Women in Latin America Confirms Fears of Abuses in Lockdown," *Reuters*, July 9, 2020, *https://uk.reuters.com/article/us-health-coronavirus-latam-violence-trf/rising-violence-against-women-in-latin-america-confirms-fears-of-abuses-in-lockdowns-idUSKBN23G2X6*.

39 Nata Davoury, Aoife Callan, Patrick Carney, and Srinivas Raghavendra, "Intimate Partner Violence: Economic Costs and Implications for Growth and Development," *Women's Voice, Agency, and Participation Research Series*, no. 3 (Washington, DC: WorldBank, November 2013), *https://openknowledge.worldbank.org/handle/10986/16697*.

40 Marcelo Vasquez Lopez, former Diversity and Inclusion Director, Sodexo, Latin America, email exchange with the author, March 13, 2021.

Chapter 7

1 Frank Dobbin and Alexandra Kalev, "Why Diversity Programs Fail: And What Works Better," *Harvard Business Review*, July–August 2016, 58.

2 Rohini Anand, PowerPoint presentation to internal audience, SWIFT meeting, Brussels, May 10, 2010.

3 Burcin Ressamoglu, CEO Benefits and Rewards Services Sodexo UK, email exchange with author, April 14, 2021.

4 Rishi Gour, CEO of Theobroma, former CEO of Sodexo India, interview with the author, June 30, 2020.

5 Anuradha Purbey, People Director for Europe and Asia, Aviva, interview with the author, July 8, 2020.

6 Excerpted with permission from Sodexo, Laura Shipler Chico, "Addressing Culture and Origins across the Globe: Lessons from Australia, Brazil, Canada, the United Kingdom and the United States," Sodexo, 11, *https://www.fi.sodexo.com/files/live/sites/com-us/files/about-us/AddressingCultureOriginsAcrossGlobe.pdf*.

7 Sodexo, "Addressing Culture and Origins," 16.

8 Sodexo, "Addressing Culture and Origins," 15.

9 Kristen Anderson, Global Chief Diversity Officer, Barilla, interview with author, August 28 and September 16, 2020.

10 AmChamFrance, "Corporate Inclusion: A Social Imperative and A Measure of Success," AmChamFrance, July 2020, 5, *http://amchamfrance.org/wp-content/uploads/2020/06/Rapport-GB-Final-01-07-2020.pdf*.

11 The Conference Board, "Engaging Employees through Employee Resource Groups" (podcast), The Conference Board, July 30, 2020, *https://conference-board.org/blog/podcasts/Barilla-Employee-Resource-Groups*.

12 Anderson, interview with author.

13 Deborah Munster, Executive VP, Seramount, email exchange with the author, April 7, 2021.

14 CEO Action for Diversity & Inclusion, "Building a Powerfully Diverse Company to Drive Business Results," CEO Action for Diversity & Inclusion, accessed December 10, 2020, *https://www.ceoaction.com/actions/building-a-powerfully-diverse-company-to-drive-business-results/*.

Chapter 8

1 Edgar H. Schein with Peter Schein, *Organizational Culture and Leadership*, 5th edition. (New Jersey: Wiley & Sons, Inc., 2017), 199.

2 Peter Brown, Group Vice President, Digital Platforms Agency, Charter Communications, Inc., interview with the author, December 16, 2020.

3 World Economic Forum, "Mind the 100 Year Gap," *World Economic Forum*, December 16, 2019, *https://www.weforum.org/reports/gender-gap-2020-report-100-years-pay-equality*.

4 International Labour Organization, "Inclusion of People with Disabilities in China," International Labour Organization, January 2013,

https://www.ilo.org/wcmsp5/groups/public/---ed_emp/---ifp_skills/documents /publication/wcms_112380.pdf.

5 "A Fine Line Teaser," *A Fine Line*, directed by Joanna James, accessed May 17, 2021, *http://afinelinemovie.com/about/.*

6 Damla Yildirim, Human Resources Director, On Site Services, Sodexo Turkey, and Ahmet Zeytinoglu, General Manager, Son Site Services, Sodexo Turkey, interview with the author, November 30, 2020.

7 Mariana Mancini, Global Talent Acquisition Center of Expertise Consultant, Dow Chemical Company, interview with the author, November 24, 2020.

8 Pragya Singh, Founder Atijeevan Foundation, India, interview with the author, January 22, 2020.

9 Women's Web, "When People Stare at Me I Smile at Them, Says Pragya Singh, Acid Attack Survivor and Activist," Women's Web, March 6, 2020, *https://www.womensweb.in/2020/03/pragya-singh-acid-attack-survivor -and-activist-atijeevan-foundation-mar20wk1sr/.*

10 WeCapable, "List of Disabilities Covered under Rights of Persons with Disabilities Act, 2016 (RPWD Act)," WeCapable, May 18, 2018, *https:// wecapable.com/disabilities-list-rpwd-act-2016/.*

11 Sreya Oberoi, Diversity and Inclusion Lead, India, and HR Business Partner Healthcare, APAC, Sodexo, email exchange and interview with author following Oberoi's conversation with Somna Singh, Human Resources, Bank of America, India, January 12, 2021.

12 Simone Grossmann, Head of HR for Brazil and the South Cone, The Coca-Cola Company, interview with the author, October 23, 2020.

13 Georges Desvaux and Sandrine Devillard, *Women Matter 2: Female Leadership, A Competitive Edge for the Future* (McKinsey & Company, 2008), 6, *https://www.mckinsey.com/~/media/mckinsey/business%20functions /organization/our%20insights/female%20leaderships%20competitive %20edge/female%20leaderships%20competitive%20edge.pdf.*

14 Erin Meyer, *The Culture Map: Breaking through the Invisible Boundaries of Global Business* (New York: BBS Publications, 2014), 200.

15 Ken Barrett, Global Chief Diversity Officer, General Motors Company, email exchange with author, April 8, 2021.

16 Jingqing Xia, Global HR Partner Commercial and HR Lead for Asia Pacific, CP Kelco, interview with the author, November 11, 2020.

17 Fu Yisheng, "Why Does Haidilao Keep the Hearts of the Employees? By Being a Half-Boss, the Employees Can Be Devastated," *Baidu*, September 19, 2002, *https://baijiahao.baidu.com/s?id=1643568133323043073&wfr=spider &for=pc.*

18 World Economic Forum, *Global Gender Gap Report 2020* (Geneva, CH: World Economic Forum, 2019), 5, accessed November 30, 2020, *http://www3.weforum.org/docs/WEF_GGGR_2020.pdf*.

19 Daniel Ornstein, Erika C. Collins, and Jordan Glassberg, "Countries Implement New Gender Pay Gap Measures," *The National Law Review* 8, no. 331, November 27, 2018, *https://www.natlawreview.com/article/countries-implement-new-gender-pay-gap-measures*.

20 PayScale, "The State of the Gender Pay Gap 2021," PayScale, accessed May 17, 2021, *https://www.payscale.com/data/gender-pay-gap*.

21 National Partnership for Women & Families, "Black Women and the Wage Gap," National Partnership for Women & Families, March 2021, *https://www.nationalpartnership.org/our-work/resources/economic-justice/fair-pay/african-american-women-wage-gap.pdf*.

22 Nancy Rothbard, "Has the Pandemic Set Female Leadership Back?" Knowledge@Wharton, March 30, 2021, *https://knowledge.wharton.upenn.edu/article/pandemic-set-female-leadership-back/?utm_source=kw_newsletter&utm_medium=email&utm_campaign=2021-03-30*.

23 Federal Ministry for Family Affairs, Senior Citizens, Women and Youth, *Parental Allowance, Parental Allowance Plus and Parental Leave* (Berlin: Federal Ministry for Family Affairs, Senior Citizens, Women and Youth, August 2019), 17–29, *https://www.bmfsfj.de/blob/139908/72ce4ea769417a058aa68d9151dd6fd3/elterngeld-elterngeldplus-englisch-data.pdf*.

24 Naina Pottamkulam, "Men Still the Exception When It Comes to Receiving Parental Allowance," I AM EXPAT, March 21, 2020, *https://www.iamexpat.de/expat-info/german-expat-news/men-still-exception-when-it-comes-receiving-parental-allowance*.

25 J. Rudnicka, "Full-Time and Part-Time Rates of Employed Men and Women with Underage Children in the Household in 2019," Statista, August 26, 2020, *https://de.statista.com/statistik/daten/studie/38796/umfrage/teilzeitquote-von-maennern-und-frauen-mit-kindern/*.

26 A.T. Kearney 361°, "Die Rush-Hour des Lebens," A.T. Kearney (January 2018), 28, *http://vaeternetzwerk.info/wp-content/uploads/2018/01/A.T.-KEARNEY-Studie-Rush-Hour.pdf*.

27 Jeanette Settembre, "Women Who Take Extended Maternity Leave Make Less Money When They Return to Work," Marketwatch, April 3, 2018, *https://www.marketwatch.com/story/women-who-take-extended-maternity-leave-make-less-money-when-they-return-to-work-2018-04-03*.

28 Rohini Anand and Mary-Frances Winters, "A Retrospective View of Corporate Diversity Training from 1964," *Academy of Management Learning & Education* 7, No. 3 (2018): 356–372.

29 Ariel, "#ShareTheLoad Journey," Procter & Gamble, accessed February 19, 2021, *https://www.ariel.in/en-in/share-the-load/the-share-the-load-journey*.

30 Rohini Anand, Rachel Sylvan, and Imraan Lilani, "Common Purpose: The Intersection of Diversity & Inclusion and Corporate Responsibility in the United States," Sodexo, accessed February 20, 2018, *https://www.fi.sodexo.com/files/live/sites/com-us/files/our-impact/CommonPurposePaperFINAL.pdf*.

31 Jonathan Woetzel, Anu Madgavkar, Kweilin Ellingrud, Eric Labaye, Sandrine Devillard, Eric Kutcher, James Manyika, Richard Dobbs, and Mekala Krishnan, "How Advancing Women's Equality Can Add $12 Trillion to Global Growth," McKinsey Global Institute, Executive Summary (September 1, 2015): 4, *https://www.mckinsey.com/featured-insights/employment-and-growth/how-advancing-womens-equality-can-add-12-trillion-to-global-growth*.

Chapter 9

1 Catalyst, "Case Study: Sodexo—Making Every Day Count: Driving Business Success through the Employee Experience," *Catalyst*, January 1, 2012, *https://www.catalyst.org/research/sodexo-making-every-day-count-driving-business-success-through-the-employee-experience/*.

2 Diversity Best Practices, "Building D&I Accountability and Representation Goals," Diversity Best Practices, November 2020, *https://www.diversitybestpractices.com/sites/diversitybestpractices.com/files/attachments/2020/11/building_di_accountability_and_representation_goals_final.pdf*.

3 Wema Hoover, Former Global Head of Inclusion, Diversity and Culture, Sanofi interview with author, July 8, 2020.

4 Mark McLane, Head of Diversity, Inclusion and Wellbeing, M&G PLC, interview with the author, July 21, 2020.

5 The International Labour Organization, "Promoting Employment Opportunities for People with Disabilities: Quota Schemes; Volume 1, Gender, Equality and Diversity and ILOAIDS Branch," International Labour Organization, 2019, *https://www.ilo.org/wcmsp5/groups/public/---ed_emp/---ifp_skills/documents/publication/wcms_735531.pdf*.

6 Jamie Warham, "Map Shows Where It's Illegal to Be Gay—30 Years Since WHO Declassified Homosexuality as Disease," *Forbes*, May 17, 2020, *https://www.forbes.com/sites/jamiewareham/2020/05/17/map-shows-where-its-illegal-to-be-gay--30-years-since-who-declassified-homosexuality-as-disease/?sh=7f0427ba578a*.

7 Lynn Pasterny, "Do Ask. Do Tell: Capturing Data on Sexual Orientation and Gender Identity Globally," Stonewall UK, 2016, accessed July 11, 2020, *https://www.stonewall.org.uk/sites/default/files/do_ask_do_tell_guide_2016.pdf*.

8 Allen Smith, "EEOC Explains How to Report Nonbinary Individuals on EEO-1 Form," SHRM, August 27, 2019, *https://www.shrm.org/resourcesandtools/legal*

-and-compliance/employment-law/pages/eeoc-nonbinary-individuals-comments -eeo-1-form.aspx.

9 Josefine Van Zanten and Alyson Meister, "Diversity & Inclusion: A Case of Targets, Quotas, or Freewheeling?," IMD, May 2020, *https://www.imd.org /research-knowledge/articles/Diversity-and-Inclusion-a-case-of-targets-quotas -or-freewheeling/.*

10 EWOB 2019 Gender Diversity Index, "European Women on Boards Gender Diversity Index," EWOB 2019 Gender Diversity Index, 2019, accessed March 20, 2021, *https://europeanwomenonboards.eu/wp-content /uploads/2020/01/Gender-Equality-Index-Final-report-vDEF-ter.pdf.*

11 Van Zanten and Meister, "Diversity & Inclusion."

12 Van Zanten and Meister, "Diversity & Inclusion."

13 Davies Review Annual Report, "Women on Boards: Davies Review Annual Report 2015," March 2015, *https://assets.publishing.service.gov.uk /government/uploads/system/uploads/attachment_data/file/415454/bis-15 -134-women-on-boards-2015-report.pdf.*

14 Procter & Gamble, "Gender Equality," 2021, *https://us.pg.com/gender-equality/.*

15 Wikipedia, "Affirmative Action," last updated May 14, 2021, *https://en .wikipedia.org/wiki/Affirmative_action.*

16 Laura Noonan, Madison Marriage, and Patrick Jenkins, "Equal Pay and Opportunities for Women in Finance: Why the Hold Up?," *Financial Times*, April 4, 2017, *https://www.ft.com/content/198abd62-1471-11e7-80f4 -13e067d5072c.*

17 Rishi Gour, CEO Theobroma India, former CEO Sodexo, India, interview with the author, June 3, 2020.

Conclusion

1 Jennifer Garcia-Alonso, Matt Krentz, Deborah Lovich, and Stephanie Mingardon, "Diversity, Equity, and Inclusion Still Matter in a Pandemic," BCG, December 17, 2020, *https://www.bcg.com/en-gb/publications/2020 /value-of-investing-in-diversity-equity-and-inclusion-during-a-pandemic.*

2 Jennifer Maloney and Lauren Weber, "Coke's Elusive Goal: Boosting Its Black Employees," *The Wall Street Journal*, December 16, 2020, *https://www .wsj.com/articles/coke-resets-goal-of-boosting-black-employees-after-20-year -effort-loses-ground-11608139999.*

3 Earl Fitzhugh, JP Julien, Nick Noel, and Shelley Stewart, "It's Time for a New Approach to Racial Equity," McKinsey & Company, December 2, 2020, *https://www.mckinsey.com/featured-insights/diversity-and-inclusion/its-time -for-a-new-approach-to-racial-equity.*

4 Kweilin Ellingrud, Mekala Krishnan, Alexis Krivkovich, Nicole Robinson, Lareina Yee, Kathryn Kukla, Ana Mendy, and Sandra Sancier-Sultan,

"Diverse Employees Are Struggling the Most during COVID-19—Here's How Companies Can Respond," McKinsey & Company, November 17, 2020, *https://www.mckinsey.com/featured-insights/diversity-and-inclusion/diverse-employees-are-struggling-the-most-during-covid-19-heres-how-companies-can-respond.*

5 Gemma D'Airia, Aaron De Smet, Chris Gagnon, Julie Goran, Dana Maor, and Richard Steele, "Reimagining the Post Pandemic Organization," McKinsey & Company, May 15, 2020, *https://www.mckinsey.com/business-functions/organization/our-insights/reimagining-the-post-pandemic-organization.*

6 Adriana Dahik, Deborah Lovich, Caroline Kreafle, Allison Bailey, Julie Kilmann, Derek Kennedy, Prateek Roongta, Felix Schuler, Leo Tomlin, and John Wenstrup, "What 12,000 Employees Have to Say about the Future of Remote Work," Boston Consulting Group, August 11, 2020, *https://www.bcg.com/publications/2020/valuable-productivity-gains-covid-19.*

7 Carolyn Dewar, Scott Keller, Kevin Sneader, and Kurt Strovink, "The CEO Moment: Leadership for a New Era," *McKinsey Quarterly* (July 2020): 1, *https://www.mckinsey.com/featured-insights/leadership/the-ceo-moment-leadership-for-a-new-era.*

8 Samantha McDonald, "Run the Numbers: These D&I Jobs Are Exploding in 2020," *Yahoo!Finance*, January 31, 2020, *https://finance.yahoo.com/news/run-numbers-d-jobs-exploding-210834475.html.*

9 Paul Ingram, "The Forgotten Dimension of Diversity," *Harvard Business Review*, January–February 2021, *https://hbr.org/2021/01/the-forgotten-dimension-of-diversity.*

10 Vicky McKeever, "Unilever Aims to Train Up 10 Million Young People for Work in Strategy to Tackle Inequality," CNBC, January 21, 2021, *https://www.cnbc.com/2021/01/21/unilever-strategy-to-tackle-inequality-includes-training-young-people.html.*

11 Colleen Jenkins and Daniel Trotta, "Seeking End to Boycott, North Carolina Rescinds Transgender Bathroom Law," *Reuters*, March 30, 2017, *https://www.reuters.com/article/us-north-carolina-lgbt/seeking-end-to-boycott-north-carolina-rescinds-transgender-bathroom-law-idUSKBN1711V4.*

Appendix

1 KPIs (key performance indicators) measure the success of the initiatives or actions.

ACRONYMS GLOSSARY

BAME	Black, Asian, and Minority Ethnic
BIPOC	Black, Indigenous, and People of Color
BLM	Black Lives Matter
CEO	Chief Executive Officer
CDO	Chief Diversity Officer
CR	Corporate responsibility
DEI	Diversity, Equity, and Inclusion
EEO	Equal employment opportunity
EEOC	Equal Employment Opportunity Commission
EU	European Union
ERG	Employee resource group
EBRG	Employee business resource group (Sodexo)
GDP	Gross domestic product
KPI	Key performance indicator
ILO	International Labour Organization
LGBTQ	Lesbian, gay, bisexual, transgender, and queer
PWD	People with disabilities
SDII	Sodexo Diversity and Inclusion Index

ACKNOWLEDGMENTS

I am grateful for my supportive community of family, friends, and colleagues. My daughters, Easha Anand and Dr. Pria Anand, are my biggest cheerleaders. Every conversation with them gave shape to nebulous concepts. Pria's work and insights on health disparities found a place in the book and I drew on Easha's criminal justice work to lend a sense of urgency to addressing racial justice. Sudeep, my spouse, has always been my rock and my anchor. Thank you for making it easy for me by taking care of all the other big and little things. My mother encouraged me throughout the process, even though it meant not visiting her in India for over a year!

I want to acknowledge the amazing, talented, and dedicated global team that worked in lockstep with me—Laura and Imraan in London, Lindsay and Sam in the US, and Arun in India.

This book would not be possible without Laura Shipler Chico. Her input, editorial support throughout, and help with writing were invaluable. She stretched my thinking and enriched the book with every review. Her attention to detail, cultural intelligence, and language precision made the book sharper and stronger. She has my deepest gratitude.

Imraan Lilani embodies diligence, commitment, and enthusiasm. His research abilities, tireless energy, and consistency were unparalleled. The book is better for his contributions. I leaned on him every step of the way. Everyone should be fortunate enough to have an Imraan by their side.

Lindsay Satterfield is a remarkable productivity coach. She not only kept me on track but also helped me with technology, provided feedback, challenged me to crystalize my message, sharpened the words, and pushed me to think big. Her versatility is amazing.

I am also indebted to Sam Wells, who enriched the writing, and Arun Teja Moduga, who somehow always found the right references to bolster my message.

Thank you to Steve Piersanti, my editor, and to the Berrett-Koehler team. Steve knew how to nudge me to focus on the core nugget in each chapter and pointed me in the right direction from the outset.

I am grateful for Liz Salett, a pioneer in multicultural counseling work, who encouraged me on this journey. Michel Landel positioned me for success and made this story possible. He has my deepest gratitude. Sophie Bellon was a consummate role model—genuinely committed and personally involved. She encouraged me both personally and professionally. Thank you!

A huge thank you to all those—over sixty individuals—who took the time to talk with me and to share their stories and insights: Ahmet Zeytinoglu, Alain Morize, Annette Mock, Anuradha Purbey, Augusto Muench, Balaji Ganapathy, Batoul Hassoun, Bruce Roche, Bruna Galvao, Burcin Ressamoglu, Carinne Brouillon, Carole Le Meur, Caroline Vaquette, Cynthia Carter-McReynolds, Damla Yildirim, Dick Macedonia, Deborah Munster, Donald Fan, Geeta Rao Gupta, Iara Santos, Irada Aghamaliyeva, James Taylor, Jeremy Solomons, Jingqing Xia, Jonny Briggs, Keysa Minnifield, Ken Barrett, Kenneth Johnson, Kristen Anderson, Lawrencia Quarshie, Lilian Rauld Campos, Lori George Billingsley, Marcelo Vasquez Lopez, Margareth Goldenberg, Margaret Johnston-Clark, Mariana Mancini, Mario Ferreira, Mark McLane, Maya Rmeity, Mia Mends, Michael Privot, Michel Landel, Nancy DiDia, Natasha Winkler-Titus, Nene Molefi, Nupur Mallick, Padma Thiruvengadam, Parmesh Shahani, Paula Espinosa, Peter Brown, Petrica Dulgheru, Reza Hariri, Rishi Gour, Roberto Cardona, Sharda Naidoo, Shelly McNamara, Simone P. Grossmann, Silvia Siqueira, Sonali

Roychowdhury, Sreya Ghosh Oberoi, Subarna Malakar, Tracy Ann Curtis, Ursula Schwarzenbart, Vijay Sharma, Vincent Meehan, and Wema Hoover. I am grateful to Alice Coulibaly, Deborah Hecker, David K. Shipler, and Bob Stern for their feedback on excerpts of the book.

Finally, my colleagues at Sodexo, and especially my DEI team, travelled this journey with me and did the heavy lifting.

Every diversity, equity, and inclusion change agent out there has contributed in some way to this book. You know who you are. This story is ours together. Keep doing the important, exhausting, and gratifying work to make us, our organizations, and our communities better.

INDEX

C

T

U

ABOUT THE AUTHOR

DR. ROHINI ANAND grew up in India, the second most populous country in the world and home to more than two thousand ethnic groups, with representation of every major religion, and twenty-two different languages. But her diversity journey really took off when, at the age of nineteen, she boarded a plane for the first time in her life and landed in North America.

In India she belonged to the majority. Surrounded by others like her, she had the privilege of not having to think about her identity. In her own naïve way, she saw herself as a citizen of the world. But in the hours and days after passing through customs, that fantasy gave way to another reality. Her identity shifted from a person who saw herself at the center of her world—a member of the educated elite—to being a minority, an immigrant, and yes, a foreigner. And she was totally unprepared for that.

But the very challenges that at first seemed like obstacles to an unsure graduate student later laid the foundation for a long and successful career as a transformational global leader respected for her cultural dexterity and ability to orchestrate and sustain large-scale global organizational transformation and influence brand recognition. As Senior Vice President and Global Chief Diversity Officer at Sodexo, she brought this expertise to her engagement with multinational leaders, working with them to transform a global organization from one that was facing a class action lawsuit to one that was considered best in class.

Under Rohini's leadership, the Sodexo brand became synonymous with a commitment to diversity, corporate responsibility, and wellness. Sodexo received the prestigious 2012 Catalyst Award and ranked in the top 10 of DiversityInc's Top 50 Companies for Diversity for eleven consecutive years.

A recognized thought leader, sought-after speaker, advisor, and consultant, Rohini currently serves on a number of boards, including WomenLift Health, a Gates Foundation initiative; Charter Communication External Diversity and Inclusion Council; Tent Partnership for Refugees, Advisory Council; and the GALT Foundation. She is a Senior Fellow with The Conference Board and chaired the Catalyst Board of Advisors.

Many years have now passed since that first plane ride. Like millions of people before her, upon arrival to this new land, Rohini took on a new identity—or, more accurately—identities. Her India-to-North America journey brought into focus how she perceived herself, how others saw her, her response to their perceptions, and, subsequently, how she reacted to the world around her. It became the core of her graduate research and today remains at the center of her work. For Rohini this work is much more than a vocation. It is a cause, a calling, and a passion. It is personal.

Residing in Potomac, Maryland, with her spouse, Rohini is the very proud mother of their two adult daughters—Easha, a public interest lawyer who has dedicated her career to reforming the criminal justice system, and Pria, a neurologist who is committed to caring for vulnerable populations.

This is how Sophie Bellon, Chair of Sodexo's Board of Directors, describes Rohini's transformative leadership: "Rohini is a bright, passionate, and inspiring leader, who quite simply makes you want to follow her. Working closely with her has been an eye-opener, and her vision has spurred my own commitment on this crucial topic."

Berrett–Koehler Publishers

Berrett-Koehler is an independent publisher dedicated to an ambitious mission: *Connecting people and ideas to create a world that works for all.*

Our publications span many formats, including print, digital, audio, and video. We also offer online resources, training, and gatherings. And we will continue expanding our products and services to advance our mission.

We believe that the solutions to the world's problems will come from all of us, working at all levels: in our society, in our organizations, and in our own lives. Our publications and resources offer pathways to creating a more just, equitable, and sustainable society. They help people make their organizations more humane, democratic, diverse, and effective (and we don't think there's any contradiction there). And they guide people in creating positive change in their own lives and aligning their personal practices with their aspirations for a better world.

And we strive to practice what we preach through what we call "The BK Way." At the core of this approach is *stewardship,* a deep sense of responsibility to administer the company for the benefit of all of our stakeholder groups, including authors, customers, employees, investors, service providers, sales partners, and the communities and environment around us. Everything we do is built around stewardship and our other core values of *quality, partnership, inclusion,* and *sustainability.*

This is why Berrett-Koehler is the first book publishing company to be both a B Corporation (a rigorous certification) and a benefit corporation (a for-profit legal status), which together require us to adhere to the highest standards for corporate, social, and environmental performance. And it is why we have instituted many pioneering practices (which you can learn about at www.bkconnection.com), including the Berrett-Koehler Constitution, the Bill of Rights and Responsibilities for BK Authors, and our unique Author Days.

We are grateful to our readers, authors, and other friends who are supporting our mission. We ask you to share with us examples of how BK publications and resources are making a difference in your lives, organizations, and communities at www.bkconnection.com/impact.

Dear reader,

Thank you for picking up this book and welcome to the worldwide BK community! You're joining a special group of people who have come together to create positive change in their lives, organizations, and communities.

What's BK all about?

Our mission is to connect people and ideas to create a world that works for all.

Why? Our communities, organizations, and lives get bogged down by old paradigms of self-interest, exclusion, hierarchy, and privilege. But we believe that can change. That's why we seek the leading experts on these challenges—and share their actionable ideas with you.

A welcome gift

To help you get started, we'd like to offer you a **free copy** of one of our bestselling ebooks:

www.bkconnection.com/welcome

When you claim your **free ebook**, you'll also be subscribed to our blog.

Our freshest insights

Access the best new tools and ideas for leaders at all levels on our blog at ideas.bkconnection.com.

Sincerely,

Your friends at Berrett-Koehler

FSC www.fsc.org MIX Paper from responsible sources FSC® C016245

Certified B Corporation